THE BASIC ARTS OF BUYING

D. E. BARKER, BEM, CEng, MIMechE, MInstPS
and
B. FARRINGTON, MSc, BSc(Econ), FInstPS, AMBIM

*Senior Lecturers in Purchasing Management
at the North West Management Centre, St. Helens, Lancashire*

Business Books
London   Melbourne   Sydney   Auckland   Johannesburg

Business Books Ltd

An imprint of the Hutchinson Publishing Group

17-21 Conway Street, London W1P 6JD

Hutchinson Group (Australia) Pty Ltd
30-32 Cremorne Street, Richmond South, Victoria 3121
PO Box 151, Broadway, New South Wales 2007

Hutchinson Group (NZ) Ltd
32-34 View Road, PO Box 40-086, Glenfield, Auckland 10

Hutchinson Group (SA) (Pty) Ltd
PO Box 337, Bergvlei 2012, South Africa

First published 1976
Reprinted 1980

Special paperback edition for the
Institute of Purchasing and Supply 1983

© Douglas Edward Barker and Brian Farrington 1976

Printed in Great Britain by The Anchor Press Ltd
and bound by Wm Brendon & Son Ltd
both of Tiptree, Essex

ISBN 0 220 66295 9 (cased)
    0 09 153131 4 (paper)

**TO KATHLEEN, ELIZABETH,
JOYCE, SANDRA AND JOANNE**
*for their encouragement and forbearance
throughout the time that this book was being written*

OTHER TITLES IN THE 'BASIC ARTS' SERIES

The Basic Arts of Management/Taylor and Watling
The Basic Arts of Financial Management/Simons
The Basic Arts of Budgeting/McAlpine

Contents

Preface *xiii*

Chapter 1 **The buying function – identifying improvement points**   1

  1.1 Elemental buying
  1.2 Define corporate objectives
  1.3 Personnel training and development
  1.4 Organisational style and environment
  1.5 Define material requirements
  1.6 Supplier provision
  1.7 Timing of supplies
  1.8 Research into total buying activities
  1.9 Economic and buying interface
  1.10 Analysis of purchase price
  1.11 Measure and monitor performance
  1.12 Summary

Chapter 2 **Organisational relationships**   20

  2.1 Buying staff relationships
  2.2 Relationships with other departments
  2.3 General comments on relationships
  2.4 Summary

viii THE BASIC ARTS OF BUYING

Chapter 3 **Systems and documentation** 43

- 3.1 Requisitioning
- 3.2 Commodity records
- 3.3 Supplier visit record
- 3.4 Enquiries
- 3.5 Quotations
- 3.6 Selection of short-list suppliers
- 3.7 Evaluating quotations
- 3.8 Purchase orders
- 3.9 Order number allocations
- 3.10 Emergency orders
- 3.11 Local purchase orders
- 3.12 Letters of authorisation
- 3.13 Order acknowledgement
- 3.14 Reconciling acknowledgements with orders
- 3.15 Expediting records and procedures
- 3.16 Rejection/discrepancy notes
- 3.17 Supplier/sub-contractor insurance and indemnity records
- 3.18 Disposals
- 3.19 Catalogues
- 3.20 Private purchases
- 3.21 Annual contracts

Chapter 4 **Sourcing and pricing** 64

- 4.1 Introduction
- 4.2 An open mind
- 4.3 The market place
- 4.4 Finding the market place
- 4.5 Visits to suppliers
- 4.6 Enquiries
- 4.7 Quotations
- 4.8 Pricing
- 4.9 Prices as a measurement of buying performance

CONTENTS ix

Chapter 5 **Financial and contractual aspects**   81

    5.1   Introduction
    5.2   Financial aspects
    5.3   General conditions of purchase
    5.4   Special conditions of purchase
    5.5   Model special conditions of contract documents
    5.6   General comments on financial and contractual aspects

Chapter 6 **Stores management and control of stock**   110

    6.1   Introduction
    6.2   What do we have in stock?
    6.3   Economic order quantity
    6.4   ABC inventory categories
    6.5   The review level system
    6.6   Exponential smoothing
    6.7   Determining the re-order level and safety stock

Chapter 7 **Global procurement**   133

    7.1   Why buy abroad?
    7.2   Locating foreign sources of supply
    7.3   Preparing an adequate enquiry
    7.4   Supplier appraisal
    7.5   Price and currency
    7.6   Payment in foreign currency
    7.7   Terms of payment
    7.8   Customs and excise requirements
    7.9   Customs clearance
    7.10   Import agents
    7.11   Insurance
    7.12   Instructions to buyer's insurance agent

7.13 Payment for imports
7.14 Progress and inspection
7.15 Terms and conditions of purchase
7.16 Summary

Chapter 8 **A review of purchasing techniques** 159

8.1 Introduction
8.2 Value engineering and value analysis
8.3 Learning curve analysis
8.4 Supplier appraisal
8.5 Quality appraisal
8.6 Supplier rating
8.7 Purchasing research
8.8 Line of balance technology
8.9 Critical path analysis
8.10 Supplier development

Chapter 9 **Measuring buying performance** 181

9.1 Over-expenditure on bought-out goods and services
9.2 Cost of failure to meet production requirements
9.3 Cost of failure to negotiate and apply adequate terms and conditions
9.4 Cost of failure to provide information to management and internal departments
9.5 Cost of applying additional efforts on expediting, transport and quality control
9.6 Cost of not satisfying outside customers
9.7 Cost of excessive stockholding
9.8 Cost of failure to dispose of surplus plant, equipment or materials at maximum prices

9.9	Cost of operating the buying department	
9.10	Cost of measuring buying performance	
9.11	Measurement — what does this involve?	
9.12	Standards of performance	
9.13	Organisational foundation	
9.14	Quantitative measurement	
9.15	Qualitative measurement	
9.16	Programmes for measuring buying performance	

Chapter 10 **Conclusions**   204

10.1	Who gets the best from price variation?	
10.2	Case studies	

References   239

Index   241

Preface

The proliferation of textbooks in many management disciplines has not been matched in the buying function where literature on buying is thin on the ground. This is indicative of a failure of the profession to establish a clear identity. Our book is intended to assist buying professionals who seek to develop their own philosophy. Frequently we see buying departments striving to cope with a flood of paperwork and, in consequence, being forced into short-term actions. It is desirable, and necessary, to devote time looking at the long-term implications of alternative buying strategies. This can only be achieved if every level of buying activity is involved. It is not the exclusive domain of management.

Our book was written in a period when economic forces were inflationary. This has placed stresses on interdepartmental relationships. The interface with the selling market place has also been difficult; resistance to price increases has been an emotive subject. The strengthening of long-term relationships with sellers has not come easy. The business cycle with its downturns and upturns results in a constant reorientation of buying activity. This dynamic change requires a flexible attitude of mind and policies reflecting movements in the market place. It is necessary also to recognise risk as an inherent feature of buying. We believe that inertia bedevils buying and therefore express the wish to see a more positive approach to risk-taking and the establishment of buying as an active entrepreneurial function.

The ideas and suggestions contained in this book are based on many years practical operational experience and consultancy work. In recent years we have entered the academic world where we have been subjected to the perceptive questioning of hundreds of buyers. We are deeply impressed with the ability and dedication of our fellow professionals. Latent talent exists and must be tapped by those organisations who seek confirmation that buying can make an impact on the success of a business. Success tends to be measured by money. This is one key dimension that can be improved by good buying.

We have attempted to write a book that can be read easily. It provides a balance between practices and techniques, recognising the problems that will exist in implementing some of them. Determination and the will to succeed are vital. Many of our suggestions do not require dramatic investments of capital, simply a change of attitude. There cannot be many professions offering the degree of interest that buying possesses. The satisfaction of searching a difficult market and locating a key material; of a successful negotiation; the ultimate delivery of a complex piece of equipment; these are features appreciated by the dedicated professional.

The inclusion of case studies is a serious attempt to create a dialogue between authors and readers. We welcome contact with our audience and look forward to receiving constructive comment on the problems discussed. Obviously we will respond. In the past there has been a singular lack of dialogue in the buying area. The future advance of the profession depends on a healthy cross-fertilisation particularly between diverse buying roles. This is encouraged on our trading programmes and has resulted in many operational improvements.

True professionalism demands accountability. Buying has a tendency to hide its light under a bushel. We would like to see a greater willingness to account for the errors and the successes. There have been many of the latter. We hope to encourage more. It can be done given the resolve.

B. FARRINGTON
D. E. BARKER

1 The Buying Function— Identifying Improvement Points

Buying is a critical activity in all public and private organisations and the profession has now come of age, in the sense that there is widespread recognition of its impact on profitability. Figure 1.1 shows how vital it is. There cannot be a more significant illustration to convince dilatory managements of the important need to control all monies spent. Expenditure on raw materials and services can be as high as 65 per cent of sales receipts and this calls for sophisticated control techniques to ensure that maximum benefit is obtained from the expenditure. Cost control is essential and extravagance must be avoided. A thoroughly professional buying department must have a positive approach when striving to make savings on existing spending. If these can be achieved, increased profitability will result. Figure 1.2 shows the relevance of a 2 per cent saving on material expenditure — the saving has increased profits directly by 10 per cent. A five-fold multiplier! the same increase in profit could be achieved by increasing productivity output but this is not simple. Assuming a profit margin of 10 per cent on gross sales, production would have to increase by £10 million in the example above to contribute the same profit. Production increases of 10 per cent cannot readily be made, nor can sales be increased at 'the drop of a hat'. It may be constructively concluded that the buying function offers considerable scope for improving the profit potential of any company.

2 THE BASIC ARTS OF BUYING

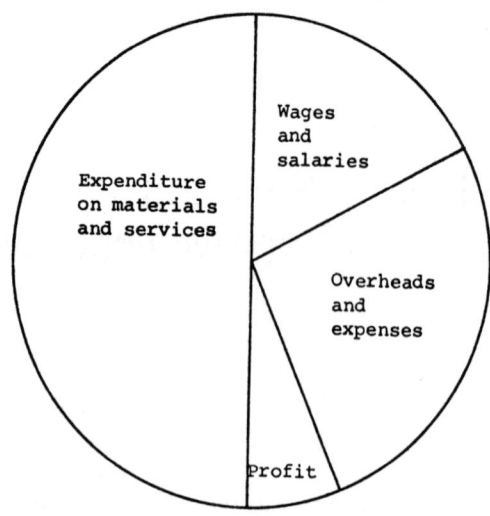

Figure 1.1 The pie represents the total sales revenue of a typical manufacturing organisation

Factor	Was	Is now	Comments
Sales turnover	£100m	£100m	Unchanged
Materials expenditure	£50m	£49m	Savings of 2%
Profit	£10m	£11m	Increase of 10%

Figure 1.2

1.1 Elemental buying

Traditional writers have stressed that buying is a matter of satisfying basic 'rights' — buying the *right* material ...
    ... at the *right* price
    ... for the *right* place
    ... in the *right* quality
    ... in the *right* quantity
    ... at the *right* time

As prerequisites these rights cannot be faulted but they represent an inadequate view of the buying function. This has been corrected by the development of 'the Stream Concept' (see Figure 1.3). The basis of this concept is that buying is a

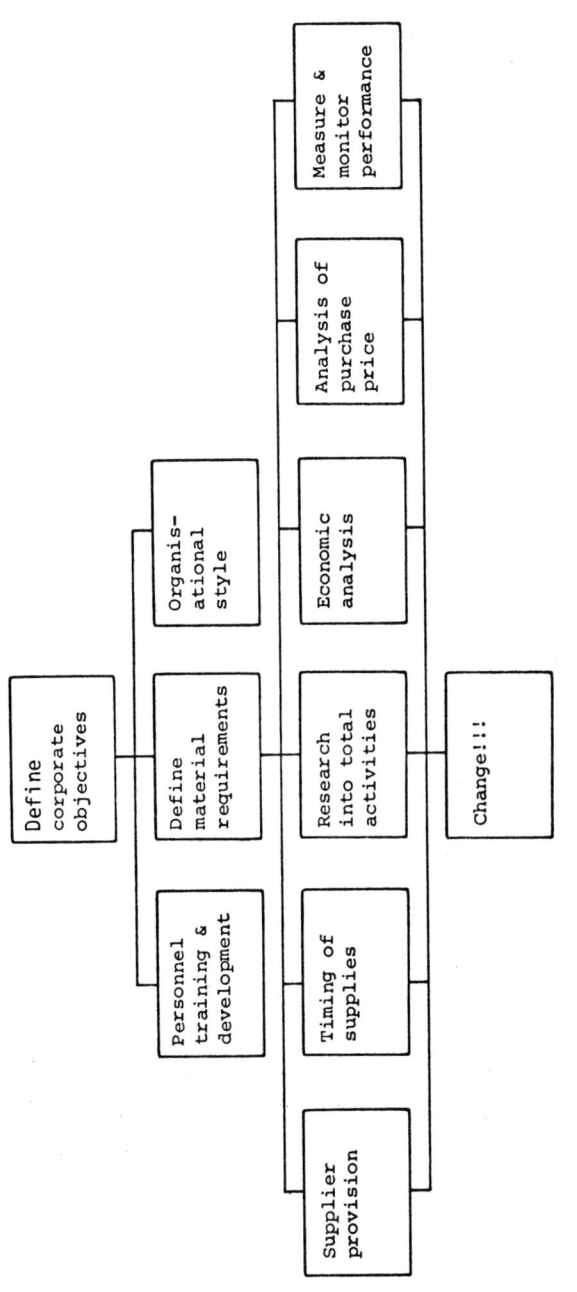

Figure 1.3 The stream concept

four-tier strategical consideration with an interdependence between each. There is a critical dependence on all being effective. A brief analysis of each element is provided to demonstrate the basic points.

1.2 Define corporate objectives

Any discussion of a functional activity such as buying must begin outside its immediate environment. There needs to be a clear definition of corporate objectives by the controlling forces — directors. It is their duty to ensure that forward planning takes place. This will represent the company's short- and long-term strategy. The period of time involved will be anything from the forthcoming year to ten years ahead. Such planning will outline development plans, product diversification, overseas potential and so on. These facts are inherently relevant to the buying office who need to be involved in the formulation of such plans. If a buyer is effective he will be considering markets in the long term. This will have to be done if he is to be involved in forecasting price and supplies availability. The emphasis on an increasing involvement in the dynamic relationships of a company is having an impact on the demand for high-calibre recruits into buying. It is also ensuring that the top echelons of buying are recognised as equals to other specialists in the organisation.

1.3 Personnel training and development

The opportunities for career development and job satisfaction are certainly present in buying. There have been many pronouncements on the qualities necessary for a good buyer. They will all, rightly, stress the involvement with people, hence the need for empathy. The buyer is the organisation's representative in the outside world and bad impressions must be avoided. It is recognised that temptations do arise — bribery is one possible form of corruption — but moral and ethical standards must be impeccable. Personal standards of dress, behaviour and commercial awareness must be of the highest order. Buying offers a challenge to those with considerable ability and the penalties for poor performance can be severe. Equally, the rewards of achievement can be highly satisfying.

Recent advertisements stress the need for high-calibre buyers:

> 'You should be aged 26-35, a graduate or equivalent, with at least three years' successful experience in a sophisticated high volume purchasing operation. Responsibilities will include control of operations of a purchasing team, budgeting expense control, on-site evaluation of suppliers' capabilities and maintaining their level of performance. Purchasing budgets at Black & Decker represent 65 per cent of manufactured cost and you will have the advantage of working in a company where purchasing is of prime importance — and a stepping stone to higher management.'

The 1969s and 1970s have seen a big improvement in the quality of training and development opportunities within buying. Traditional training patterns have been extended to include intensive courses. These were established at the North West Regional Management Centre in St Helens, Merseyside, in 1973 and have since been supported by many international companies. The basic buying course consists of block release, residential courses where course members are participating in a highly intensive pattern of training and development. The total duration of the course is eight weeks, followed by a detailed in-plant research study aimed at giving the course member an opportunity to apply his newly developed skills. Other unique training programmes are also available at St Helens.

1.4 Organisational style and environment

Buying may be organised in many different ways. These alternatives have to be examined and related to the environment of the firm. Centralisation of all buying may be considered by large geographically scattered companies. Such an approach will contrast sharply with a decentralised organisation where each operating company is responsible for its own buying. Within a department there will be a choice of employing specialist commodity buyers or expecting each buyer to buy a wide range of commodities. The latter will not be a specialist in any commodity whereas the former may develop such an expertise.

There is no ideal organisational pattern that will suit all buying activities. It is however realistic to say that they should all be striving to maximise the value obtained from their outlay. When like items are bought in two or more locations in a multiplant situation, someone should be held responsible for coordinating that outlay. This will ensure that the savings are maximised, providing appropriate techniques are used.

The environment of the company is crucial to these considerations. If, in a large company, decentralisation is the style, buying will find it difficult to adopt a style contrary to this.

Figure 1.4 shows how a merchandise buying department is organised at Gallahers Limited, the cigarette, cigar, tobacco and snuff manufacturers.

A good organisational style will have many attributes. Specifically it will:

1   Provide clear lines of communication from top to bottom whereby everyone has adequate information for his level of decision-making.
2   Provide scope for the employment of those with expertise in the areas of largest outlay.
3   Provide an opportunity for training, particularly junior members of staff.
4   Be compatible with other functions to develop career opportunities where salary levels reflect the skills inherent in an effective buying function.
5   Provide for an appropriate division of responsibilities to avoid confusion in decision-making.
6   Provide sufficient flexibility to avoid excessive work loading without overall performance being reduced.
7   Be readily understood by those in other departments who need to call upon the services of buyers.
8   Be such that no member of the department is expected to control more than six people in a direct supervision chain.

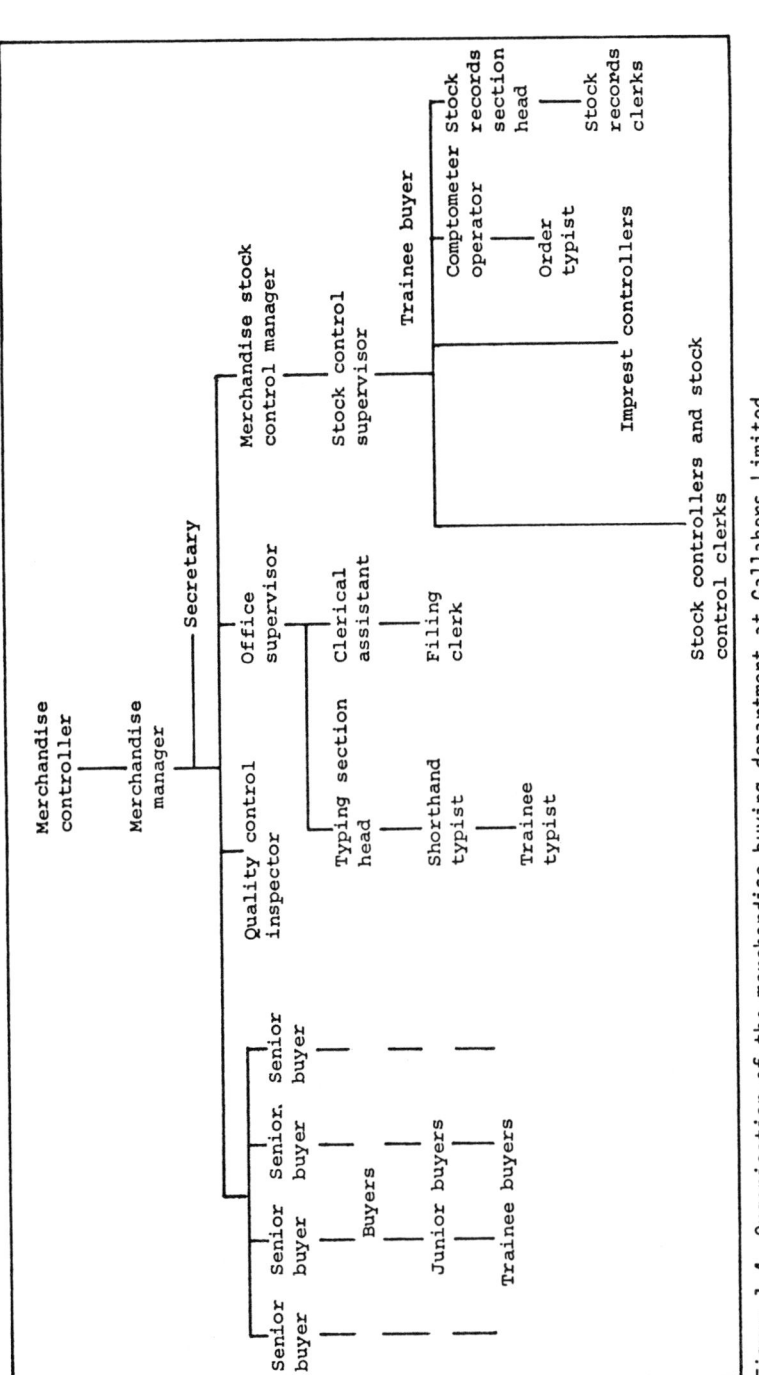

Figure 1.4 Organisation of the merchandise buying department at Gallahers Limited

There will be situations which call for re-organisation of a department. When this becomes necessary morale may be affected. It is therefore vital that announcements are made at the appropriate times. This should restrict rumour and malicious gossip.

Many organisations have a choice between centralisation of the buying activity or its decentralisation. Again there is no ideal form. It is necessary to ensure that whatever form is adopted meets the requirements determined by policy. There are advantages in centralisation, the more important being:

1. It enables expenditure on all items of a like nature to be coordinated, thus enabling negotiations to be made from a strong position. The aggregation of requirements of a like nature is essential.
2. It enables the department to be organised in a way that promotes the most capable personnel rather than adopting a system based on age.
3. It permits the employment and use of specialists. Commodity specialist buyers will become a possibility. Of equal importance is the use of support services for the buyers. All too frequently they are asked to cope with situations that have not been adequately researched for effective decision-making. This can be avoided by using purchase analysts who vet all requisitions before the buyer receives them.

In simple terms the analysts will check that all information is provided, for example:

    Financial authorisation given
    Realistic delivery date specified
    Specifications complete
    Drawings enclosed
    Relevant design information provided
    Usage figures given
    Stock position provided
    Authorised signature used
    Previous price history given

These are come of the vital pieces of information which, if not given, will delay the buyer and prevent him carrying out his task to maximum effect.

Purchasing research specialists can be gainfully employed

in the larger departments. They will be responsible for researching price levels, market supply changes, new materials, new manufacturing methods, suppliers' financial viability, international trading conditions, etc. These factors will be monitored and reported to the buyer who will be expected to take them into account when he is looking for sources. This type of information makes the buyer's job more specific and prevents him being diverted and turned into a creature of routine.

1.5 Define material requirements

Reference to the 'steam' concept will show that this element is seen as the central core of the second tier. From this factor other basic essentials of good buying are derived. It is patently obvious that every company should know what materials, goods and services it intends to buy. Life does not run in logical patterns, which accounts for the fact that day-to-day crisis problem-solving occurs too frequently. The buying office should be systemised in such a way that forward requirements are specified clearly. This will require long-term planning and the active involvement of other departments.

The definition of material requirements is a vital consideration. It is useful at this point to consider Pareto — an Italian philosopher. He studied the distribution of wealth and discovered that 80 per cent of the wealth in Italy was held by 20 per cent of the population. He did this many years ago and thereafter all management functions have referred to the '80/20' rule. It is not irrelevant that the same consideration applies to the buying activity. Fortunately we are able to generalise here. If one examines the amount spent in a buying department it will usually be found that approximately 80 per cent of expenditure is accounted for by 20 per cent of the items bought. The relevance of this must not be underestimated. What is really being argued is that the buyer can control four-fifths of expenditure by controlling one-fifth of the items. If he believes management by exception to be a sensible maxim he will ensure that this policy is adopted. Let there be no excuses for not doing so because it has been adopted in many organisations with considerable savings.

1.6 Supplier provision

There can be no more basic role for a buyer than to ensure that he provides the best supplier for his company in every single purchase. Rightly, this should be viewed as a demanding responsibility. To meet company requirements the buyer must take many factors into account. The detailed bases of appraisal systems are included in the chapter dealing with Sourcing and Pricing. For this reason, broad issues only will be considered at this point. The buyer would be well advised to ask:

1 With whom are we dealing? For example, is he a producer, a merchant, a stockholder, an agent, a wholesaler or what? These are vital considerations. The buyer who thinks he is dealing with a producer but is, in fact, dealing with an agent could be asking for trouble. Two examples should suffice. The agent may be including a commission which inflates the price. In times of difficult production circumstances the buyer needs direct access to the manufacturer when production schedules are changing.

2 Have we considered make/buy? Some buyers are able to buy something from a supplier or have it made within their own organisation. Which they do will obviously depend on manufacturing capabilities but the buyer should always check that his source is the most competitive and that the sourcing strategy conforms to the policy established by his company. For instance, internal manufacturing capabilities are made to compete with external sources. There should be some predetermined method for effective cost evaluation.

3 Do we know where our items are being made? This is a fundamental thought. It would be folly to assume that because an order is placed with a supplier he is in a position to fulfill it. On the contrary, he may have to sub-contract part or all of the order. This has legal connotations should anything seriously jeopardise delivery. It is essential that the buyer takes all the necessary steps to familiarise himself with the manufacturing capabilities of the nominated supplier.

Selection of suppliers is a key task of the buyer. The points detailed above are basic but must be reinforced with a formal, appraisal system. In this context the buyer must ensure that he is familiar with the market place. This can involve a good deal of work, including:

1. Keeping a detailed library of catalogues, trade journals and relevant professional literature. This should be international in character and not limited geographically.
2. Ensuring that the buyer samples a reasonable proportion of the available market place. This demands the abolition of restrictive sourcing practices, perpetuated by some buyers who insist on a sampling of a maximum of six possible suppliers with major requirements. Statistics put this practice in perspective. If it is assumed that potentially there are one hundred suppliers and the buyer asks six to tender, he has in effect lost a 94 per cent chance of finding the best one.
3. Continual questioning of existing suppliers' capabilities to avoid complacency. There should be continual checking to ensure that current prices paid are the most competitive and that existing suppliers are the most effective.

1.7 Timing of supplies

It is a prime responsibility of any buying activity to ensure that supplies are available when required. This is not a simple task, because of the vagaries of supply. Late deliveries are the bane of a buyer's life. Rightly the recalcitrant supplier is held to task and probably is penalised in some way when further business is being considered. The same attitude does not appear to prevail when suppliers make deliveries before the due date. This situation, however, causes problems which should be recognised. The name of the game in manufacturing companies is profit and it needs to be recognised that early deliveries have serious implications:

Cash flow Early deliveries mean early payment and a correspondingly longer period between the arrival of goods and their subsequent conversion to finished goods, ultimate use or sale. In this context the buyer should be aware that the finance activity must provide for its cash requirements as far ahead as possible. If this pattern is not adhered to, it could mean costly borrowing of short-term money at high rates of interest.

Storage space This is usually at a premium in most organisations. Unplanned deliveries may cause bottle-necks and wreak havoc on planned storage. In extreme situations it may be necessary to hire expensive warehousing capacity on a temporary basis.

Cost of storage It has been determined in many companies that it costs 30 per cent per annum of the total valuation of stocks, to hold stocks. This is a serious point and an explanation is necessary. The major cost is the opportunity cost of capital. If the money was not tied up in stocks it could be profitably employed elsewhere. In addition there is the cost of providing space to keep the stocks (a considerable figure), wages and salaries to supervise the stores, risks and actual deterioration and obsolescence which will vary according to the nature of the company concerned. Insurance is a factor often overlooked when stocks are considered. The usual overhead costs will obtain: lighting, heating, cleaning, etc. It is also necessary to consider the major implications of late deliveries.

Production delays This is clearly of major concern to manufacturing companies who are concerned that they do not stop production lines. They will need to plan ahead and it is the duty of buying functions to ensure that costly delays do not occur. The buyer should not underestimate the effect on morale when workers have to be laid off. It is also likely that industrial relations problems may arise in these circumstances.

Increased administration costs Whenever supplies become overdue there will be an increase in administration costs. Routine expediting methods will become ineffective and will be replaced by expensive telephone calls. Visits to suppliers will become more frequent and costly.

Increased carriage cost The buyer may be tempted to resort to more costly forms of transport in an effort to hasten deliveries. Road transport may be replaced by air freight. There are legal overtones here which basically assert that the seller should pay because of his delays. Life is never so simple, however, and it may be contractually impossible to recover these extra costs.

Loss of goodwill The absence of materials when required may mean the loss of orders from customers. It is always difficult to assess the long-term implications arising from a customer's loss of confidence. The risks are certainly inherent in the situation and the buyer must recognise his responsibilities in the marketing and selling functions.

1.8 Research into total buying activities

Complacency is cancerous in any buying department. Existing procedures should be continually challenged — as should the use of purchasing techniques, sourcing decisions, and all other aspects of the buying function. In the small departments this presents a major difficulty due to staffing problems. The larger departments are more fortunate — they should be in a position to allocate staff who can devote their energies to the studies that may be undertaken by a purchasing research activity. It is vital that such an activity be established on correct management organisation lines. In terms of purchasing research this would mean an organisation similar to that shown in Figure 1.5. In such an instance the whole purchasing research section should be seen as a staff function. This is important because it is a support function and does not take buying decisions. Its task is to study any of the aspects detailed above plus those identified as requiring research studies. If it is made clear to the buyers that their tasks will be enhanced they should not be suspicious of the purchasing research function. The latter should be at pains to provide a service, giving the detailed information of use to the buyer. Examples of what can be undertaken are detailed below.

Market studies These should deal with existing purchased commodities. The duty of purchasing research is quite simple — to undertake a full market study to reveal all potential suppliers with whom the buyer may conduct future negotiations. This aspect of the function is a key duty involving necessary travel and expense.

Statistics The buyer's job is becoming increasingly dependent upon the use and presentation of statistics. One major need is the monitoring of all statistical data regarding indices relevant to key areas of spending. At the minimum this will involve labour and material index movements. This is essential because these elements are certain to be the basis of suppliers' price increase requests.

Reporting Management will require basic information from the buying function. This should be collated centrally and the purchasing research function is ideally placed to meet this demand. It can, for instance, work closely with the finance department to produce reports of price movements and forecasts. These are of potential use to the marketing people who may have to change price levels if price movements are to the disadvantage of the buyer's company.

Price analysis Whenever major negotiations are due to take place the buyer will require a detailed background on the whole basis of likely price discussions. This is time-consuming and he would be well advised to share the responsibility with purchasing research specialists.

Systems analysis Existing systems should be challenged continually since they may need changing to meet what is always a dynamic environment.

1.9 Economic and buying interface

Economic events have a continuing, direct interface with the buying function — a fact that is ignored in many organisations. The buyer who operates in ignorance of economic events is

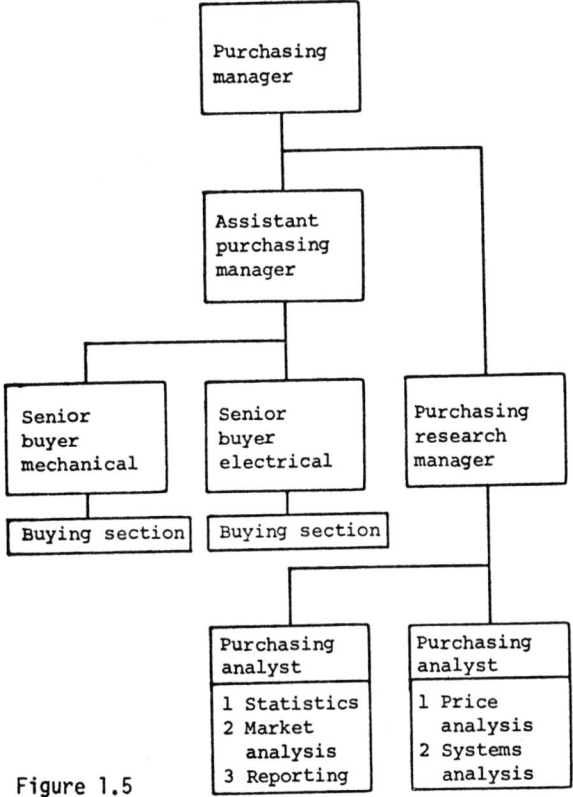

Figure 1.5

hindering or preventing normal trading conditions. A watchful eye is needed to ensure that maximum advantage is obtained from foreign trade.

Multinational organisations   The industrial trend is towards conglomerates and multinational organisations. These, in many ways, can have an impact on the buyer's efficiency. Pricing can be abnormal because of transfer pricing arrangements. In some instances the buyer will need to be wary as to who owns a particular company. This could have contractual overtones. If it becomes necessary to sue a trading organisation whose headquarters are overseas, serious problems could arise, because of the conflict of national commercial laws and their interpretation.

ignoring an influence on his job which may eventually catch him unawares. There are many examples that could be used to illustrate this point but those that follow have arisen recently.

Trading blocs The European Economic Community is a further trading bloc to come into prominence. In line with other similar communities they are establishing revised trading barriers which affect those outside the Community. This is not unique to the EEC. It is a feature throughout the world, which serves to demonstrate the considerable influence that policies have on foreign trade. There needs to be a serious appraisal by the buyer of likely interference in the market place in which he operates.

The laws of supply and demand In a perfect market the laws of supply and demand would fix the price of a commodity. Unfortunately the world does not operate in such a way to suit the economists' more ideal theories. The laws are interfered with in many ways. Tariffs, quotas and other import restrictions are all designed with a view to promoting.

1.10 Analysis of purchase price

A welcome trend in recent years has been the increasing awareness that the buyer should attempt to know as much about a selling price as does the seller. This is a vital principle for all buying departments. They are spending their organisations' monies and should expect to be held fully accountable for spending it wisely. A hypothetical — but typical — example can serve to illustrate the point.

The buyer receives six tenders for a vital piece of capital equipment — see Figure 1.6. At face value all six suppliers can meet the specification. To whom would you award the contract? The majority would select supplier D on the basis that all things being equal he offers the best price and the best delivery. So far so good. Assume that the contract is awarded to supplier D. How does the buyer know that his price is the best possible? On the facts above, he doesn't. It may be that the right price should be £35,000, conversely it could be supplier B whose price is appropriate.

If the buyer is doing his job properly he should have an estimated cost before he invites tenders. Any selling price consists of a number of elements — Material, Labour, Overheads, Profit.

Obviously this explains matters in their simplest form. In many instances the buyer's organisation will be in a position to estimate the likely cost of materials in his contract. This will also apply to the labour element. The situation gets more involved when the seller's overheads and profit elements are concerned. Let there be no misunderstanding, these are the concern of the buyer. He should ensure that the seller, normally, makes a reasonable profit but not an excessive one. The buyer is also concerned that the seller apportions only those overheads applicable to his contract to the final cost. It is in this area that much scope for negotiation may arise because the allocation of overheads very often cannot bear close scrutiny.

It is the buyer's role to create an environment whereby the seller is prepared to discuss his costs in detail. This demands from him a recognition that he will honour such confidences and will not divulge them to third parties. Given this cooperation it is always possible that the buyer can offer genuine help to the seller to reduce his costs. Two examples may be cited here. The seller may not have a professional buyer and may thus spend excessive amounts on raw materials. By considerate counselling the buyer may be in a position to advise a more competitive source. In this way the seller benefits twofold. The contract under discussion becomes

Supplier	Price, £	Delivery, weeks
A	55,160	20
B	60,107	18
C	87,206	36
D	45,305	12
E	51,000	40
F	67,511	16

Figure 1.6.

more competitive and similar products may be reduced in price. The seller may, unwittingly, be using outdated methods of manufacture. The buyer may be able to advise on more modern techniques of production. He would not do this in isolation, of course. Production management specialists and possibly quality control personnel could advise on the methods of keeping rejects within acceptable limits.

It should now be evident that buying departments who have put themselves in an advantageous trading position are those who have adopted purchase price analysis techniques.

1.11 Measure and monitor performance

There is an urgent need for the buying function to develop ways of measuring the effectiveness of its role. This is essential if any form of credibility is to be obtained. The measuring of performance must include failure, in addition to success. Only in this way can there be an environment whereby failures are critically appraised. For example, stock-out situations may be caused by ineffective expediting methods. If so the cause needs to be examined. Perhaps it was a faulty material release system. This can be changed for the good of everyone concerned and this is the environment that should be created. If people can see that there is no witch hunt taking place and that there is a singleminded intention to improve methods, co-operation will be obtained from all involved. Detailed views on measuring and monitoring performance are included in Chapter 9.

1.12 Summary

This opening chapter has concentrated on establishing an outline philosophy for any buying function. This philosophy applies to all levels of management, from the board of directors to the most junior staff. If everyone adopts a positive attitude that declares an intent to make all the aspects of the 'stream concept' work, there will be obvious improvements in performance. This sets the scene for the remainder of the book which is aimed at a practical demonstration of the ways in which anyone can improve his ability and make an increased contribution to the profitability of his company.

2 Organisational Relationships

How can buying make an effective contribution to an organisation's financial viability? What should be the buyer's role? Obviously, his role and scope will vary greatly depending on the size and nature of the organisation. A managing director's view of buying within the total procurement function will have a significant bearing on how it may be supported and developed. The function may be represented by one person responsible for buying a limited range of commodities with low annual expenditure. At the other end of the scale, buying may embrace purchasing research, expediting, material control and stores. Such a department may have a large staff responsible for an annual expenditure exceeding £100 million and may be located at group, division and works sites.

We are heartened by evidence that directors of many organisations are taking an increasing interest in buying. There is a greater awareness that as 50 per cent or more of an organisation's total expenditure may be accounted for in bought-out goods and services, such expenditure must be efficiently and effectively controlled. As a result of this awareness, enlightened managements are directing efforts to organise and adequately staff their buying departments with trained, higher calibre staff. This enables them to make greater progress to meet their objectives of buying plant, equipment, materials and services to meet an organisation's requirements at the minimum economic true total cost.

For buying to make its required contribution to an organisation's financial viability, it must be allowed to play a full and effective role within the organisation. What sort of foundation is required from which to build, to achieve this objective? The chief executive must take the first action. He has to decide precisely what the role of buying should be. He will be faced with a greater organisational problem when buying is more than a singly housed department but is dispersed across group, division and works sections in two- or three-tier structures. The degree of centralisation or decentralisation will have advantages as well as disadvantages. When centralisation is undertaken, lines of communication with works or site offices will extend. Directors of purchasing and their purchasing managers must pursue policies to avoid or at least to minimise the development of staff frustration and morale problems, particularly at works or site offices where buyers are actively concerned in meeting day to day requirements. Group, central or divisional buying departments must not be so managed that they develop a 'head office' complex and become too remote and isolated from their works or site staffs.

Much restructuring of buying is taking place in many companies and public undertakings at the present time. This activity inevitably results in the transfer and movement of staff with consequent personnel problems when staff are relocated in other offices, particularly in other parts of a country, with attendant disruption to home life. Managements must plan well in advance when such restructuring is envisaged. They should arrange preparatory discussions with staff representatives at the earliest possible stage to explain how they propose to minimise staff problems. Good communications are the basis of good relationships and managements must set the example and inform staff on matters of concern as quickly as circumstances allow. Where centralisation of divisionalisation takes place, this will result in the transfer of work loads. Such re-organisation frequently presents a works or site purchasing manager or buyer with divided responsibilities. They may be responsible to a central purchasing, divisional or group purchasing director or manager for policy, and at the same time be required to provide a works or site manager with the day to day service he needs to meet his operational commitments.

Staff career prospects are an important aspect to which much thought must be given, particularly when an organisation embarks on a buying development or restructuring program. Staff should be given reasonable opportunities for training and development so that their knowledge, experience and skills can be harnessed to the full mutual benefit of their organisation and themselves. Whilst it is important to have a career development program for existing staff, a realistic staffing policy must cater for an influx of new staff into buying from other functions and from outside the organisation too. Buying needs this widening of experience and the stimulation of new ideas which newcomers may bring. Such a policy has to be explained to existing personnel so that new staff can be quickly and smoothly integrated into the organisation.

The buying role must be defined in clear unambiguous terms. This would take the form of a buying or procurement document. This document would include not only terms of reference for the buying department, but it would include also, terms of reference for associated departments involved in the total procurement function. This is a sound first step but is only meaningful if the policy document has the full and continuous backing of all directors, and secondly, and equally importantly, buying has full and effective representation at board level. In a large organisation, a purchasing director may be responsible for a function which could vary from buying only, to a broader materials management concept. The position would be somewhat different in a small organisation where the director with responsibility for buying might also control other functions such as engineering, projects or estimating. Whatever the director's span of control, buying policies and procedures must also have the full and active backing of his fellow directors. Only with such support at board level, can a buyer under the direction of his purchasing manager, have scope to achieve his objectives.

Buying departments cannot provide an effective service, as some managers may believe to be possible, by operating in isolation. They must not restrict their activities to receiving and processing documents, making decisions and placing purchase orders without necessary consultation with specifying and using department staff. Buyers must have an understanding of the needs of users. The buying department must be a fully integrated member of an organisation team from which positive constructive attitudes are developed, each department co-operating with one another to achieve common objectives. Within such an environment, buying cannot be inward-looking. It must provide the service demanded of it and, therefore, win the respect and confidence of other departments. Buying must develop and retain a professional image. It must have credibility.

2.1 Buying staff relationships

Let us assume that a buying policy document has been issued which has the full backing of the directors. If the buying department is now to fulfil its role, it must be soundly organised and adequately and competently staffed. Staff capabilities must be developed to the full and efforts harnessed and directed under good leadership. The buyer's relationships with his colleagues in other departments must also be developed and improved. There are greater opportunities for achieving this objective when internal relationships within the buying department are satisfactory.

2.1.1 *Communications*

The basis for good relationships is good communications. A purchasing manager may have the same basic communications problems that face his colleagues in other departments. He must, therefore, first select, train and develop the members of his departmental team. He has to evaluate the work load of his department and then delegate and share the work fairly, defining also the duties and responsibilities of each member of his staff. To assist him in this task, he must prepare job descriptions and ensure they are updated as job content changes. Each member of his staff thus knows what his own duties and responsibilities are and, therefore, what is expected of him. Staff should also have a reasonable knowledge of the duties and responsibilities of their section heads, colleagues and assistants. This information can be provided in the form of an office manual which includes all buying department job descriptions.

A buyer must know within what limits he is able to take action and make decisions and in what circumstances he needs to refer to his section head or manager for guidance or action. Good communications are essential and they must operate vertically and laterally. The manager must inform his staff on matters of interest or concern to them. He would also expect that in return, his staff would not allow problems to develop, including deterioration in relationships, but they would inform him promptly, thus giving him reasonable time to deal with such problems at an early stage and take corrective action. A manager must have good communications with his staff and know when a situation is deteriorating. Such a departmental environment, coupled with a demonstrated concern for the well-being of his staff, will result in a manager winning their confidence and trust. He can then build from sound foundations to train and develop an effective team.

2.1.2 *Buying and expediting*

A buyer may be responsible for buying and expediting functions but it is frequently the practice to divorce expediting from buying and to handle it under a separate section which may or may not come under buying control. In some organisations, expediting may be controlled by material control or production control managers. Buying and expediting are related activities which require the exercise of different skills. Nevertheless, the two activities are closely associated and complementary within the total procurement function, irrespective of where the functions are carried out and who controls them. When expediting comes within the buying sphere the manner of its performance directly affects the latter's image. Buyers and expeditors need to work closely together and learn how they can assist each other to avoid or to minimise procurement problems, simplify work load and increase combined effectiveness.

The buyer's task can be simply stated even though it may be difficult to carry out. He has to source, negotiate and place orders with suppliers whom he has assessed to be capable of meeting his requirements on quality, deliver, price and after-sales service. Once the buyer has placed his order, an expeditor may then take over responsibility to progress or expedite it with the supplier. It is normal practice for the expeditor to receive a copy of all purchase orders placed. His job is to plan when and how he will progress orders with suppliers to meet required or agreed delivery or completion dates. He must keep the buyer concerned informed of suppliers' delivery performances so that the buyer will be better informed when he negotiates future orders. The expeditor may be unsuccessful in his attempts to get a supplier to deliver in time. Such a situation may become all too frequent in times of national or international economic difficulties. The expeditor can seek the buyer's assistance to press a supplier to take more positive action to retrieve or to improve on an unsatisfactory delivery promise. The buyer's scope for such action will depend to a great extent on his personal standing with the supplier and the value of future business he may have to place. The buyer may need to find an alternative source of supply. He may be able to transfer the whole or part of an order from the existing unsatisfactory supplier where such action is possible and desirable. The buyer/expeditor relationship is a key one. The buyer is able to appraise more adequately an existing supplier when information on his delivery performance has been received from the expeditor.

The expeditor may occasionally find it necessary to take special action with a supplier either to obtain deliveries to time, or to minimise delays. Before taking any action which might affect price or quality, he must first consult with the buyer. This is important because to retrieve a slippage situation, a supplier might propose to introduce overtime working, process the order on higher costed machines, or sublet the whole or part of the order, at increased cost, to another supplier. The expeditor's task is to progress orders to meet delivery requirements without incurring additional charges. Where he finds it impossible to achieve this aim, he must consult with the buyer concerned and with using or requisitioning staff as necessary.

2.1.3 Line and staff

In addition to buying and expediting activities, many buying departments, certainly in the larger, more enlightened organisations, operate purchasing research as a separate staff function. This is an area of buying in need of much greater development. Where the scope exists it should be a separate staff function. A purchasing research specialist heading a small team, or working as an individual, can undertake the work of locating new sources of supply, forecasting price and availability, purchase price analysis and value analysis in conjunction, as necessary, with technical staff. Purchasing research staff should not be involved in day-to-day buying activities. Such work should be done by line buyers who have to learn to cope with the daily pressures associated with their jobs. Buying performance can be greatly improved when purchasing research provides an effective complementary service.

Inevitably, when two such staff groups work closely together within a department, viewpoints may be strongly expressed on the relative contributions made by each group. The purchasing manager must ensure that these two aspects of buying are properly coordinated and that the staffs concerned clearly understand what their separate but complementary roles are. They must work closely together in the best interests of their department and their organisation as a whole. Satisfactory working arrangements must be established between line and staff functions. Buyers have an obligation too. They must co-operate with their purchasing research colleagues and provide the necessary data to enable them to investigate areas for achieving cost savings — savings that would be in their mutual interest. Purchasing research staff must appreciate the nature and the pressure of demand on busy buyers and so, in seeking their co-operation, they must demonstrate the type of service they can provide and the advantages to be gained by looking broadly and deeply into supply problems. Purchasing research staff must sell their service: they have to show tangible and significant results achieved; they must stimulate buyers' interest in the task of raising buying standards, achievable by their combined efforts to tackle procurement problems of quality, delivery, price or inventory, to increase departmental productivity and effectiveness.

2.1.4 *Commercial versus technical background*

What should a buyer's background be? What qualifications does he need? Should he have been trained in the technology of his firm? Much will depend on the specialised nature of the plant, equipment, materials or services bought and on the support technical staff give buyers. The reasons for selecting buyers with particular experience or qualifications may be traditional. It is important that a buyer should have a flair for buying and be a competent and an enthusiastic person. He must have an open mind and always be prepared to learn. Buying departments may have a policy to employ commercially or technically trained staff. They may combine the two. Individual buyers, whatever their backgrounds, should work together to achieve an effective total result. We know buyers with very different backgrounds who are equally successful doing similar jobs. In one particular buying department, the general buyer is commercially trained; his colleague, the engineering buyer, came from engineering into buying. Each gives invaluable assistance one to the other, increasing their knowledge and appreciation of engineering or commercial aspects. This is how buyers should work — together — irrespective of previous experience or qualifications. In so doing they inevitably help themselves as well as increasing their contributions to the work output and effectiveness of their departments.

2.2 Relationships with other departments

Buying is at the very centre of the total procurement function. Good relationships developed within the buying department must be extended to embrace other departments within the organisation, particularly requisitioning and using departments, financial and accounting, stores and material control, production control, sales and marketing, EDP and the typing pool. Buying must have close links with all these departments.

2.2.1 Production

High on the list of a production manager's priorities is the desire to have sufficient quantities of materials to support his production program. He and his staff will be concerned that material supplies will be assured and, of course, they look to buying to provide an efficient and effective supply service. The nature of pressures exerted on a production manager will determine how much he in turn applies pressures on buying. His lack of confidence in buying will encourage him to build up his material stocks and to demand too high a quality of material to avoid possible production delays which could result from material delivery or quality problems. An optimum balance is required in terms of operating costs, production lost time, production yield and capital tied up in material stocks. In the latter case, it will be appreciated that in times of inflation or anticipated scarcity there may be an obvious advantage to build up stock levels. However, whatever circumstances exist, there will be an optimum level for operating stocks.

In some organisations, efforts are coordinated to investigate and report on production lost time, production yield and stock levels within the framework of a sound economic policy so that proper emphasis is given to material stock levels in a given market or production situation. Not all organisations, however, give sufficient time and attention to the full economic considerations and consequently undue pressure may be applied on a production manager to increase his material stocks or to increase his material quality. He may thus adopt an over-cautious attitude on stock levels and apply pressures to buying accordingly. Such a situation can and does so easily develop. The buying department faces a particular problem in these circumstances. Having selected existing suppliers by supplier appraisal, the buyer may be forced to re-source to locate other possible suppliers who may be better able to meet production requirements, but at increased cost. The buyer is on trial. He must demonstrate the quality of the service he can provide and so convince production managers that stock levels can be reduced to acceptable economic levels and quality standards can be set at acceptable minimum standards. This is a selling job for the buyer. He has to convince the production manager he can operate on tighter margins. Of course, such target reductions cannot be achieved overnight. The process of convincing the production manager may be a slow one. The buyer has to win and retain his confidence in buying's ability to provide specified materials to time. Such confidence, once gained, must not be lost otherwise the buyer may face a long uphill struggle to regain the future co-operation of the production manager.

The buying/production relationship is two-directional. Production managers and their staffs can and must provide assistance to the buyer, particularly when production schedules have been revised or are to be revised. The buyer must be informed properly so that he can take necessary action (in conjunction with the expeditor where he is involved) to defer, suspend, cancel of advance deliveries to meet revised programs. Where the production department is responsible for quality control, it must co-operate with buying and inform the buyer concerned immediately quality problems arise. Where the production department requisitions materials, buying must keep it informed of current delivery periods, certainly for items of significance so that requisitioning staffs can, in turn, seek to give the buyer adequate notice of requirements.

2.2.2 Engineering

The engineering department is concerned with design, development and maintenance and thus is responsible for preparing specifications or checking existing ones. Engineering staff may have decided views on equipment or material specifications which give the buyer little or no scope to seek competitive quotations, with consequent loss of opportunities for achieving savings. There may be suitable lower priced alternatives available in the market which meet specification requirements but because an engineer is satisfied with the quality of goods previously obtained from established sources of supply he is, therefore, loath to agree to change suppliers. Good engineering means economic engineering. A buyer may need occasionally, to persuade an engineer to be less restrictive and to prepare and submit specifications which are adequate but no more for their intended purpose, giving the buyer scope to source more widely. It is in this area, particularly, where engineers and buyers need to co-operate to achieve advantageous buying.

'Value in use' is the criteria against which buying performance is ultimately measured. Buyers must not seek the lowest prices to the detriment of quality, delivery or after-sales service. Value in use must include the cost to production which results from equipment and material delays or defects. Buyers must not have a restricted outlook if they wish to have credibility and to obtain co-operation from engineering staff. They should keep engineers informed of anticipated changes in supply and delivery periods of significant items and of new sources of supply, new materials and processes which may provide opportunities to reduce equipment or material costs.

Engineers, for their part, must give buyers adequate scope to buy keenly by ensuring that, in addition to preparing adequate specifications, they enable buyers to source widely to obtain competitive quotations. During technical discussions with suppliers' representatives, engineers must avoid giving information which might jeopardise the buyer's scope for negotiating commercial aspects, particularly on price. Having satisfied themselves a supplier can meet the specifications required, technical staff will undermine the buyer's position if they say to the supplier 'when you get the order' instead of 'if buying places the order with you'. One simple word 'when' inadvertantly used, will result in higher prices being paid or in a loss being incurred in some other way. Engineers and other requisitioning staff must give the buyer as much time as possible to procure. A combined operation can then be mounted, with the aid of the expeditor, to plan and tackle an effective procurement program. This is another area where 'Pareto's Law' (the 80/20 law) should be applied. All staff concerned should identify the '20 per cent of items which are likely to cause '80 per cent' of their problems on quality, price, delivery, after-sales service on inventory.

Buying and engineering are complementary functions within total procurement. The engineer designs, specifies, installs and maintains; the buyer sources, negotiates and buys. The two may jointly carry out an appraisal of possible suppliers. It may be necessary in some circumstances, particularly where complex plant, equipment or materials are being ordered, for the engineer to be involved with the buyer in commercial negotiations. Frequently, project and contract engineering staff may be involved in lengthy discussions with suppliers and sub-contractors on projects which may or may not materialise into contracts. There is a need in such circumstances for an understanding to be reached between engineering and buying so that the buyer is kept informed of developments and can become involved in commercial negotiations at the appropriate stage. Certainly, buyers must appreciate that they need technical assistance, support or even lead occasionally, when negotiating particular commercial aspects on special orders. For example, where the organisation is placing orders for major site work of complexity, buyers must not only familiarise themselves with contractual aspects relating to site work and particular site regulations in force, but be prepared to work closely with technical staff during negotiations and to plan an agreed strategy for dealing with such aspects.

2.2.3 Accounts

Virtually every purchase order placed involves an accountancy transaction; invoicing, charging out to stores, work in progress or to contract. The buyer must ensure that each requisition he receives has the correct cost allocation 'capital', 'revenue', 'contract', 'stores', so far as he is able to determine, and that this allocation is typed on each purchase order to facilitate subsequent financial control by accounts department.

In negotiating the purchase order, the buyer may occasionally, have to accept special terms of payment including a down payment with order. When buying abroad, he may have agreed payment in a foreign currency. A buyer should consult with his accountant colleague before entering into any commitment with a supplier that requires the accountant's sanction or approval. There are many areas where buying and accounts need to work together including reconciling invoiced and order prices to facilitate the clearing of invoices.

Where the stores function is a buying responsibility, buying will be concerned that goods received notes are cleared promptly by stores and routed to accounts for reconciliation with invoices. With such responsibility for stores, buying would also be involved in inventories, stocktaking and audits. It would, therefore, have to work closely with accounts providing necessary assistance on these activities.

Another area where the two departments may have to work together is on the disposal of surplus plant, equipment and scrap material (where the sale of such items is a buyer's responsibility). Here the buyer reverses his normal role and becomes the seller. Accounts will provide him with the book valuations of plant and equipment and cost allocations against which to credit scrap material sales. Once the buyer has negotiated a sale, he must notify accounts immediately in writing so that the items of plant or equipment can be deleted from the plant list (for plant revaluation purposes) and so that credit for scrap sales can be correctly allocated and charged. Accounts would then raise invoices and post to the merchant or scrap dealer.

To enable a buyer to harness his negotiating power he needs to know the value of annual business placed with suppliers of main commodities. Accounts can provide him with such information showing a comparison of expenditure over previous years with current 'year to date' figures. This sort of information is also very useful to purchasing research staff in assisting them to decide where their efforts should be concentrated, i.e. such statements will identify commodities of high annual expenditure. The accountant can also assist the buyer on supplier appraisal by investigating financial viability in conjunction, as necessary, with financial specialists.

2.2.4 Stores

When stores is a separate function and not combined with buying within an integrated supplies function, close links must be established between the two departments who share responsibility for minimising inventory levels. Stores must set stock levels in conjunction with buying and other departments concerned, agreed for each commodity but subject to revision to meet anticipated changes in usage and replenishment rates and financial policies. The stock controller must requisition promptly once re-order points are reached. Jointly, stores and buying must develop and operate satisfactory procedures which best serve their mutual interests.

In addition to normal procedures operating for goods-receives notes, stores staff must notify expeditors promptly when urgently required items are received into stores so that they can delete such items from their action lists to concentrate effort to outstanding items. Communications must work in both directions. Expeditors must notify storekeepers of anticipated deliveries of special loads so that prior arrangements can be made to receive and offload. Such requirements may include the use of cranes or manpower not usually available outside stores normal working hours. Buyers and expeditors must keep suppliers informed of the times during which deliveries can be accepted. Special efforts may be needed to contact suppliers to hold deliveries prior to holidays or when labour problems or other restrictions affect normal arrangements for receiving goods. Consignment and delivery instructions must be clearly stated on purchase orders, and may include labelling instructions, advice note and lorry ticket requirements, item descriptions and reference coding numbers. Requirements may also cover all material and equipment consigned to stores from suppliers including free issue, samples and returned, repaired or reconditioned items.

2.2.5 Sales and marketing

Sales and marketing sell an organisation's products. They assess their probable share of a given market, increase or maintain business with existing customers and try to win new customers. These departments are, therefore, ideally placed to advise buying on forecasted budget production levels so that they can formulate long-term buying policies, particularly on high-value, high-volume items or those in short supply. Buying must be informed of anticipated changes in product demand which will affect the quantities or qualities of commodities purchased.

Where buying plays an effective part in an organisation's corporate planning activities, it is in a sound position to advise sales and marketing on the anticipated availability of key materials and components required for production, and also on probable price movements. Without such involvement in corporate planning, buying can make little or no contribution to assist sales and marketing in an integrated team effort.

Reciprocity of trade may be another area where the two departments can coordinate activities to work for the best interests of their organisation in both the long and the short terms. Resulting from anticipated changes in product demand, there will also be the need to identify anticipated obsolescence of plant, equipment and materials. Such an exercise may require production or engineering staff to co-operate with purchasing and sales to reschedule, phase-out materials and to minimise the value of such stocks.

2.2.6 Quality control

Quality control may frequently be involved with buying at the supplier appraisal stage before a purchase order is placed, to assist in determining to whom orders should be issued. Quality control staff will make supplier visits to investigate methods of manufacture, equipment standards and quality control inspection and test facilities. Following his inspection, the inspector would submit a report, the format of which will depend on requirements. Where contract specifications involve meeting the requirements of inspection authorities for say, welding, pressure vessels, cranes and lifting tackle, then inspectors may have to complete and submit standard supplier appraisal forms to the appropriate authorities to satisfy them on the capabilities and facilities of suppliers.

The paths of the two departments converge on purchasing research, value analysis and other cost reduction areas. Quality control must specify minimum standards of quality. Subsequently, quality control staff have to ensure that these standards are being achieved and maintained. Buyers must pass copies of relevant purchase orders promptly on quality control so that its work load can be planned with a knowledge of order commitments.

The quality control inspector must report to the buyer immediately he rejects items at the supplier's works or on receipt at the organisation's premises. The expeditor too, should be informed promptly so that he is aware what his outstanding commitments are. Quality control inspectors will, of course, assist suppliers to overcome manufacturing problems, to speed the rectification of defective items or to replace such items promptly. With the information he receives from quality control on suppliers' quality performance plus the information he receives from the expeditor on delivery performance, the buyer is better placed to negotiate future orders with suppliers with knowledge of their capabilities and reliability.

2.2.7 Material control

Material control may form part of production control or stores functions. It may be a buying responsibility. Where it is a separate activity, satisfactory working arrangements have to be developed between the two departments so that production commitments are met within minimum inventories. Material control will have data on standard and non-standard materials, usage rates, current stock levels, commited and free stocks, balances of outstanding quantities on order (and when due), and outstanding requisition quantities waiting to be placed on order. In consultation with production control, they will assess future commitments. Buyers must inform material control promptly on current and anticipated changes in delivery periods so that they can determine when and how much material to requisition.

The two departments must co-operate with stores to phase out stocks of materials not required for future production, to reduce obsolescent stocks to a minimum and to ensure, where it is economic to do so, that existing non-standard stocks are used and so avoid unnecessary ordering of standard materials.

2.2.8 Transport

Transport is an element of cost that buyers and expeditors may not always fully appreciate when they place or expedite orders. They need to be conversant with current transport rates related to size, weight and distance, full and partial loads and with regulations relating to drivers' working hours and wide load restrictions. Transport charges can be minimised when buyers and expeditors utilise their own organisation's vehicles returning from outward journeys empty or part loaded. The activities of buying and transport departments must be coordinated to avoid incurring unnecessary transport charges when bought-out goods are being consigned. The buyer must give a supplier clear consignment instructions so that his drivers will deliver goods accompanied by satisfactory documents. Lorry tickets should be correctly filled in and the goods labelled with correct descriptions, reference numbers, order and contract numbers as specified in the purchase order. On receipt of the supplier's vehicle at the buyer's premises, the transport department can then direct the driver to stores or other specified destination for offloading.

Transport insurance is another aspect in which a buyer should take special interest where his own transport department is using hired vehicles to carry the goods he has bought. He must satisfy himself that the various transport companies used carry adequate insurance to protect his organisation in the event of accident, loss or damage to bought-out goods being carried by those companies. The buyer should consult with the transport manager to obtain the names and addresses of transport companies used. He should write to each haulier and instruct them to submit copies of their insurance policies with evidence of premiums paid. He must know policy renewal dates and follow up to ensure that policies are renewed by due dates.

2.2.9 Electronic data processing (EDP)

Buying is ideally placed at the centre of the total material supply function to receive information generated from within and outside the organisation. The extent to which EDP is used in buying will depend on the size and nature of the buying commitment. Buying procedures should be automated only where an investigation shows that economic advantages will be gained by converting from manual operation.

Buying is perhaps one of the last functions to appreciate the possibilities of applying the computer as an aid. Purchasing managers, buyers and expeditors are not (generally speaking) oriented to systems and procedures and certainly not to data processing. However, where EDP is used, there is need for buying department staff to understand its application to buying and therefore, to be able to discuss problems with EDP staff and to evaluate any possible results from recommended changes. Computers are ideal machines to handle volume work, assess variables and to compute when and how much to buy to enable an organisation to operate with minimum inventories. Computers however, are as good as the quality of their input. Files have to be maintained, from accurate gathered data. This requires regular updating and the involvement of the buying department with a number of other departments including EDP, stores and material control.

Computer time has to be used economically. Computers serve many users. Allocation of computer time required for buying has to be discussed and considered against the needs of other major users. Buying staff must state their case and use negotiating skill to obtain a reasonable allocation of computer time. Purchasing managers, buyers and expeditors must co-operate with EDP staff in the design of viable, economic, flexible systems. This must not be a one-sided partnership. All parties concerned must make adequate contributions to the ultimate advantage of the buying function.

2.2.10 *Typing pool*

Typing arrangements vary from one organisation to another. Buyers, expeditors and purchasing research staff may have the services of typists, working ideally within their own department. However, typing might be a separate section operating as a centralised typing pool serving a number of departments. Purchasing work directed to a typing pool would include the typing of enquiries, purchase orders, amendments to orders and general correspondence. Buying staff passing work to typists must aim to simplify the latters' task by ensuring that handwriting is legible, instructions are clear, adequate and unambiguous, and presented in such a way or format to speed and ease work flow. Typists must be given priorities so that they can process work in the required sequence. Buyers and other departmental staff should, therefore, indicate required release dates for manuscript drafts they pass to typists.

A well typed and presented buying document enhances the buying image. Typists should, therefore, be selected and trained to specialise on buying work, wherever this is possible. They must produce neat and accurate work to minimise the possibilities of misinterpretation of order requirements by suppliers. They should be encouraged to work to high standards and to refer back to buyers and other staff on doubtful points in drafts. The partnership between buying and typists must be developed (certainly in a business sense). A good, experienced typist, able to specialise on buying work, familiar with the terminology and details normally included on buying documents, is an invaluable ally to the busy buyer, expeditor or purchasing research staff by providing a further check for clerical or other errors.

2.3 General comments on relationships

Buying must generate a positive and dynamic image through the actions of its managers, buyers, expeditors, purchasing research and other staff to provide an efficient and effective service to other departments. It must separate the important from the unimportant. Problem areas must be identified and priorities set. Urgent commitments must be dealt with promptly. Buyers, expeditors and purchasing research staff must concentrate efforts in areas which will yield the maximum return to their organisation. In addition to carrying out their actual buying, expediting or purchasing research activities, buying staff must provide the necessary information on a regular basis to requisitioning, using or other department staffs. Such information will enable recipients to note aspects of concern and to take necessary action. Such aspects would include material delivery periods, new sources of supply, new materials, products and processes.

Buying staff cannot establish good relationships unless they make sufficient efforts to avoid creating unnecessary problems for other staffs. They must demonstrate a capacity for logical, thorough and unbiased evaluation of, and for providing solutions to, supply problems. They must demonstrate competency. Considered judgements must be made on situations, not snap decisions taken on the basis of biased opinions or unsubstantiated facts. At the same time, buyers must demonstrate an ability to assess risk and the courage to act on evidence available. They must, however, be sensible and consult with knowledgeable and interested parties who may be able to contribute to good decision-making.

Buying is a key function which has not yet acquired total international or national status and recognition. Greater efforts must be made to train and to educate buyers and their colleagues in associated departments. Many staff may be involved in the complete procurement cycle from requisitioning to invoicing of goods and services. Buying cannot, therefore, operate within rigid lines of demarcation. It must seek to understand and appreciate the problems facing others. Buyers, particularly, often feel that many of their problems arise from the shortcomings of others (not planning work or consulting with buying). Other staff may become involved with suppliers on commercial aspects because of tradition or circumstances. The buyer has to demonstrate clearly and firmly that he is the person best equipped to handle procurement requirements. He is the person to obtain the goods at the right place and quality, and perhaps with an expeditor's assistance, to time.

Specialists, designers and other requisitioning staffs have their problems too. They may not always be able to give the buyer reasonable notice of requirements. Emergencies may arise outside their control. Within limits, this must be accepted as part of the way of life, certainly within industry. Buyers, however, can and should educate and convince requisitioning colleagues to plan their work more thoroughly in the interests of all concerned. With more time at his disposal, a buyer can then provide them with a more effective service.

A buyer must work hard to win co-operation from other staff. He must go beyond half-way in assisting colleagues to get work on the move. Where he knows a particular important item should have been requisitioned and there is a delay in the system, he should investigate. He must not sit back feeling that as the delay is not of his making it is not of his concern. A positive, dynamic attitude taken by a buyer is to his ultimate advantage. His reputation will grow and interdepartmental relationships will improve as he shows interest and active involvement in matters of mutual concern. Obviously a buyer can lean too far in attempts to assist others, to the detriment of some of his other work. There must be a sensible limit to which any person goes to co-operate with others. The buyer requires a good commonsense approach. He needs to think as an organisation team man.

Because of the very nature of buying, staff from other departments may become involved in strictly buying activities, reducing the buyer's scope to source and negotiate. In such circumstances, management should take corrective action. Purchasing managers should draw the attention of 'offenders' to the organisation's buying policy and give them the opportunity to avoid infringements in future. Where such involvement by other staffs is not corrected, not only does inefficient buying result, but buyers may lose confidence and become frustrated and aggressive in their attitudes. They may become less likely to co-operate and not take corrective action to minimise the effects of the shortcomings of others. Such lack of responsible action is to be deplored but it is understandable. The buyer, can do much to overcome this type of problem, prevalent in many organisations, by striving to be more competent, by learning about the commodities he buys and the uses to which they are put. He must learn more, too, about his major suppliers, their facilities and their capabilities. His manager must allow him reasonable time to visit suppliers' works for this purpose.

The buyer's colleagues in other departments must, for their part, try to give reasonable notice of requirements and to notify him promptly when problems arise which require his action. They must be constructive in their criticism of his apparent actions or lack of actions, first establishing the facts before making comments or accusations. The buyer may not have been aware of a particular need. He may have been severely restricted by pressure of work from carrying out a task. The buyer must have reasonable time and scope to source. A specification must not, therefore, be over-elaborated or be an unnecessarily restricted brand obtainable from one supplier only. Requisitioners must specify their quality-standard requirements and state what assurance or test certificates may have to be provided. They must give the buyer, also, adequate consigning and labelling instructions.

2.4 Summary

Organisational relationships must be fostered and developed to a high standard. To achieve this desirable, indeed essential, objective:

1 The buying role must be clearly stated.
2 Directors must give full and continual support to the buying policy.
3 An organisation team must be developed within which buying can be an effective member.
4 Buying must be well organised, adequately staffed,

trained and well led.
5 Buying staff must be outward looking in order to gain the confidence, support and co-operation of other departments.
6 Buying must be professional in its approach. It must have credibility.

3 Systems and Documentation

Purchasing managers, generally, need to give more thought to systems and documentations. Effective purchasing is impossible unless satisfactory procedures are implemented and documentation designed to meet departmental needs. Purchasing managers must appreciate, however, that the needs of other departments must also be taken into account as many staff may be involved in the total procurement cycle. Over-elaboration must be avoided. Systems have to be operated and documentation used by less experienced junior staff as well as by their senior colleagues.

An essential first step towards introducing and operating effective buying procedures and documentation is to list all forma and documents used within the buying department including the input and output documents which it handles. We have concentrated on the more important documents required in a buying department. Whilst actual sample documents are not provided, a descriptive account is deemed essential. This should be used as a check list. It is futile plagiarising other firm's documents. The ideal document is one specifically designed to meet all one's needs. Documents required and used include:

1 Purchase requisitions
2 Stores traveller requisitions
3 Suppliers records
4 Supplier visit records
5 Enquiries

6   Quotations
7   Purchase orders
8   Local purchase orders
9   Letters of authorisation
10 Order acknowledgements
11 Expediting records
12 Supplier visit reports
13 Advice notes
14 Disposals
15 Catalogues
16 Annual contracts

   All tasks undertaken by staff, the format and routing of documents should be included in written draft buying procedures. The purchasing manager may require assistance from his organisation and methods colleagues to set down the details of current procedures as a basis for investigation and discussion with all interested parties from which to formulate effective procedures. Failure to tackle the assignment in a logical and practical manner will inevitably result in essential information not being provided, or being provided inadequately. Also, duplication of effort may result between departments or within sections of a department. Purchasing managers must avoid taking procedures or documents successfully used elsewhere and attempting to use them without considering modifications necessary to meet the specific needs of their own departments. The successful operation of a procedure or use of a document will depend on the receptive attitudes of those staff within or outside the buying departments who are required to use them. The purchasing manager has a selling job; he has to convince all parties concerned with procurement of the necessity for their implementation.

   He should convince them that the advantages of implementing his proposals will outweigh alternative proposals which may be suggested. We have seen many examples of inadequately operated procedures resulting from failure to consider the views of interested parties prior to implementation. Take as an example, a purchase requisition. Should this be a form designed to meet the needs of the requisitioner and buyer only? A number of other staff may be concerned in the design of this document. Typists have a particular interest because the greater part of their working day may be spent typing purchase orders from requisitions. Where the format of the two documents is dissimilar this will automatically slow the rate of typing as the typist has to pick out sections of information from the requisition and type them in different locations on the order document. Where a requisition is similar in format to the purchase order, this enables the typist to maintain a smooth flow of words with greatly increased output and reduced errors. Stores and material control too, may handle requisitions before they reach the buyer to check if items requisitioned can be supplied from existing stocks and thus avoid duplication of orders or over-ordering. Stores will, of course, be particularly concerned with form design, especially when the requisition is a 'traveller' which passes between stores and buying providing a complete record of commodity quantities, dates requisitioned, order numbers, quantities ordered, order dates and suppliers. Stores may well have an equal say with buying in the format of this type of requisition.

Many aspects must be considered in the design of forms and documents. Quality of paper or card is important. How frequently will the form or document be handled? Will it be used once or will it need to be made from stiff paper or card to facilitate frequent handling. What size and shape should it be? Has it to be accommodated in existing filing cabinets? Where the document details are to be typed, are the lines and boxes so spaced to meet typewriter spacings to avoid time being wasted by typists who have to reset their machine to type within boxes or spaces.

3.1 Requisitioning

Requisitions sent to buying can be of several different types, depending on the nature of the requirement and the frequency of requisitioning.

3.1.1 *Purchase requisitions*

The purchase requisition form may be printed vertically or

horizontally lengthwise and may or may not be similar to the format of the purchase order form. The design of the purchase requisition and the extent of pre-printed details may vary appreciably. A compromise solution has to be reached. Requirements need to be adequately specified including cost allocations, authorisations or material reference under specific box or line headings as a guide to requisitioners to reduce recording time to a minimum but at the same time to produce an adequate document which is not over-elaborated and can be used for the majority of commodities or services being requisitioned. One sees many examples, particularly in industry, where requisition headings and instruction notes cover so many aspects that space available for the requisitioner to write his actual requirements is severely restricted. In a large organisation, demands on buying may be so varied that it may be advantageous to use two or three different requisition forms for the different applications and so optimise their use.

How many copies of a requisition are required? Some organisations use duplicate pads with requisitions numbered sequentially. The top copy is passed to buying. The carbon copy remains in the pad as a record of what was requisitioned and when. Other organisations prepare master requisitions from which several copies are produced for issue to engineering, production control and contracts estimating sections.

For a variety of reasons, what is finally ordered in terms of specification, quantities, delivery point and date may be different from what has been initially specified on a requisition. In our opinion, the number of requisition copies should be reduced to the minimum. In the case of the stores 'traveller' requisition a copy may not be required.

3.1.2 *Stores traveller requisition*

The stores traveller requisition is the ideal document to use for replenishment stock items. The form should be made of card to facilitate frequent handling. On reaching the order point, stores or material control enter the quantity, date requisitioned and required delivery date. The information is then recorded on the stock record card and the traveller sent to buying. The card must bear an updated, accurate specification of requirements. The names of previously approved and used suppliers would also be stated — possibly varying from one supplier (where there was only one known source) to six or more suppliers. Buying must, of course, re-source but the extent to which it does may depend on time available, probable annual expenditure or supply problems experienced. The card would detail a history of previous quantities requisitioned and ordered together with names of suppliers.

As a duplicate copy is not retained, it is particularly important to ensure prompt routing and action. Plastic wallets are ideal. They can be used to carry travellers between stores and buying, thus minimising possibility of misplacement or loss.

3.2 Commodity records

The buying department is the recipient of requisitions and other requests for enquiries. To deal with such documents, the buyer concerned needs a system that enables him to place requirements expeditiously at minimum cost and effort. To achieve this objective he must have adequate commodity records. Such records would be classified under commodities and include names and addresses of suppliers, prices and price increases and when introduced, an indication of quality and delivery performance. These latter details would be received from quality control and expediting. It is particularly important that buyers have adequate clerical support so that such records can be maintained up to date and information made readily available to the buyer when he receives a requisition or a request to issue an enquiry.

The commodity record may take the form of a record card or a loose-leaf sheet.

Another useful buying record is the suppliers' address card whose use simplifies and speeds the work of typists. All changes of suppliers' names and addresses received in the department must be passed promptly to the person responsible for maintaining the supplier records.

3.3 Supplier visit record

Where buying is responsible for making regular supplier visits the reports of such visits should be routed to the buying records section so that information can be abstracted. Supplier appraisal cards should be maintained giving details of the appraisals and the dates undertaken. Target dates for re-appraisal should be entered and a signalling system introduced to trigger off follow-up checks on suppliers.

3.4 Enquiries

The important points relating to the issue of enquiries are the time available for a thorough market search, existing knowledge of suppliers and the dates quotations are required. Where time is short, possible suppliers must be contacted by telephone or telex. It is important that the buyer concerned keeps a record of actions taken (attached to the requisition or enquiry request), so that in his absence such actions can be readily determined.

Where the buyer does not have a list of known approved or possible suppliers he may have been given a recommended name by the requestee. He must adequately source the market and check other possibilities from his directories — Kellys, Kompass, Sells, Rylands and Jaeger and Waldman or from any other avenues open to him.

3.5 Quotations

The initial requirement is to progress outstanding quotations not received by the closing date stated on the enquiry. Where the situation demands, a prior check should be made with suppliers to see if they will quote by the stipulated date. Should an extension to time be required, the buyer must check promptly with the requisitioner or others concerned to see if this can be allowed. This concession will depend on whether or not the delivery period likely to be given by the supplier will exceed the time which can be allowed for contract execution. Where an extension is granted to one supplier, others should be granted the same privilege.

3.6 Selection of short-list suppliers

Where there are a number of quotation details to evaluate, such details should be recorded on a quotation analysis sheet and would include supplier's name and address, what has been offered (additions, alternatives or exclusions against the specification), price(s), delivery and completion dates, terms of payment and any particular conditions of sale to be challenged. The extent to which technical staff or requisitioning staff need to be involved in the presentation of the analysis depends on the degree of complexity, i.e. determining technically what has been offered against what is actually required.

3.7 Evaluating quotations

Buying and requisitioning staffs should co-operate as necessary to evaluate technical and commercial content to compare offers made, rejecting initially those quotations which cannot be short-listed because of obvious unacceptability on specification, delivery or price. Where quotations have to be passed to technical staff for technical appraisal or evaluation, details of this action must be recorded and filed with enquiry documents giving date of release and the person to whom quotations have been passed. The buyer should note the dates by which decisions should be reached which allows time to place orders to meet required delivery/completion dates. Pending quotations must be progressed with those responsible for evaluation or authorisation so that requisitions (or other authorisation) can be issued to buying by agreed target dates to enable purchase orders to be placed to obtain required deliveries.

Where technical staff recommend placing work with a favoured supplier or contractor who has not submitted the lowest price, they must justify such selection (endorsed where necessary by their section heads) to the satisfaction of the buyer.

3.8 Purchase orders

The requisition is a key document because on receipt, the buyer has to prepare it for use as the order draft from which the typists can produce the purchase order. The draft document must be accurate, clear and unambiguous and be so set out to facilitate the typists's task of transferring information to transmit to the supplier. The buyer must indicate to the typist that he has processed the requisition into a draft order from which he or she can now type the order, i.e. he has completed all necessary information including order number, price and delivery.

3.9 Order number allocations

Order numbers are normally allocated sequentially, series of numbers sometimes being allocated for different categories of work such as 'stock', 'capital', 'contracts' and 'revenue'. To facilitate ready identification of goods by stores, expeditors and cost accounts, separate series of numbers may be allocated to individual major capital projects or contracts, etc. Four-, five- or six-digit numbers may be used to differentiate between different categories of orders. Changes in initial digits may be used as further sub-divisions between say, different types of contract.

The number of copies of orders normally required depends on the type of order and the organisation's requirements. The top copy is normally issued to the supplier. The buyer concerned requires an office copy which is normally filed sequentially by order number. The expeditor, accounts and stores require copies. Using, requisitioning, production, planning and EDP departments may require copies. The buyer's customer may require a copy where significant materials or items of equipment are being ordered for one of his contracts. Normally, unpriced copies of orders are issued to 'customers' and stores as it is normally considered to be undesirable to divulge prices paid. This approach is understandable in the case of the customer's copy. However, in the case of the stores' copy, there are two schools of thought. If stores is to be treated as an essential and responsible department then storekeepers should be aware of prices paid so that they too can apply Pareto's Law and devote adequate time to safe-guarding items of high value. The existing approach, unfortunately common in many organisations, is that storekeepers should not be aware of commodity prices. However, order prices must be treated in the strictest confidence and priced order copies not left lying around for perusal by third parties.

Purchase orders are usually prepared against requisition requests. In the case of blanket orders, the buyer determines the anticipated requirement for a contract period (usually a year) and gives the supplier some indication of the minimum and maximum quantities required. Once the contract terms have been agreed, the purchase order is issued and the buyer calls off quantities throughout the year on request from stores or material control. This call off can be done by telephone, telex or postcard, the supplier dispatching the goods and quoting the blanket order number on consignment notes. Subsequently, he submits his invoice for payment. As the cost of producing a purchase order can vary from (approximately) £2 to £6 there is a good case for considering the use of blanket orders for large quantity consumables. Paperwork is simplified and the buyer has increased bargaining power to negotiate acceptable discounts or annual rebates by aggregating his quantities in a blanket order.

3.10 Emergency orders

Whatever systems are introduced for purchase orders, allowance must be made for dealing with emergency requirements. Situations do arise in the best regulated organisations which necessitate suppliers being instructed to proceed with work before receipt of an official purchase order. The requirement may arise outside normal working hours when a contract or maintenance engineer needs material which he can obtain from a local stockist or wholesaler. He may require the service of a sub-contractor who is available to assist him in an urgent site job.

In such circumstances, the engineer concerned must be empowered to instruct a supplier to issue goods, or a contractor to provide a service, against an undertaking that buying will follow up promptly and issue an official purchase order. To cover such an eventuality, buying may need to allocate one or more order numbers to engineers for use only in emergencies together with an emergency order procedure instruction sheet. Scope for non-buying staff to place orders with suppliers must be restricted to a minimum for legitimate emergencies. Requisitions bearing allocated order numbers must be sent promptly to buying so that the suppliers can be given properly authorised purchase order documents, copies of which will go to stores and accounts for their information and subsequent action.

3.11 Local purchase orders

An organisation may have staff working on customers' sites in various parts of the home country or abroad and situations may arise where materials are required urgently and time does not allow normal procedures to be followed. Take, as an example, a contract engineer working on a customer's site. He may be unable to proceed with the contract for a number of reasons. The materials or equipment he requires may have been bought by his organisation and sent to the site, and lost or damaged on the way. It may not have been sent to the site and lies several hundred miles away in the main stores. There might have been an oversight at the requisitioning stage resulting in the required materials or equipment not being ordered. Such materials or equipment may be obtainable locally. To enable an engineer on site to deal with such circumstances he can be issued with a pad of local purchase orders, printed in triplicate and numbered sequentially. This allows him to contact local suppliers or sub-contractors and place local purchase orders with them. The local purchase order form would state that he is authorised to act on behalf of the purchasing manager up to a stated financial limit as stated on the local purchase order. Invoicing instructions to the supplier would also be stated on the document.

3.12 Letters of authorisation

Occasions may arise when it is not possible to release a purchase order promptly to instruct a supplier to proceed with work. Such occasions include the supplier requiring instructions immediately either to hold a price firm, to allocate work in his production programme or to release a suborder for an item on long delivery. To give the supplier a firm commitment, it would be necessary to send him a letter of authorisation. This letter (or telex) would specify requirements, the price or prices to be paid including discounts and the required delivery or completion dates. The buyer would also include details of agreed terms of payment and any other special terms and conditions of purchase which had been agreed for the proposed order.

It has been our experience that many suppliers do not act expeditiously on receipt of letters of authorisation because they are not certain that an official order will be forthcoming and that the buyer would stand costs incurred up to the time of such notifications or for losses sustained by the supplier, should he not be able to fill his production capacity because he had turned away other possible orders to undertake the buyer's work.

The buyer should therefore ensure that not only does he state precisely on what agreed terms and conditions the proposed order will be issued, but also when he expects to release the order. He should also state the order number allocated so that the supplier can book charges against the contract. The buyer must also state in his letter of authorisation that if he does not subsequently place the purchase order for reasons outside his control, he will reimburse the supplier for all reasonable and justified charges incurred by him up to the time of such cancellation. The buyer should also instruct the supplier to acknowledge promptly his receipt and acceptance of the letter of authorisation in accordance with the requirements. The buyer must set a target date and if the supplier does not acknowledge the letter by that date, he should not actively progress with him.

3.13 Order acknowledgement

Opinions may differ on how an order acknowledgement system should operate. Purchase orders fall into many categories, ranging from very important to relatively unimportant. Certainly, for important orders, a system is required to ensure that suppliers acknowledge receipts or orders with acceptance also of the price, delivery, specification and terms of conditions of purchase. Orders of significance should be treated as 'pending' until acknowledgements have been received. The buyer should include as a final clause to his order:

> '*Acknowledgement to Order*
> Please confirm promptly (or by stated date) your acceptance of this purchase order and your acceptance also of the specification, price(s) and delivery/completion and the stated special conditions of purchase.'

The buyer must set a target date for submission of acknowledgements to orders and introduce a signalling system through his own section or through the expeditor to expedite them if not received by the due date.

3.14 Reconciling acknowledgements with orders

The two documents must be compared and efforts made immediately to reconcile differences to the buyer's advantage, where this is possible. Unresolved differences may ultimately lead to contractual problems.

3.15 Expediting records and procedures

The essential first step is to ensure that a copy of each purchase order is passed promptly to those responsible for expediting. The buyer himself, or his buying clerk may be responsible for expediting or a separate expediting section may be responsible. It may not be policy to expedite every order placed and in such circumstances it may be decided to pass copies of every order to the person responsible for expediting who would discard copies not to be progressed. Normally at least two copies of a purchase order are distributed within the buying department; the sequential numbered order copy retained within the buying section on which price variations and other details would be recorded and a second expediting copy retained by the expeditors and filed alphabetically by commodity and supplier.

Orders for action may fall into two distinct categories; those which are progressed on a routeing basis by office-based expeditors and those which are progressed by expediting engineers who are required to visit the suppliers' works.

3.15.1 Initial action

On receipt of the purchase order copy, the expeditor must determine what the form of his initial action will be and when. Expediting systems can fall into the following forms:

1. Purchase order copy filed by next action date. The problem is to locate the order copy if required.
2. Purchase order copy filed by commodities and subdivided into suppliers alphabetically. The next action date would be marked on the copy and the order number recorded together with details of supplier and commodity in a diary. The expeditor can then progress all orders which fall due for progressing in a particular week (or day).

Some expeditors plan their intended expediting program and enter all the dates in their diaries. For example, consider an order being placed for delivery in ten months time. The expeditor would enter in the diary the first action date say, in six weeks time with subsequent actions dates at say, six-week intervals. The weakness of this system is that the expeditor may wish to completely revise his expediting program as a result of the information gained from his first action. There may be obvious signs of a supplier's failure to process work at a satisfactory rate so that checks must be made at monthly, three-week or two-week intervals in an effort to bring the supplier back on to target.

A card system can be used instead of a diary but this is really a diary used in an exploded form. To operate this method, a card is required for each week of the year and the expeditor enters the order number on the appropriate weekly card for action. As a back up to such a system it is more convenient to file order copies numerically to facilitate speedy location.

Computers are playing an increasing role in expediting.

3.15.2 *Contracts*

Expediting systems may also have to cater for expediting by contracts as a whole and not by individual orders. In these circumstances, a contract register is required on which the expeditor can record the details of all orders placed for the contract which would include order number, supplier, date of order, order description, date required, quantity, progress action and order requirements. Where an organisation is involved on its own capital plant project or on a major contract for a customer, it is essential that a contract register is prepared. All orders placed should be progressed with the knowledge of what is required in total. For example, should a delivery of a particular item need to be advanced. Similarly, should there be some delay to a particular item or replanning of the project a number of items may not now be required by dates previously given to the suppliers. The expeditor needs to be informed of such revised requirements so that he can replan his work load to deal with priorities and defer action on the less urgent requirements.

3.15.3 *Supplier work load*

Where a number of orders have been placed with one supplier, it is important for the expeditor to have a full picture of the work load so that he can determine the sequence in which orders should be processed for completion. It is important too, that all contact with the supplier on delivery is channelled through the expeditor responsible to avoid a clash of interests and confusion.

3.15.4 *Notification of deliveries to requisitioners and users*

Expeditors must keep appropriate staff informed of deliveries. This can be achieved by issuing a daily statement to production control, material control or contract engineers as necessary to inform them of items delivered the previous day. The daily return should also include details of revised promises received from suppliers. The expeditor would request the staff concerned to confirm if the revised dates were acceptable or not and to reply promptly. This daily return sheet would augment any urgent verbal contact which an expeditor had with requisitioning and using staff to deal with emergencies.

3.15.5 *Supplier visits*

Where expeditors or expediting engineers are required to visit suppliers' works for progress action, they should complete visit reports for appending to the progress file with copies to appropriate staff for information or for comment. Delivery may be running behind schedule or the supplier may be seeking information on some aspect which the expeditor cannot give. (The economies of planned deliveries are shown in Figure 3.1.)

3.15.6 *Advice notes*

Purchase order instructions would normally require suppliers to issue advice notes by post within 24 hours of goods being despatched. On receipt, the expeditor would note the details and pass the documents to stores (or vice versa) so that they could be tied up with delivery notes accompanying consignments. Discrepancies between advice notes, delivery notes and actual consignments would be noted and the supplier informed promptly so that he could take action, with his carrier if necessary, within the stipulated 10 to 14 days period.

Once stores and expeditors had dealt with the advice notes, these notes or 'goods received' copies of orders would be released by stores and forwarded to accounts to be checked against invoices when received.

3.16   Rejection/discrepancy notes

On receipt of goods into stores two checks would normally be made against delivery notes and advice notes (against which a supplier's invoice will be raised), the first on quantities and the second on acceptability against specification and quality standards including possible damage in transit, method of packing or anti-corrosive treatment. Where there are discrepancies a rejection/discrepancy note should be raised (a minimum of three copies), one to be sent to the supplier, one copy to the buying department so that the expeditor is aware that although stated quantities of items have been received or have been advised as having been received, there are shortages or damaged or reject items which need to be replaced.

3.17   Supplier/sub-contractor insurance and indemnity records

A separate file should be raised for all purchase orders which require insurance cover:

1   In the joint names of the supplier and the buyer for the period of manufacture where the buyer is making substantial progress payments in advance of delivery and for which he has transfer of title to the goods.
2   For sub-contractor employer liability, public liability and contract works all-risks insurance where the sub-contractor is engaged to work on site on behalf of the buyer.

In both cases, the buyer needs to satisfy himself that the supplier or sub-contractor has taken out adequate insurance which protects the buyer's interests in the event of accidents,

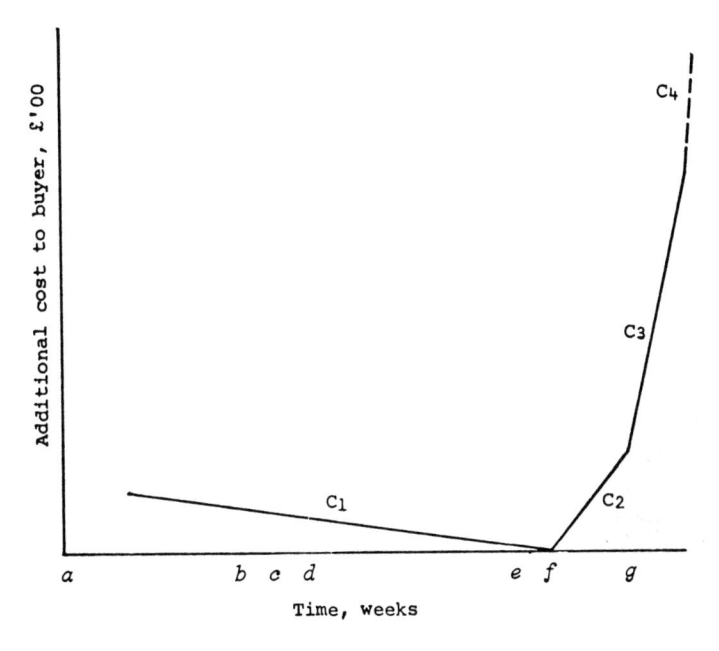

a Enquiry issue date
b Quotation required date
c Requisition release date
d Order release date
e Possible target date given to supplier
f Required delivery date (ideal economic date)
g Latest possible acceptable delivery date

Costs incurred

C_1 Losses resulting from early delivery loss of investment earnings, and possible loss, deterioration and damage, stockholding and possible double handling.
C_2 Losses resulting from replanning involving overtime working, utilisation of high-cost machines, additional work or sub-letting.
C_3 Lost production of liquidated damages to customer.
C_4 Cancellation charges to customer.

Note: the example assumes that the supplier will not increase his price during the period d–g.

Figure 3.1 The economics of planned deliveries

loss or damage. Copies of insurance documents should be obtained and filed with the appropriate orders, or letters obtained from the suppliers/sub-contractors' brokers confirming the extent of their clients' cover. Buyers should satisfy themselves that premiums are paid by renewal dates where these fall within the period of the contract.

3.18   Disposals

Where buying is responsible for the disposal of surplus plant, equipment and material, it is necessary to lay down strict procedures to avoid, or at least to minimise, the possibilities of malpractice. Buyers must take particular care to select reliable merchants, who in the event of their offers being accepted, would enter the buyer's premises to remove materials expeditiously avoiding interfering with other work and taking only those items selected for disposal.

Items for disposal can fall into a number of separate categories such as:
- Plant and equipment
- Ferrous materials
- Non-ferrous materials
- Commercial vehicles and cars
- Office equipment
- Surplus stores items
- General scrap

In the case of plant and equipment, Board approval may normally be required for disposal. Where the organisation is associated with other companies within a group, details of items of possible interest must first be circulated within the group before they are offered to merchants. Items may have plant item reference numbers and book values. Market values may, of course, be greater than book values and the buyer, with possible assistance from his technical colleagues, may need to determine the disposal target prices at which he must aim. The buyer would write to potential buyers and inform them what is being offered for disposal and ask them to phone to make an appointment to view.

The buyer should prepare his disposal sheets and record

details of the merchants, dates of inspection and prices offered. Where the best prices submitted fall short of the target prices, the buyer should negotiate to seek improvement. Finally, once a sale has been agreed, a standard letter would be sent to the merchant confirming the sale (with copies to accounts and transport), requesting the supplier to submit his invoice promptly. Transport would be instructed to raise the necessary consignment notes for collection by the merchant's driver.

3.18.1 Scrap material

The person responsible for disposal must agree schedules of rates per tonne for the different qualities of materials such as ferrous and non-ferrous metals. It is important that efforts be directed at the production stage to segregate the different qualities of scrap to simplify the work of disposal.

3.18.2 Commercial vehicles and cars

Usually, quite separate arrangements may be made to dispose of commercial vehicles and cars. An agreed list of approved dealers must be established and details of items for sale circulated inviting inspection and submission of offers.

3.18.3 Office equipment

Items for disposal are normally handled by the buyer responsible for buying the new equipment. He would negotiate to trade in the old equipment at agreed trade-in prices related to age, condition and market demand.

3.18.4 Surplus stores stocks

Stores items fall into two main categories — items of common use for which there may be a re-use value and items specifically designed for use within the organisation for which there is only a scrap value once they become obsolescent or surplus.

3.19 Catalogues

All catalogues and leaflets received from suppliers should be filed alphabetically by commodities, and the details entered on a register. A separate register should be raised alphabetically by suppliers and cross-referenced to commodities. Where a catalogue included a range of commodities it should be filed under the main commodity and cross-referenced sheets inserted in the appropriate sections of the file.

3.20 Private purchases

Policies vary on the subject of private purchases. Some organisations do not assist their staff in any way. Others may have arrangements with particular suppliers which enable staff to obtain discounts for purchases which they make direct on producing evidence that they are employees of the approved organisations. Some organisations operate a private purchase order system in a limited form and issue purchase orders to suppliers on behalf of the staff. Staff are required to give an undertaking that on receipt of the invoice by accounts from the supplier, they will immediately pay the amount due to accounts.

Normally a separate order number series is used to identify private purchases. A register should be maintained to identify the individuals and the orders issued on their behalf.

3.21 Annual contracts

A register should be maintained of all annual contracts placed. The register can be in the form of separate cards or an open-leaf book. Details to be recorded will include a brief description of the contract, the company, starting date of the contract, the contract period, notice due for renewal and the renewal date, agreed prices or schedules for rates, and price adjustments.

There are two basic methods in use. Some buyers phase all contracts to commence on 1 January and negotiate initially interim contracts for renewal by annual contracts operative from 1 January next. This method simplifies the buyer's task of knowing when contracts are due for renewal but it concentrates his work load into a short space of time. The alternative is to negotiate annual contracts as the need arises with commencement dates phased throughout the year. Whichever method is used the buyer concerned must contact requisitioners to ascertain if they wish contracts to be renewed on the terms being offered. A complete copy of contract register details should be circulated (at the contract renewal stage) to directors concerned to ensure that contract renewals are made in accordance with the current organisation requirements and policies of the company.

4 Sourcing and Pricing

4.1 Introduction

Sourcing is a vital aspect of buying. Buyers stand or fall by the calibre of suppliers with whom they place contracts. This is an inescapable fact and makes it essential to devote considerable energy to the sourcing aspect of the job.

4.2 An open mind

Too many buyers are conditioned by experience and, for this reason, they support the same suppliers irrespective of their performances. This is a foolish policy to adopt and in the long term is destined to fail. Irrespective of the items being bought one needs to start with certain basics.

What is the item? There are certain features which will probably establish parameters. For instance there may be a design stipulation that calls up a brand name. This means that there may be little choice but to use the nominated source, although as a matter of buying policy the design department should be asked to consider alternatives. The onus rests with buying to locate possible alternative materials.

The design characteristics of the item may determine the selection of supplier in that special manufacturing responsibilities may be required. If so, this will restrict the choice.

The quantity required will also be a major influence. If

very few are used it may be necessary to deal with a stockist or merchant rather than a producer who basically needs large quantities.

Patents may well also restrict the buyer to particular sources as he must not infringe patent rights under any circumstances.

There are some of the constraints to be faced. Even so there is still considerable scope for sourcing studies. The buyer retains the right to challenge anything that is put in front of him. He does not, however, retain the right to change anything without reference to the appropriate authority. It is important to recognise this because any unilateral attempt to force change may create problems and will be resisted.

The buyer must seek out, as a matter of routine, all available sources of supply for the product range for which he is responsible. With this detailed knowledge of sources he will be in an advantageous position when flexibility of sourcing policy is required.

4.3 The market place

There are four basic choices when sourcing any product:

1 Local suppliers If these are used there is an advantage of supporting local industry but this should not be permitted to over-ride other commercial considerations.

2 Make or buy This demands a realistic appraisal of all the relative costs. If the buyer's company has the facility to make a product which can also be bought out, there should be a company policy for assessing the relative merits. The policy of one major company requires that all internal manufacturing capabilities must compete with external sources. The issue is however more complex than this. If an item is suddenly switched from a supplier to in-plant, it may cause redundancies with the consequent human misery that follows in its wake. This also applies conversely.

3 National buying It may have been decided to source all

the items in the home market. The motivation to support domestic industries is excellent. It is necessary, however, to recognise that this is a restrictive outlook which limits the choice of supplier. In many countries there are artificial trading barriers which make buying abroad more difficult. This can result from tariffs and quotas or from special agreements made by trading blocs such as the European Economic Community.

4 Worldwide buying This is international, where buying has literally worldwide potential. Obviously one may expect problems here because of language barriers, stretched lines of communications and documentation requirements. These potential problems must not be minimised but they must not deter an active search for potential sources abroad. This subject is dealt with fully in Chapter 7 where detailed advice is offered on sourcing abroad.

4.4 Finding the market place

This should be a key part of the buyer's job. It will be time-consuming but it is essential. There are many sources one can use and outline comments are made here for guidance.

4.4.1 Representatives

The buyer may receive many visits from representatives of potential and active suppliers. He should derive as much benefit as possible from such visits. Consider the first visit of a representative. He will ask for information concerning the organisation products bought, frequency of need and other relevant information. Full co-operation is important otherwise the buyer may miss a potentially useful source of supply in the future. At this juncture the representative should be asked for detailed information on his organisation. This can be done either formally by working through a checklist, or informally. A record of the interview should be kept. This may be useful to the buyer, or his colleagues, in the future.

4.4.2 Trade directories

These are useful but rarely comprehensive. One needs to recognise trade directories for what they are, which is, advertising media. The publisher attempts to convince the manufacturers that his trade directory is the one that matters. Some will be attracted to it but not all. These should be treated with caution. There must not be too much reliance placed on trade directories as the sole source of information. It is vital, nevertheless, that they form a part of the buying library.

4.4.3 Exhibitions and trade fairs

These are most useful because they concentrate many suppliers from the same industry in one place at a particular point in time. Some trade fairs have an international reputation, whilst others are local in nature. The buyer should monitor such events and make periodic visits. This will ensure that a serious attempt has been made to be aware of any changes in technology or of new suppliers who may have entered the market place. Some of the less enlightened companies may not encourage such visits. This is regrettable because the trade fair can be an important source of information.

4.4.4 Other buyers

The profession of buying is inherently introvert when it comes to disclosing sources of supply. This is understandable to some extent but not completely. Some commercial confidentialities must be respected. This should not stop buyers talking to other buyers about mutual experiences in certain product groups. This gives both parties the advantage of increasing their fields of knowledge. Efforts should be made to establish relationships between buyers in a district and on a broader front, in the same product buying area.

4.4.5 Embassies

Many foreign countries maintain embassies in the buyer's country. They usually have a trade or commercial attache whose task is specifically to encourage trade between the two countries concerned. He is likely, therefore, to have detailed information of manufacturers in his homeland. If he hasn't he should be able to get names and addresses through his contacts. We have experienced difficulties with this source but it can be useful and should be tried.

4.5 Visits to suppliers

The buyer should make determined efforts to visit key suppliers frequently. This has many advantages but primarily it keeps him in touch with production developments and any changes that may take place in management or in any other area. Such visits may be time consuming, particularly when long distances have to be travelled and this makes it imperative that one makes every minute count. Haphazard and unstructured supplier visits are to be deplored. They waste everyone's time — a valuable resource. So visits must be planned. The supplier must be told of the purpose of a proposed visit to enable him to provide whatever facilities may be required.

4.6 Enquiries

Potential suppliers need to be given adequate information. This is achieved by sending an enquiry document which invites the source to make an offer to supply. When sending an enquiry one should ensure that detailed, accurate information is provided. Specifically one needs to stipulate.
    Off-take — monthly and annual
    Specifications
    Relevant drawings
    Quantity control standards
    Trading conditions

SOURCING AND PRICING 69

    Any special instructions or invitations
    Delivery points
    Packaging requirements
    Payment requirements
    Contact point for selling queries
    Discount points

One should remember a basic premise; the seller cannot really have too much information at this point. It may well prevent problems in the future if the buyer works closely with him when quotations are being prepared.

Depending on the items that are to be purchased, it may be useful to ask the seller to quote based on the buyer's specifications. Additionally, however, he can be asked to offer any alternatives he may have, or any items which may save costs. He may be a specialist in his particular field which the buyer is not. It is, therefore, likely that he has met and resolved a particular type of problem before. The vast majority of sellers are anxious to help, but they have to be given the opportunity.

It is essential that conditions of purchase are included with the enquiry. These are dealt with in Chapter 5. Conditions of purchase, should, clearly and concisely, advise the seller of the buyer's legal stipulations and thus help to avoid or minimise problems arising in the future.

An important decision to be made is how many sellers should be invited to tender. A reasonable percentage of the total market must be sourced. If the item is a repeat buy at least two new sources should be asked to quote each time the repeat buy occurs. This will ensure that a check is maintained on the market place and avoid complacency and inertia.

It may be necessary to decide on a closing date for receipt of tenders. This must be realistic. The seller must be given sufficient time to gather all his information and prepare his detailed tender. It must be appreciated that he will have to contact his raw-material suppliers to ensure his pricing is up to date. If a final closing date is fixed it should be adhered to. There may be some suppliers who will delay to the very end of the time allowed in the hope of obtaining further advantageous information. Buyers must not fall into this trap. This is a vital aspect of ethical behaviour in buying. All suppliers should be given equal treatment. This applies to the need for adherence to prices tendered. If negotiations are undertaken with one supplier, all others should be given similar opportunities.

4.7 Quotations

Ideally, the seller will be asked to provide written evidence of his offer to supply the goods required. This is an essential document for the buyer. It is certainly relevant to the legal commitment that may be entered into. It is evidence that cannot be denied or challenged in the same way as that of verbal undertakings.

When he receives a quotation the buyer must scrutinise all the information provided. It is folly to assume that the seller's proposals will agree with all requirements in every detail.

Some of the key points to be checked are shown below:

1 Specification Is there adequate information? For instance in buying a chemical and the tender states 'Our Brand XY 2579', this must be questioned. Details of the formulation will be required if not already available.

2 Price Is it clear on what basis this is given? Is the price a 'delivered' one to the usage point. If it is not, there will be freight charges to meet which could be costly if air freight has been used. The buyer must not make assumptions. The word 'assume' is interesting, divided into three elements it makes an ASS-U-ME! Buying abroad will bring its own variety of delivery/price methods. FOB, FOQ and FAS are examples of price-basing points.

3 Delivery The seller's offer on delivery must be carefully checked. It is pointless for him to state '12 weeks' and then to exclude on the reverse of the tender form, in his conditions of sale, any responsibility for late delivery. 'Circumstances outside his control' and vague statements such as '12-18 weeks' should be challenged. A definite date should be obtained otherwise expediting staff will not stand any chance of attaining the desired date.

4 *Exclusions* The seller may, for various reasons, exclude certain items from his quotations. In the building and civil engineering industry we know of an example where a contract was placed for spraying asbestos on the roof girders in a building. This was done for fire protection. The contractor who tendered for this work specifically excluded the hire of his scaffolding and the hire of temporary lighting necessary for the interior work in darkness. These two items were thus the responsibility of the buyer and he had to assess the likely cost of the hire. It is, of course, a buying responsibility to check quotations for any exclusions. Such exclusions may be intended or they may be accidental. It is also quite common for the seller to exclude processes or treatment to materials over which he had no control. This is a regular occurrence in the engineering industry and the alert buyer will spot these exclusions when they occur.

5 *Capacity* Wherever possible the buyer should ensure that the seller has adequate capacity to cover his requirements. If he has not, he will delay execution or pass on the work to a third party, known as the sub-contractor. This may create considerable risk for the buyer because of the seller's reduced control over that contract. It is also necessary to check the legal position if work is passed on to a third party. Conditions of purchase should include a clause which informs the seller that he must obtain permission if he intends to sub-contract any part of a contract. The importance of this requirement must be stressed to the seller.

4.8 Pricing

Buyers have been accused of making price their only criteria in assessing quotations from potential suppliers. This is unfortunately largely true. Price is important but it does not over-ride all other considerations. All aspects must be put in perspective. It must also be appreciated that price does not necessarily reflect cost. Some sellers may sell a product at a loss to attract other business, e.g. supermarkets with loss leaders intended to attract customers into their store. Other sellers may be adding a net profit margin of 50 per cent onto all known costs. They will only do this to take advantage of a seller's market, e.g. where total demand exceeds total supply. This brief introduction shows that price is important and that there are many aspects to be considered before placing contracts.

4.8.1 Where do we start

Ideally, the buyer will have some knowledge of the product pricing, based on personal knowledge or purchase price analysis, before he goes out to tender. Let us assume the following information shown in Figure 4.1 is gathered. This amount of information would represent the buying company's opinion of the commodity costs. They may be right or wrong but it certainly provides a basis from which to assess the seller's quotation when it arrives.

There are however other factors to be considered on this aspect.

4.8.2 Discounts

The basis of any price should be determined. It is trade custom in many industries to offer discounts which have the effect of reducing the gross price. These discounts will be of various types, the more important being detailed below.

1 Original equipment manufacturers discount   This is offered by the seller to the manufacturer of original equipment as an inducement for him to specify a particular product. A typical example is that of a conveyer manufacturer who will be offered special discounts by the makers of bearings, chain drives, and conveyor belt. This discount would not normally be available to the buyer of the original equipment. It is very important that this discount is claimed, the buyer making it known to the seller that he is buying the

		%
Powder feed		23.58
Mixing		
Direct wages		0.85
Factory overheads		2.22
Includes: Factory wages and salaries	0.94	
General power and light	0.21	
Plant depreciation	0.13	
General overheads	0.94	
TOTAL COST OF MIXED POWDER		26.65
Pressing		
Direct wages		3.40
Factory overheads		15.30
Includes: Factory wages and salaries	2.50	
General power and light and power for presses	0.65	
Plant depreciation	5.10	
Toolroom wages	3.90	
Toolroom plant depreciation	0.65	
General overheads	2.50	
TOTAL COST OF PRESSING		18.70
Sintering		
Direct wages		2.55
Power for furnaces and atmosphere		4.25
Factory overheads		7.35
Includes: Factory wages and salaries	1.92	
Plant depreciation	2.55	
Maintenance material costs	1.00	
General overheads	1.88	
TOTAL COSTS OF SINTERING		14.15
Sizing		
Direct wages		1.28
Factory overheads		3.32
Includes: Factory wages and salaries	0.94	
General power and power and light to presses	0.17	
Plant depreciation	0.22	
Toolroom wages	0.93	
Toolroom plant depreciation	0.17	
General overheads	0.89	
TOTAL COSTS OF SIZING		4.60
TOTAL FACTORY COSTS		64.10
Administration:		
Salaries	4.90	
General overheads	3.30	
TOTAL COSTS OF SELLING		8.20
PROFIT MARGIN		14.90
FINAL SELLING PRICE		100.00

Figure 4.1 Breakdown of costs as a percentage of the average selling price per pound of sintered items (hypothetical example)

products for resale. This is an important bargaining point for the buyer who is, in fact, assisting the seller to widen his market.

2   *Turnover discounts*   Generally speaking, sellers are interested in increasing their total sales volume. Assume, as an example, that Jones Corporation buys products from the Ashburn Trading Company to the value of £780,000 in each of the last two years. It also spends £520,000 on the same product with Robinson Supplies Limited. It could be in the interests of Ashburn to increase Jones Corporation's spending to £1 million in the next year. For this value of business they could for example offer 9½ per cent discount if that figure is reached. Such an offer deserves serious consideration. Obviously, it would be necessary to look at the impact of such a reduction on Robinson Supplies Limited. It is important that opportunities for negotiating such discounts are recognised with the realisation that the initiative rests with the buyer. The seller will not beat the drums to make such offers.

3   *Quantity discounts*   This is another way of reducing prices. Assume that the seller publishes a price list offering the following prices:

Quantity	Discounts applicable to base prices, %
0-100	0
100-1000	2½
1000-10000	5
10000-50000	7½
50000-100000	10
100000-250000	20

The buyer may be in the habit of ordering this product in quantities of 9500, because of the stock control system in his plant. He will recognise from reference to the table that by increasing his order to 10,000 he will obtain an additional 2½ per cent discount. He must beware the cynics in his profession who will say that this is such an insignificant amount it is not worth investigating. Not so! The repeat of this level of saving all helps to reduce a buyer's expenditure figure. He should have available an up-to-date list of such quantity discounts, for all the sellers with whom he has a trading relationship.

4 Payment discounts   In a world where liquid cash resources, generally, are never sufficient there will always be sellers who offer discounts for prompt payment of bills. Typical of such arrangements are those who offer 2½ per cent discount for payment within four weeks of submitting the invoice. Another example is 3¾ per cent discount for payment within ten days of submitting the invoice. It may not be the buyer's decision to agree to such arrangements but it is his duty to co-operate closely with the finance activity to examine the potential benefits of such arrangements to their company.

5 Trade discounts   There are examples where manufacturers of certain ranges of goods prefer to deal through trade wholesale outlets. This offers them the advantage of dealing through an orderly distribution system and prevents the manufacturer from having to handle many small accounts. The wholesaler will probably ask for business to be placed with him for which he can offer a trade discount, e g. 20 per cent. This would not be available to a buyer if he were to approach a third line trader — one who had previously bought off a wholesaler. Here again the moral is quite simple; he must ask!

4.8.3 Negotiation

It would be wrong in any serious discussion on prices to omit the possibilities of negotiation. As a topic, negotiation can arouse passions. In many public buying institutions it is outlawed because justice must be done; whilst this point of view must be respected there is another one which actively encourages negotiation between buyer and seller. Clearly it is essential that a buyer is familiar with his organisation's policies.

It is our belief that he must continually appraise any situation which affords the opportunity for negotiation. The following points are intended as a check list:

1 Complexity of the 'buy' Common sense decrees that the more complex the buy the more chance there is of serious debate on some aspect of the pricing. Purchase price analysis will provide a considered opinion of the worth of a product. However, the seller's figures may be at variance with the buyer's. This should not be unexpected and need not lead to ill feeling. There will always be an inter-relation between the technical functions of a product and its price. Perhaps the seller has included within his specification some feature which is providing a performance in excess of that required. If so it provides the buyer with an opportunity to ask for a change in the specification with a possible consequential reduction in the price. His responsibility is to obtain the best buy for his company and this involves technical features.

2 Renewal of existing contracts It is poor practice to allow, unchallenged, the seller to renew a contract based on a new price. Complacency is a major problem encountered with some sellers who feel that contracts are theirs by right. The prices being offered must be checked. It is likely that there are some indices which can be checked. If the seller's increase exceeds the indices he should be asked for an explanation. This is a buyer's entitlement.

3 Suspicious price levels tendered Occasionally, a number of quotations may be submitted all stating the same price. Various explanations can be offered. It may be a coincidence but it may not. Past collusion among sellers is not unknown and will no doubt recur in the future. In some industries there may be a price leader who sets the pace for other producers in the same industry, who are content to follow his price leadership because he is usually the largest in the field and carries large overheads. The smaller producers tend to make higher levels of profit in these circumstances. Negotiations will not be easy in such instances but the buyer must not be deterred. It is always possible that one producer will want the business and will make this quite obvious in his selling tactics. This offers opportunities to the buyer which he must seek.

4 Internal manufacture There may be occasions when there is the opportunity to make an item internally within the plant rather than buy out. This presents the buyer with an excellent negotiation weapon which he should use. If the potential source of supply refuses to discuss contract price revision he can be informed that he may lose the contract. It is vital, however, to avoid bluff in this, or any other situation but to deal only in facts. The threat of the loss of a large contract is usually sufficient to get both sides talking again.

5 Where certain points need finalisation There will be other occasions when the finer points of a contract require a thorough discussion. This could be on any aspect of the contract. Negotiation should proceed on all the points on which the buyer or the seller are dissatisfied. A typical instance is provided by capital equipment buying. The seller may ask for a down payment of 40 per cent of the total value of the contract, with the purchase order. The buyer may feel that this is not in his interests and will wish to negotiate to make progress payments based on the valuation of work done at certain points in time. The seller may also want the price to be on an *ex-works* basis which excludes his responsibility for transport and insurance. Here again this may not be acceptable to the buyer and he may ask the seller to tender a *delivered* price whereby he assumes the above responsibilities.

6 Dutch auctions A good buying maxim is to do to all suppliers what is done to any one of them. Therefore if one of six bidders is given the chance to revise a tendered price the other five should be given the same opportunity. However, one should not continue giving all six more and more chances to revise their prices. This can only lead to eventual anarchy when tenders are invited. Firm dealing is important in such circumstances. The seller should be allowed a chance to revise his tender only if there is a good reason for doing so.

7 *When a buyer has not met contractual requirements* The emphasis so far has been on controlled but dynamic buying practices where one seeks opportunities of negotiating improved contractual terms and conditions or product improvements. This approach needs to be tempered with the fact that a buyer's own organisation may occasionally fail to honour its commitments. Assume that a company has contracted to take 50,000 tonnes of a chemical. This was based on a sales forecast which proved to be very optimistic, to the point where at the end of the contract period there is a shortfall in off-take of 25 per cent. If there is no possible chance of eventually taking this from the seller it is equitable to negotiate a revised price with the seller if he so requests. The buyer must seek to establish long-term relationships and this should put the whole matter in perspective.

It is our belief that negotiation is an excellent and vital area for buyer involvement. It is certainly an interesting facet of buying. It requires serious training and is not something that should lightly be entered into. We have trained many hundreds of buyers in the art of negotiation and have made observations based on these training programs.

There is an important psychological side to negotiation. This is probably amply demonstrated by the buyer who insists that the seller visits him because it makes the buyer 'feel better'. Such a view signals an important training need. The quality of negotiation will be determined by preparation, a grasp of a situation and the use of facts. If a buyer is confident in these then he should have little hesitation in visiting a suppliers' plant to negotiate. He must think positively and act accordingly.

The planning of negotiations will be improved by an ability to determine all the salient points of the forthcoming negotiation. This places the onus on one to spend the sppropriate length of time planning his approach. Experiments suggest that approximately six hours of planning are required to support one hour of negotiation. This 6/1 ratio is important because it is rarely adhered to in industrial negotiations where critical discussions are held on the basis of scant pre-planning.

One should not be afraid to hold an inquest when he has

completed a tricky and complex negotiation. One should critically appraise the way it was conducted and by so doing flaws in strategy or tactics may be spotted. This then gives the buyer the chance of remedial action before any further negotiations are undertaken. One should aim to learn something from every task undertaken.

4.9 Prices as a measurement of buying performance

It is becoming increasingly fashionable to use prices as the basis for measuring buying performance. It should not be the sole criteria as will be shown later in the book, but it is a crucial pointer to buying effectiveness. An example is shown below to demonstrate its practical use.

Let us assume that a buyer is responsible for the purchase of a range of production materials which are in continual use. His manager wishes to use prices as an equitable basis to measure his efforts. He therefore asks to be given two pieces of information:

'*Part A*' This element takes every item in the amount spent and gives the following information:

Part number	Brief description	Annual quantity	Current price	Forecasting price for next year	Annual impact on present volume

It will be noted that the document requires a forecast from the buyer regarding the possible price in twelve months time. Obviously this will be difficult for the buyer but he is the person on whom the organisation depends for knowledge of the market place and its likely movement. Everyone will agree that the forecast represents his opinion on what may happen in the market place in the forthcoming year. He will be expected to discuss his views with the section leader and manager who may have some constructive comments to make which will help him finalise the total forecast.

It is essential that the buyer realises the information requested above is necessary for other functions in the firm. The marketing function will have a close interest in the likely movements of materials; if they become markedly different, selling prices may have to be changed. At the end of the year to which the forecast refers it will be capable of being measured against actual achievements. This must be done objectively. It must be accepted that some of the forecasts may have been inaccurate. Good managements will discuss these variances with the buyer and establish the reasons. On some occasions there could be censure of performance but there could equally be recognition of success.

'Part B' This requests an estimate of the cost savings the buyer intends to make in the forthcoming year. This is an entirely reasonable request for any manager to make. What he is really saying is this: 'Despite the market changes which have an influence on price there will still be opportunities for cost savings'. An alert buyer will be continually seeking these and monitoring where such opportunities may next arise. Some examples are detailed below:

    Substituting one material for another
    Reductions in transportation costs
    Savings in packaging costs
    Changes in the method of buying, e.g. seasonal buying rather than a monthly equal total
    Changing the source of supply
    Specification changes
    Variety reduction
    Changes in re-ordering quantities
    Discontinuation of the need to buy; this may be far fetched but it has occurred a number of times, so the buyer can usefully ask 'Do we really need this item?'

All these instances provides opportunities for cost savings. These will rarely be achieved operating in a vacuum. Cooperation will have to be the keyword with other departments. Everyone in the firm has a part to play in cost reduction but where materials and services are concerned, the buyer can act as the pivot and usefully coordinate all the various investigations for more effective control of material prices.

5 Financial and Contractual Aspects

Too few buyers are sufficiently involved in either financial or contractual aspects. The buyer must familiarise himself with these needs otherwise he will find that he becomes little more than an order clerk, unable to buy efficiently or to safeguard his organisation's interests. A thorough understanding is, therefore, essential. Few buyers will be qualified accountants or legal experts, but they can seek assistance when the situation demands. The accounts department is usually only a telephone call away or perhaps a short walking distance from the buyer's office. There will be many occasions when the buyer has to deal with financial aspects as part of his normal work. He must, therefore, be self-supporting to some extent and refer to his purchasing manager or accountancy colleagues for assistance or guidance when the need arises. Similarly, on contractual aspects, the buyer may need to seek information from his manager or legal experts from within or outside the organisation.

Inadequate consideration of financial and contractual aspects of buying will result in many problems developing with resulting financial loss to the organisation.

5.2 Financial aspects

The finance function is concerned with the provision of long-term funding. In their planning of adequate financial resources they must be made aware of all the financial requirements associated with purchases, particularly price and the cash flow implications of terms of payment. Of equal importance is the need to plan for financial resources to meet inventory plans. Cash is required to support any strategic inventory policy. This must not be planned ahead on an *ad hoc* basis. The main points for consideration are as follows.

5.2.1 Price

Price and the function of buying are automatically related in one's mind, but what do we mean by price? A price quoted by a supplier may be an all-embracing one or it may be a price each for a number of items, a rate per stated quantity, or a rate per unit of weight or volume. An estimator may have produced an estimated or budget price within which the buyer is expected to buy. The supplier submits his quoted price and the buyer then negotiates to obtain the keenest price possible within estimate. Ideally, this price should be at least as low as his competitors would pay in similar bargaining and market conditions. The price may be delivered, 'Ex-works', 'FOB', 'CIF' or other specified basing point price.

The agreed price must be stated on the purchase order. It will be paid by the buyer's organisation to a supplier or contractor in consideration for the supply of specified goods or for providing a specified service. The buyer is concerned with obtaining the best value in use for the price paid. The agreed price must, therefore, be a satisfactory one to the buyer. It may be firmly fixed for the duration of the contract or it may be variable, subject to adjustment related to movements in material and labour indices. Where the goods are being bought abroad, payment may be stipulated in an agreed currency subject to price increases should there be an adverse fluctuation in rates of exchange. Buyers must be absolutely clear on the price basis agreed for the order and under what particular circumstances and to what extent, a supplier would be justified in claiming an increase in price. The accounts department (responsible for making payment against approved invoices submitted), the estimator or cost engineer, and the buyer must, therefore, have an agreed common understanding of the basis of the order price so that each is aware of the actual commitment. Where discounts or rebates apply, these must be clearly stated on the order. Discounts may be related to quantity, value or for prompt payment. Rebates are normally related to the value of annual business placed with a supplier and may be retrospective.

5.2.2 Price variation formulae

We have said that one of the buyer's main aims is to place orders at the keenest prices possible and where advantageous, fixed firm for the duration of a contract, where this is negotiable. In times of inflation the supplier is not likely to quote a fixed price to a buyer for an order of significant value, or where the time for execution is lengthy, unless he builds into his price an adequate element to cater for anticipated increases in material and labour costs which may arise during the contract period. The buyer can seek a choice of two prices: one firmly fixed for the duration of the contract or alternatively, a variable price based on datum costs at date of quoting, which would be subject to price variation in accordance with an agreed formula. This presents the buyer with the task of comparing the two prices and deciding which one to accept. This is a speculative exercise where the buyer assesses the extent to which he expects prices to rise within the timescale of the contract.

Price-variation formulae have been prepared to cater for the needs of various industries, whose particular 'mix' of material and labour content for contracts may vary. Normally, proportions of fixed charges, material and labour charges are established and states as percentages of the total order price. Price indices for materials and labour are specified and movements in them are related to the quotation data and a time-scale expressed as a percentage of the contract period. The price variation formulae caters, of course, for a fall in prices and is sometimes, therefore, referred to as a 'rise and fall' formula. Typical forms of price-variation formulae are shown in the final chapter.

Buyers should examine price-variation formulae to be applied to their contracts to satisfy themselves that such formulae are not weighted in the supplier's or contractor's favour.

Where a buyer is dealing with a foreign supplier he should ensure that the agreed formula is proposed by the supplier, operates on recognised and approved indices, details of which are published regularly in the supplier's country and are readily accessible to the buyer.

5.2.3 Terms of payment

Payment is usually to be made on a specific date in the month following receipt of goods. This information is normally stated on the reverse sides of the enquiry and purchase order forms. In the case of high value plant and equipment, special materials or contract work carried out on the buyer's or his customer's site, special terms of payment are usually agreed. Ideally, of course, the buyer would prefer to make a single total payment for goods supplied or for contract services rendered on completion of the contract (which may include a maintenance guarantee period) when he was satisfied that specification requirements had been met. Such an ideal situation rarely exists. A buyer must be prepared to make progress payments at various stages of the contract related either to a stated time-scale or to completion of identifiable stages of work carried out. For example, where a large machine has been ordered, the buyer may agree to make a down-payment with subsequent progress payments when the supplier has received all the main castings and forgings; has machined them; has completed assembly; has delivered; has installed and commissioned with perhaps a retainer (for example, 5 per cent of the total price) to be paid on completion of the maintenance guarantee period.

Both buyer and supplier are concerned with cash flow, and they may have to reach a compromise agreement on the extent and rate at which progress payments will be made. The supplier must justify his claims for payments related to work done or expenditure incurred. The buyer and his colleagues must satisfy themselves on receipt of an invoice for progress payment, that the claim is justified.

Progress payments may be made at various stages of the contract. Where the contract is for civil engineering work it is normal practice for payment to be made weekly or monthly to cover wages paid to the contractor's men from the time work commences on site. There will also be monthly claims for materials placed on site.

A buyer must avoid financing his supplier or contractor beyond what he considers is an acceptable or necessary level. Where the buyer is placing orders for a customer contract he will try to ensure that progress payments made to suppliers or contractors (expressed as percentages of the order value) are not more favourable (to them) than the progress payments agreed with his own customers for main contracts. The buyer must negotiate the best terms possible. He will appreciate that a progress payment made three months earlier than could have been negotiated, may result in loss of investment earnings of 3-6 per cent of the value of the payment.

Terms of payment are important but they cannot be considered in isolation. A buyer has to decide which is the most fruitful course of action to take. Should he, initially, state his proposed terms of payment and then negotiate the keenest price possible, or should he negotiate the price first and then negotiate terms of payment? Satisfactory results have been obtained by buyers who have used the two approaches. A buyer has to carefully consider alternative courses of action and decide on his negotiating strategy which will be influenced and possibly be directed by his organisation's cash flow position.

Whatever terms of payment have been agreed, the buyer, accountant, engineering or other colleagues concerned must adopt agreed satisfactory procedures for verifying invoice claims submitted by suppliers or contractors. Claims may be for work in progress at the supplier's works, for goods delivered or for work in progress or completed on the buyer's site or his customer's site. A nominated person, e.g. a quantity surveyor, may need to confirm, as a service to the buyer, whether or not a particular claim is justified.

5.2.4 Supplier's financial status

A buyer must satisfy himself on a supplier's facilities and capabilities to undertake a given order. Equally, he needs to satisfy himself that a supplier has the financial resources to execute the order. A buyer will not wish to trade with a supplier who is likely to have his material deliveries suspended pending payment of outstanding accounts, or more seriously still, to become bankrupt. The extent to which a buyer requires to investigate a supplier's financial position depends on many factors such as value of contract, contract timescale, experience of the supplier, supplier's financial association with other companies, any adverse information he receives concerning the supplier's financial position and the current economic situation. Where the buyer feels the need for financial investigation, he can seek the assistance of the finance department, who will have established contacts with financial investigators or local trade protection societies who specialise in investigating companies with particular reference to credit rating, taking account of published company statements and details of directors and their financial interests. Where a major contract is proposed with a supplier or contractor of whom the buyer has no previous experience, he can engage financial investigators of international repute, such as Dun and Bradstreet.

It may be difficult to determine a company's financial viability but where such an investigation is deemed necessary it should be undertaken. Financial investigators should, at least, be able to comment on such ratios as net sales to working capital, net sales to inventory, long-term liabilities to working capital and net profit to net sales and therefore, to indicate if there is doubt on a supplier's financial status. This information should assist the buyer to make sound decisions. Buyers should avail themselves of such services, as an additional safeguard when they consider a need exists.

5.2.5 Bank guarantees

The buyer may need to take an additional safeguard of obtaining a bank guarantee from the supplier's bank whereby any payments made will be refunded to the buyer in the event of a supplier failing to execute a contract. A bank guarantee is particularly necessary when the buyer makes a substantial down payment with order to a supplier with whom he does business for the first time. A 'title to the goods' clause if negotiated, would be of little value to the buyer at this initial stage of a contract unless there were goods in existence to which he has title.

Even with a bank guarantee, the buyer may still have a problem. Whilst his money may be refunded in the event of a supplier's failure to execute the contract, nevertheless, the buyer may not be able to place the work elsewhere at an acceptable price or to meet his required programmed dates and thus his company could suffer appreciable consequential losses.

5.2.6 Performance bonds

Occasionally a buyer places an order where the consequences of non-fulfilment of contract by a supplier or contractor would be so serious that the buyer requires a definite undertaking (in the form of an agreed sum deposited with the bank) that in the event of failure to execute the contract, this sum will be paid to the buyer. There may be a strong case for obtaining a performance bond when the order is being placed with a new company, particularly when it has a parent company, foreign based. The supplier or contractor may want to write a force majeure clause into the contract to protect his interests should he fail to execute the order because of circumstances beyond his reasonable control, e.g. national strikes or natural disasters.

5.3 General conditions of purchase

Can you state your general conditions of purchase? Ask a buyer this question and note his response. Some organisations may have twenty or more clauses in their general conditions of purchase. Many buyers would find it difficult to list a third of that number. Buyers with many years experience may well be included in their ranks. Of course, a buyer may pose a counter question and ask 'If general conditions are so important, how have I been able to buy goods and services for many years giving them little or no attention?' This is a reasonable question which we would answer as follows: Because a buyer has paid little attention to general conditions and no serious problems have arisen, does not mean that he is efficient. A serious problem might easily have arisen. One could occur in the immediate future. If a buyer has been lax in checking a supplier's conditions of sale he has been very fortunate in not incurring loss to his organisation. He has certainly not taken effective measures to safeguard its interests. There is however a need to be selective. The buyer will not have time to read all the small print on every quotation he receives but he should reconcile differences between conditions of sale and purchases for all orders of significance he places.

General conditions of purchase are normally printed on the reverse of the buyer's enquiry and purchase order forms. The attention of existing or potential suppliers is drawn to them by instructions printed on the front of these documents. These instructions usually state that an order must be accepted subject to acceptance of these general conditions of purchase, augmented where indicated by specified special conditions of purchase.

General conditions may include the following clause details.

5.3.1 *Definition of terms*

Terms used by the buyer in his conditions are defined. These may include 'Organisation', 'Company', 'Contractor', 'Contract' and 'Goods'. Some general conditions do not include the necessary introductory clause. Where this is the case, buyers should consult with their purchasing managers on the advisability of arranging their inclusion.

5.3.2 Conditions

A statement may follow that the conditions govern all requirements for goods and services placed by the buyer with a supplier or sub-contractor unless modified by special conditions agreed for an order, and that no variations to order will be accepted unless agreed in writing by the buyer.

5.3.3 Acknowledgement to purchase order

The buyer makes known his requirement to the supplier that the order must be acknowledged promptly using an acknowledgement slip or form (where this has been enclosed by the buyer with the order). The supplier is required to confirm his acceptance of order, price, delivery and terms and conditions of purchase.

5.3.4 Standard of supply

The buyer requires that goods supplied or services provided against the order shall be the best of their respective kinds and of the specified quality. The buyer reserves the right to reject the whole or part of the order should defective goods be supplied. Such goods received shall be returned to the supplier and be replaced promptly by him at his expense.

5.3.5 Prices

Attention is drawn to the fact that the buyer will not be liable to pay for goods delivered unless covered by an official purchase order, duly signed and authorised on behalf of his organisation. Claims for extras will not be accepted unless submitted to the buyer and authorised by him by amendment to order. The buyer shall not pay for weights or quantities delivered in excess of amounts specified in the order.

5.3.6 *Variations to order*

No variations to purchase order shall be accepted unless authorised by the buyer's amendment to order signed on behalf of his organisation.

5.3.7 *Dispatch and delivery*

All goods are to be delivered to the stated destination, normally carriage paid unless agreed otherwise. Advice notes and delivery notes must clearly state the purchase order number, job/account number and other necessary information as requested in the purchase order. Advice notes should be posted to the buyer on the day goods are dispatched.

5.3.8 *Packing*

The supplier may be required to supply packing cases or packing materials free of additional charge unless otherwise agreed for the order. On request, the buyer will use his best endeavours to return empty cases to the supplier at the latter's expense. Damage to goods during transit to the buyer's premises or other specified site shall be made good at the supplier's expense.

5.3.9 *Drawings, patterns and tooling*

The supplier may be required to check patterns supplied by the buyer for the order against drawings and to satisfy himself that there are no discrepancies. Where he finds these, he must apply to the buyer for instructions before proceeding with that particular part of the order. The supplier is to take care of all patterns and tooling which are the property of the buyer. The buyer's drawings must be treated in confidence and not be reproduced or their contents disclosed to third parties, without the prior written consent of the buyer.

5.3.10 Payment

It may be the normal practice for the buyer to make payment against invoices submitted, by a specified date, e.g. the 15th day of the month following the month in which the invoice is received. Instructions on submitting the invoice may be stated on the front of the order.

5.3.11 Infringement of patent

For the bulk of purchase orders there will be no problems of infringement of patent. To cater for the occasions when protection is required a suitable clause might state that the supplier shall indemnify the buyer (and where applicable, his customer too) against all claims, damages, costs and expenses for infringement of letters patent or registered design or similar rights by the use or the sale of any article or material supplied against the order.

5.3.12 Completion

Buyers frequently include a clause stating that completion of contract by the date specified in the order is an essential requirement. In some clauses the buyer states he has the right to withdraw from the contract if it is not completed by that date. Where the buyer has made progress payments, or where he cannot find an alternative source of supply, such a clause however, may give him little or no safeguards, because of costly litigation.

5.3.13 Force majeure

A buyer will normally state in his force majeure clause that he can only accept delays to delivery occasioned by legitimate force majeure circumstances such as 'Acts of God', national strikes, storm, fire or explosion, which are beyond the 'reasonable' control of the supplier.

5.3.14 Cancellation

The buyer may reserve the right to cancel the order or any part of it should the supplier or sub-contractor fail to deliver the goods or fail to complete the contract as stated under 'Completion', and also in the event of a supplier's bankruptcy or where he has a receiving order filed against him.

5.3.15 Arbitration

In the event of a dispute arising between the parties to the contract, the buyer may wish the dispute to be referred to arbitration. Where the parties fail to agree on the choice of an arbitrator within a specified time, e.g. 14 days, then the dispute would be referred to the president of an appropriate institute or association, e.g. mechanical, electrical, civil, structural or chemical engineers, who would be empowered to appoint an arbitrator whose findings would be binding on each of the parties to the contract.

5.3.16 Legal interpretation

Should a dispute arise which has to be referred to a court of law for judgement, it would be necessary to agree and specify that a particular country's laws would apply. A dispute would, therefore, be referred to the Courts of that country for settlement. Legal interpretation problems may arise when the buyer and supplier are located in the same country. A greater problem may arise however, when the buyer places an order with a foreign supplier, as the practice is increasing for international trading bodies to recommend that the law of a supplier's country shall apply to an order. The buyer should however, negotiate to modify this clause where he has scope to do so.

5.4 Special conditions of purchase

General conditions of purchase printed on the back of enquiries and purchase orders need to be augmented from time to time with selected special conditions of purchase, because of the value, nature and complexity of the plant, equipment, materials or services being provided or because of special importance of meeting delivery or completion dates. Buyers must determine their special needs and negotiate with suppliers or contractors to reconcile differences between conditions of sale and purchase. Buyers may have to consult project or contract engineering staff to seek information of their own organisation's contractual commitments, where the goods to be supplied or services provided are for a customer contract.

Many buyers may be content to drift along taking a limited interest on the subject of special conditions. They may have an inadequate list of clauses from which to select from time to time to apply to purchase orders. Responsible buyers will recognise the need to safeguard their organisation's interests and they will seek specialist assistance to compile adequate and relevant special conditions of purchase. Having seen the two different approaches made, our advice to purchasing managers and buyers is to familiarise themselves with the organisation's requirements. Study conditions of sale submitted by suppliers and contractors, study standard contract documents issued by various professional bodies so that you can select adequate and relevant clauses to apply to purchase orders.

There are many clauses which can be included in special conditions (some may be included in general conditions of purchase) but the following should be of particular interest to most buyers.

5.4.1 *Guarantees*

Guarantees generally take two forms; material quality and plant (or equipment) performance guarantees. When a buyer places an order for the supply of goods or the provision of a service, he expects to receive reasonable satisfaction in the goods supplied or services provided. Where goods fail to perform to a stated level of performance under normal 'fair wear and tear' conditions during a specified period of time, the buyer would rightly expect the supplier to make good any defects by replacing sub-standard components or materials (or repairing them, if acceptable to the buyer).

A problem faces a buyer when the supplier offers a restricted guarantee related to the intensity of work to which goods are put, e.g. he may give a twelve month's guarantee for plant working on a single day shift but only give four month's guarantee for plant working on a three-shift basis. The date on which the guarantee becomes operative is also important. Some suppliers may agree that the guarantee period can commence from the date the goods are put into operation but most suppliers give a start date operative from delivery. Where the supplier buys out components or materials from other sources for the order he will normally only pass on to the buyer the guarantee terms granted to him for such goods. Buyers must, therefore, negotiate the best guarantee clauses possible in line with accepted custom and practice within a particular industry or public undertaking or in line with what their sales colleagues have accepted for a customer contract.

Important as start dates and periods of guarantee may be, buyers must also determine what is actually covered by guarantees. When a part fails under guarantee, costs incurred may include the actual cost of replacing or repairing the item, dismantling, transport and installation charges. Consequential loss may also be incurred including production, lost time or secondary damage to other components as a result of a part's failure. Most suppliers, naturally, restrict their obligations under guarantee to replacing or repairing only. Where transport charges are relatively small, a supplier may bear these. A supplier is normally reluctant to give more than a limited guarantee because he cannot control the use to which the goods are put. Whilst he will accept responsibility for his materials and workmanship, design may not necessarily be his responsibility as he might be supplying goods to the buyer's specification. Operating responsibility will rest with the buyer (or his customer). The onus would normally be on the buyer to prove that in the event of failure or defect, the supplier was at fault.

In making the best buy, a buyer must take into account possible costs which might be incurred by his organisation through component or material failures or through defects arising during the guarantee period. He must seek to negotiate an acceptable guarantee clause which affords reasonable safeguards, but at the same time, avoids increasing the order price. He and his colleagues may also need to confirm that the goods are suitable for a particular application and to consider interface problems. (See Figure 5.1).

5.4.2 Transfer of title

Buyers frequently have to make progress payments in advance of delivery of goods. Irrespective of how much time and attention have been devoted to determining a supplier's financial status, there is always the risk that a supplier may have financial difficulties, perhaps through cash-flow problems, which might result in bankruptcy. When such a catastrophe occurs, the receiver takes control of all materials and equipment not identified as being the property of entitled organisations. He is empowered to dispose of all such goods to raise funds to make limited payments to all the bankrupt supplier's creditors.

Where the buyer makes significant progress payments prior to delivery, he should ensure that he has title to the goods, and that such goods are clearly identified with his order. The acknowledgement of order should confirm the supplier's acceptance of the transfer of title clause. The buyer requires full title to the goods subject to lien for unpaid purchase money — because he may for example, have paid £10,000 in progress payments against an order valued at £20,000. If the supplier goes into liquidation and the value of work done is assessed by the receiver to be £12,000 then to take possession of the goods to which he has title, the buyer has to pay the receiver the 'lien', or balance of unpaid purchase money, i.e. £2,000.

5.4.3 *Insurance during manufacture*

Where the buyer has negotiated a transfer of title clause he has gone part way to safeguard his organisation's interests. He has to consider, however, what his position would be, if following a supplier's bankruptcy, the goods were lost or damaged by fire or from any other cause on the supplier's premises (or his sub-contractor's premises). Title to the goods may be of little value unless he had arranged with the supplier that, in addition to having transfer of title, he has also had the goods insured to their total value in the joint names of the supplier and himself for the requisite period. The buyer should negotiate such a clause and satisfy himself that insurance cover has been arranged and that policies are renewed by due dates. Buyers should always aim to negotiate 'transfer of title' and 'insurance during manufacture' clauses together to safeguard their organisation's interests.

5.4.4 *Variations to contract*

It is one thing to have issued a specification of requirements with an order for an agreed price, but often a buyer is faced with claims for price increases because of variations to contract instigated by his technical colleagues without prior consultation. A clear policy is necessary on variations to orders. The purchase order should include a clause which states that variations to contract must only be done against written amendments although allowance must be made for dealing with emergency situations. Circumstances will arise when urgent action has to be taken which is particularly relevant where site work is concerned. There must be some flexibility of policy which allows responsible staff to take prompt action in an emergency. Such work should be restricted to immediate requirements and the buyer concerned, informed promptly and given an authorised requisition from which he can issue the order amendment to regularise the situation.

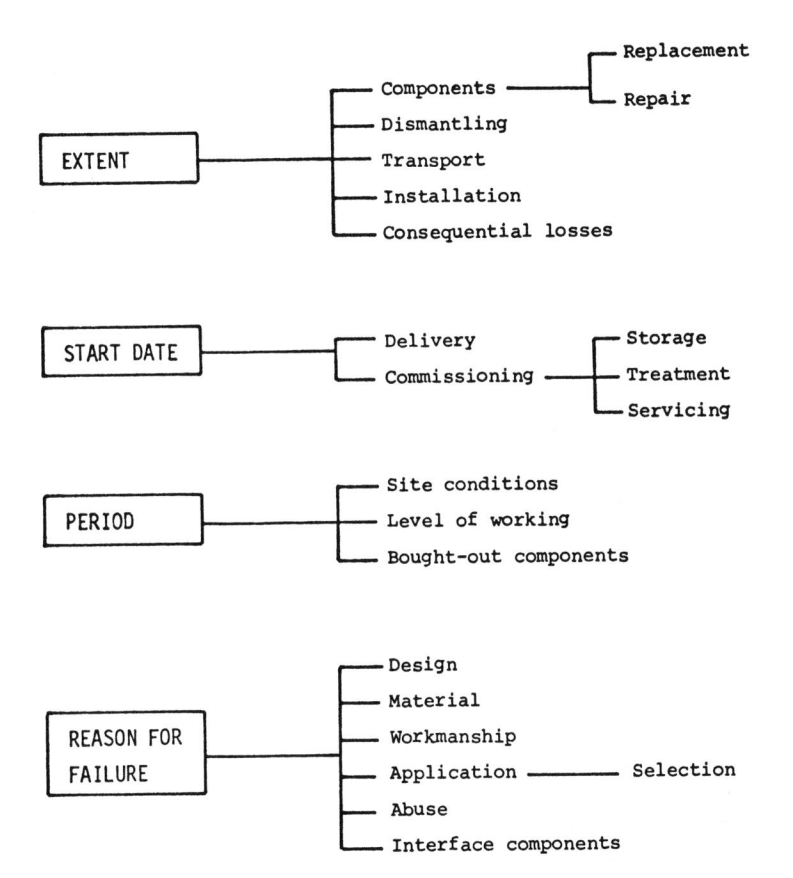

```
                          ┌─ Replacement
              ┌─ Components ─┤
              │              └─ Repair
              ├─ Dismantling
[EXTENT] ─────┼─ Transport
              ├─ Installation
              └─ Consequential losses


                  ┌─ Delivery                ┌─ Storage
[START DATE] ─────┤                          │
                  └─ Commissioning ──────────┼─ Treatment
                                             └─ Servicing


              ┌─ Site conditions
[PERIOD] ─────┼─ Level of working
              └─ Bought-out components


                    ┌─ Design
                    ├─ Material
[REASON FOR         ├─ Workmanship
 FAILURE]    ───────┼─ Application ──────── Selection
                    ├─ Abuse
                    └─ Interface components
```

Figure 5.1 Material guarantees

5.4.5 Sub-letting of work

The supplier will be selected probably with assistance from technical colleagues, based on assessment of his facilities and capabilities. Whilst the buyer would accept the supplier sub-letting certain portions of work in accordance with his normal practice, supplier appraisal is rendered void if the supplier sub-contracts work which the buyer expects him to process. Circumstances can change after the supplier has received an order, which could not have been foreseen. This may require an alternative sub-contracting to a company who have the technical capability to work to specification and to deliver to time. An assurance should be sought that the supplier will not sub-contract work without the buyer's prior approval. One reason is that for specific customer contracts he may have to obtain the customer's approval of the revised proposal.

Copies of such sub-orders placed should be obtained as a condition of contract with a clear statement that there would not be an unreasonable withholding of consent to such work being sub-let.

5.4.6 Inspection and progress

The supplier would be required to allow the buyer's representatives access to the supplier's works (or the works of his sub-contractors) to progress or inspect work during reasonable hours to satisfy themselves on quality standards and progress made. If it is necessary to witness tests, the supplier must give reasonable notice when such tests or stage inspections are due thereby providing the buyer with the opportunity to send representatives.

5.4.7 Job programmes

The nature of the goods on order will determine the form of job programme the buyer requires from the supplier. A schedule of quantities with planned delivery dates may be adequate. In some cases a simple bar chart may be required. Such a bar chart may compare 'actual' with 'planned' progress and indicate possible effects on the completion date. When major plant, equipment or steelwork, are bought there may have to be a clause which requires the supplier to produce a detailed bar chart or network diagram within say, one month of receipt of order which compares 'actual' and 'planned' progress of design, drawing, bought-out materials, manufacturing and site work (where applicable). The buyer may wish such programmes to be up-dated and submitted fortnightly or monthly. (See Figure 5.2).

5.4.8 Documentation

Where a supplier is to provide drawings, manuals, certificates or correspondence which has to be dealt with formally, the buyer may wish to include a 'documentation' clause. The supplier may be instructed to submit drawings to the buyer's technical colleagues for approval before proceeding with manufacture or placing sub-orders. The drawing may have to conform to a particular standard, to meet the buyer's requirements or his customer's requirements, where this applies.

Where drawings are provided, possibly with specifications, he will not wish the supplier to deviate from them without prior agreement. Should there be any discrepancies between drawings and specifications the supplier will be required to apply for instructions before proceeding with that particular portion of the work. The clause would also include a statement that all drawings or specifications provided by either of the two parties to the contract shall be treated in confidence by the other party. Their contents must not be disclosed to third parties without prior agreement in writing.

5.4.9 Free issue material

Where he is supplying free-issue material, the buyer may include a clause which states that the material shall remain his property for the period of the contract and it must not be removed from the supplier's premises (or the premises of an agreed sub-contractor) without the buyer's prior written consent. Where the material is of high value or of special importance, the supplier would be required to identify it as the buyer's property whilst it is in his possession.

The buyer should also satisfy himself that his own organisation's insurance will cover such material during the period it is in the supplier's possession.

5.4.10 Packing and preservation

Where goods to be supplied such as machinery, electrical equipment or instruments are liable to deterioration or damage in transit or during the anticipated period of storage following receipt, the buyer should include a clause which safeguards his interests. Exposed machinery surfaces may need to be coated with some proprietary fluid, unexposed machined surfaces may need to be greased or oiled, equipment vulnerable to moisture such as instruments may need sealing from the atmosphere and sachets of silica gel enclosed with the items to absorb moisture.

5.4.11 Indemnities for site workings

When the supplier is to install, erect or commission plant, equipment or steel-work he is supplying (or is being supplied by others), the buyer must satisfy himself that the supplier or contractor takes out adequate insurance to indemnify the buyer against all claims for accidents, loss or damage which might result from the negligent acts of the supplier's or contractor's men working on site. The forms of insurance include employer liability, public liability and third party, and contract work (all risks). The amount of insurance cover required would be stated. Where the site work was of a minor nature to be carried out on an unrestricted site free of complications, then the public liability and third party insurance might be £50,000 because possibilities of accidents occurring were limited. On the other hand, work may be carried out on a

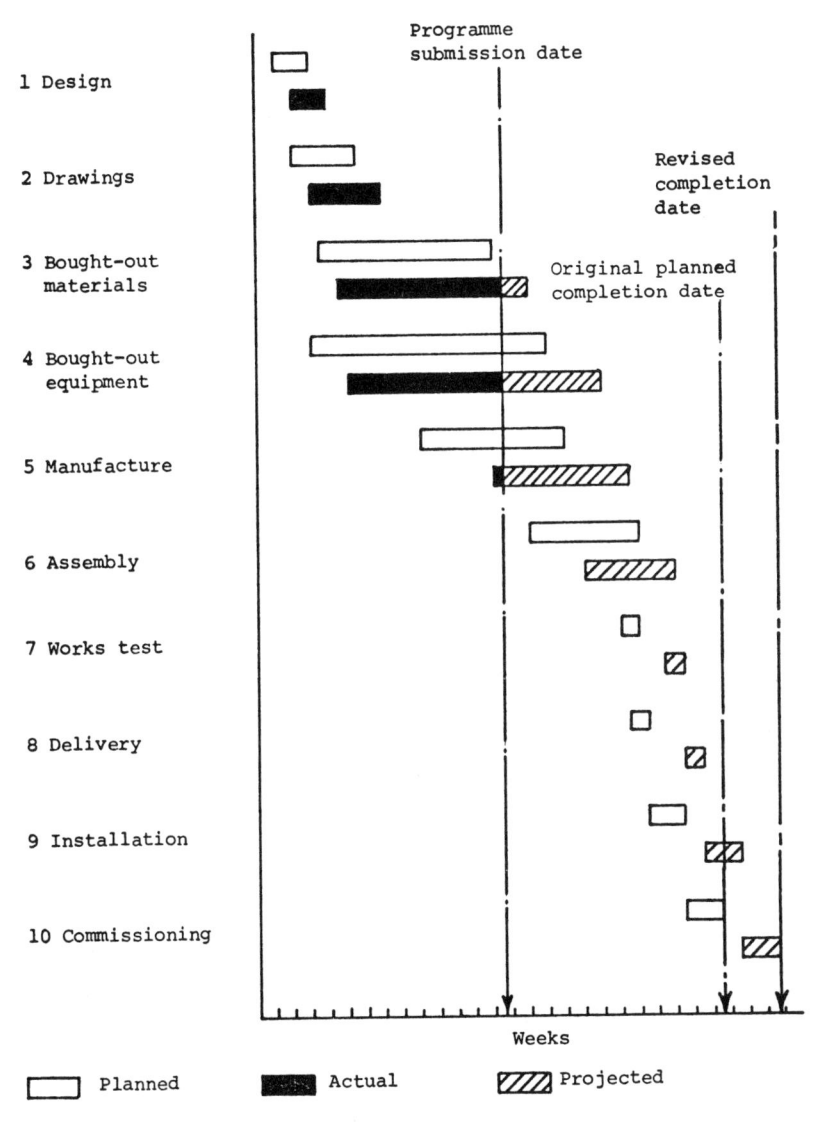

Figure 5.2 Bar chart job programme

large scale under more difficult site conditions where possibilities are much greater of accidents occurring and the nature of such accidents could be far more serious, perhaps catastrophic. Insurance of £2 million or more may be required to be specified for the contract. This cover would protect the buyer's organisation (or his customer) against accidents to persons other than the supplier's or contractor's employees (covered by employer liability insurance). It would also cover loss or damage to plant equipment or material other than that being supplied for the contract.

Where the buyer or his customer are not taking out insurance to cover possible loss or damage to items supplied for the contract from the time received on site to hand-over on completion of commissioning, then the buyer must arrange for the supplier or contractor to take out Contract Works (All Risks) insurance for this period. The amount of insurance cover would be related to the maximum loss which could occur to the goods on site.

The buyer must satisfy himself that the suppliers' or contractor's policies are adequate and have not lapsed, i.e. premiums due are paid by renewal dates. The policies must cover the whole period of the contract work on site including the maintenance guarantee period as men may return to site after commissioning to carry out remedial work. Insurance policies should be checked before work initially commences on site where the supplier delivers plant, equipment or material which he has to insure on Contract Works (All Risks) insurance. The buyer must ensure that such insurance is satisfactory before he allows the goods to be delivered to the site and specify that copies of all the relevant insurance policies and premium payment slips are submitted for his scrutiny. Alternatively, the supplier can instruct his insurance broker to submit a letter to the buyer stating the extent of his client's insurance for the contract together with policy renewal dates.

When checking policies, a buyer must note exceptions and limitations. We have knowledge of one particular contractor's public liability and third party insurance policy which was only valid for work carried out on his own premises. Subsequent enquiries disclosed he was sub-letting site erection work (a fact unknown, initially, to the buyer).

5.4.12 Storage of goods

There may be occasions when it is necessary to negotiate a contract with a firm delivery date but which also includes a proviso that if, for reasons outside the buyer's control, he cannot accept delivery on the stated date, the supplier would store the goods free of charge or for an agreed additional charge for a specified limited period. Ultimately, the goods must be delivered by the agreed revised date in a satisfactory condition. If the goods were liable to deterioration through lack of servicing or maintenance, then it must be specified that any remedial work must be carried out by the supplier. A large electric motor, for example may need its stator shaft turning at periodic intervals to equalise the loading on bearings. In another case, rust-inhibited fluid may have to be applied periodically.

Whatever arrangements are made for storage, the supplier must be instructed to direct his full efforts to meet the specified delivery date (against which failure to meet may result in liquidated damages). The proviso on storage is a precautionary measure for application in special circumstances.

5.4.13 Notice of delivery

When an order is placed on a 'time is of the essence of the contract' basis, the onus is on the buyer to notify the supplier when he cannot accept delivery at his premises or other specified site because of lack of facilities or lack of manpower, he should include a clause which states that the supplier must first check with the buyer before consigning goods. Should the supplier not make this prior check, and his driver be unable to off-load the goods and has to make a second journey, then there would be no liability to the buyer for additional transport charges incurred.

5.4.14 Liquidated damages for late delivery or late completion

Where it is important that the supplier meets a stated delivery date or that a contractor completes his work to time, the buyer should seek to negotiate a 'time is of the essence' clause. However, suppliers or contractors would only agree to such a clause in special circumstances because of the high risk they would be required to take. Suppliers or contractors may be prepared to consider a liquidated damages clause which would make them liable to pay agreed sums as compensation for late delivery or late completion of contract. Liquidated damages must be a predetermined and realistic assessment made of the probable losses that would be incurred should there be delay. The damages would be related to a stipulated amount for each week of delay increasing to a maximum figure after a specified number of weeks.

Many industries, institutions and associations use their own special conditions of purchase which include a standard liquidated damages clause of 'a half per cent of the total contract price for each week of delay up to a maximum of five per cent operative after ten weeks delay.' This formula, universally accepted and applied, cannot possibly be a realistic assessment of the buyer's probable loss. By sheer chance in a particular situation this formula might produce a realistic assessment but this would be the exception, not the rule.

A supplier may anticipate the application of liquidated damages and accordingly build an amount into his price to cater for a possible claim for late delivery. A second problem is that a supplier may only be prepared to accept liquidated damages related to that portion of an order which may run late. This must be examined closely because there would be virtually no disadvantage to a supplier if the delayed item cost say £5. If the total value of the order was £50,000 and the buyer could not commission the plant or equipment without the outstanding item then a liquidated damages clause should be applied on the total order value.

5.4.15 Liquidated damages for inadequate plant/equipment performance

When an organisation buys plant or equipment this is normally against Board sanction given on the expectation of obtaining a given level of performance. Industry expects a given return against capital outlay. Such plant or equipment purchased should, therefore, operate to a stated level of performance and a buyer would wish to apply a liquidated damages clause to an order as an 'incentive' to the supplier to meet his obligations in this respect.

Consider the purchase of a conveyor required to carry 20,000 units per day to be economically viable. Technical staff may, therefore, specify that the conveyor has to carry 21,000 units per day. If subsequent performance was below 20,000 units per day, the buyer would have the right to reject the conveyor and to cancel the contract, any progress payments made being refunded. To seek to achieve his objectives, the buyer might apply liquidated damages at the rate of half per cent of the total contract price for each hundred units below specified performance up to a maximum of five per cent of the total contract price where performance was one thousand units below the specified figure of 21,000 units.

Similarly, the buyer may wish to apply liquidated damages for excessive fuel or electricity consumption needed to operate plant and equipment related to the specified standards of consumption.

5.4.16 Spares

When plant or equipment is being purchased some consideration may be needed on possible spares. Spares fall into two categories. Firstly, there are those spares which must be available for possible use from the day plant or equipment is put into operation, such spares being called insurance or emergency spares. In a contract for a steel rolling mill, for example, a spare main drive shaft would be required with the new mill, though not necessarily supplied on the same order.

The second group of spares are general spares required for use during the first year or so of operation of the plant or equipment.

Normally the contract would include a clause requiring the supplier to submit a schedule of recommended spares in each category, possibly within two or four weeks from receipt of the order. The buyer can then consult with his technical colleagues to decide on actual requirements and to obtain authorisation to place an amendment to order or an additional order.

5.4.17 Force majeure

Force majeure may be included in general conditions of purchase but there should be careful scrutiny on how force majeure is to be applied and interpreted on major orders where a supplier has accepted a liquidated damages clause. The latter may make a sustained, determined effort to meet his delivery obligations but fail for reasons completely beyond his control. He may be late on delivery because of government action, industrial action, abnormal climatic conditions, fire, explosions, etc. A supplier would not expect liquidated damages to be enforced if the delay results from one of these causes.

Government action could include legislation, intervention, commandeering or requisitioning of raw materials, production or transport facilities. Industrial action could include national strikes (local strikes are normally excluded as buyers feel that suppliers could precipitate these), civil commotion, insurrection or malicious damage. A supplier too, may have reasonable grounds for claiming disruption of his raw material supplies as legitimate force majeures. A sudden stoppage, internationally, of supplies of rubber, copper, nickel or other key material needed for the order might well be submitted as a valid claim.

The supplier may claim force majeure because of an Act of God which is defined as some unforseen accident occasioned by the elementary forces of nature unconnected with the agency of man, the occurrence of which could not have been foreseen and the consequences of which could not have been prevented by a reasonably competent supplier taking reasonable precautions. Abnormal climatic conditions, epidemics, plagues, fire, explosion or loss at sea are normally accepted as Acts of God although a supplier's actions or lack of actions may influence, in some circumstances, the development or the extent of such occurrences.

Finally, some suppliers may seek to include under a force majeure clause, delays resulting from breakdown of major production plant, late deliveries of components or materials from their suppliers or because of local strikes. The keen buyer must resist such proposals and negotiate a reasonable but realistic force majeure clause which does not give the supplier such scope that it would be virtually impossible to apply liquidated damages for late delivery.

5.4.18 Publicity

When a supplier or contractor is awarded a particular contract he may wish to publicise the fact that he has been successful. There may be good strategic reasons however, why this fact should not be advertised. It may not be the organisation's policy to publicise that work is proceeding on this contract, certainly not that it be generally known that they were unable to carry out the work themselves, but had to sub-let it.

To avoid such difficulties arising, a clause should be inserted which requires the supplier not to make prior announcement and not to issue any publicity material in connection with the contract without prior consent in writing.

5.5 Model special conditions of contract documents

There are a number of model special conditions of contract documents drawn up by various professional bodies such as mechanical, electrical and civil engineers and architects. These model conditions apply to the supply and installation or erection of plant, equipment or steel work and civil engineering and building work, and are modified from time to time in an attempt to give a reasonable balance between the interests of the buyer and the supplier or contractor. They have been developed after many years of experience in particular fields. Where extensive site work is involved, it may be advantageous to use the appropriate model contract document for a contract, augmented as necessary with the buyer's own selected special conditions and general conditions of purchase.

5.6 General comments on financial and contractual aspects

We have dealt with a number of aspects which buyers may have to consider when placing purchase orders. They must gain a better understanding of financial and contractual aspects and take all reasonable steps to safeguard their organisations' interests. More time and attention must be directed to negotiating relevant financial and contractual aspects at the pre-contract stage when the buyer has maximum bargaining power. Differences between conditions of sale and purchase should be reconciled to his advantage. It is certainly true, however, that disputes can and do arise after an order has been placed irrespective of the quality and depth of effort previously applied. The two parties to a contract may each have a different interpretation of what was meant or intended. There may be requests for clarification on particular points. When disputes arise which the two parties cannot resolve, they can take recourse to arbitration or law. These courses of action may be costly and lengthy to both parties with consequent publicity not helping an organisation's image. Nor is there any certainty that the arbitrator or judge would rule in the buyer's favour.

In spite of difficulties which may arise, there will be a clear advantage in devoting sufficient time and effort to agreeing special conditions of purchase and negotiating associated financial aspects, particularly where the value or nature of the order warrants this. Both parties have much to gain because each then knows where he stands, what is expected of him, what his obligations and liabilities are. Both parties gain a clear insight at the outset of what is in each others' minds and thus many grey areas can be eliminated. A planned informative approach by all concerned in contract negotiating does much to avoid, or at least, to minimise the possibilities of disputes arising at a later stage. Those responsible for negotiating contracts may not necessarily be available for consultation at later stages in a contract and their intentions should, therefore, be adequately and clearly defined in the purchase order or other contract document.

Where the buyer is placing a major contract, it is advantageous for him to prepare an order draft which includes all terms and conditions. This should be submitted to the supplier immediately negotiations are finalised to obtain his confirmation that he would accept an order in accordance with the draft order document. This increases the possibilities of the supplier subsequently acknowledging the order promptly, and in its entirety.

Where the buyer wishes to be certain that what has been negotiated will be accepted by a supplier or contractor, he should draw up a contract agreement document (in duplicate) and present it to the final negotiation meeting for signatures of acceptance by the two parties to the contract. A formal purchase order document can be issued later with an order number against which consignment notes, lorry tickets, advice notes, work sheets, invoices and general correspondence can be submitted, identified and processed.

6 Stores Management and Control of Stock

6.1 Introduction

There are many buying departments who do not have responsibility for the stores or stock control function. Despite this, the role of buying is inexorably linked with both functions. Every organisation has some stock which must be cared for and which represent money. If only organisations would see all stocks as cash lying on a shelf with all the attendant risks. Some may be stolen if not adequately supervised; imagine a bank where you could help yourself! It is not uncommon to find a stores where this can be done. Money could deteriorate if exposed to extremes of dampness. This would render it useless and the same applies to stocks. Obsolescence would be a possibility; imagine having money that no one else wanted. The money would need to be in a form acceptable to everyone. It would be futile having gold bars when everyone was demanding silver coins. Equally, incorrect stocks are quite unacceptable to those in industry.

The major reasons for holding stocks are:
1   Insurance against higher-than-average demand.
2   Insurance against longer-than-average supplier lead time.
3   To take advantage of quantity discounts.
4   To take advantage of seasonal and other price fluctuations.
5   To minimise delay in production caused by lack of parts.

Generally, large stocks cost money; it is difficult to be

precise but latest estimates suggest 30 per cent per annum approximately as the cost of holding stock. This means that for every £100 of stock held for a year it would cost £30 to keep it there. Some buyers are bewildered at the origin of this figure. It really is quite simple.

1 The opportunity cost of capital If the cash represented in stocks, was not tied up, it could be invested in many forms to earn interest rates in excess of ten per cent. This latter figure depends on the state of the money markets and varies from time to time.

2 Storage space Cost is incurred to provide space for holding stocks; this applies to inside and outside storage compounds. The apportionment of overheads will take account of the space used. This is frequently the largest single item of expense after the opportunity cost of capital.

3 Wages and salaries These are a necessary expense but need to be taken into account when the final assessments are made.

4 General overheads allocation The stores and outside compound will require expenditure on things such as lighting, heating, maintenance, handling equipment and so on. These will increase in proportion to the amount of stocks.

5 Deterioration and obsolescence These are very real risks which will occur in varying proportions according to the type of industry. The electronics industry is notorious for obsolescence — resulting from a rapidly changing technology.

6 Insurance It is accepted that this may be a form of overhead but it needs to be singled out for attention, particularly where stocks are held in warehouses belonging to third parties.

The objective of all companies must be to minimise stockholdings consistent with all operational requirements. This is, of course, easy to request but difficult to practise. There are occasions when stocks will appreciate in value because of rising prices, and at these times companies will make windfall profits on any excess stocks. However, they need to temper stockholding with some degree of caution where prices may fall thereby reducing profitability.

This chapter is devoted to those areas of stores management and control of stock which offer scope for improvements.

6.2   What do we have in stock?

There has to be a starting point for any investigation of existing methods. In terms of stores management, it makes good sense to expect an accurate record of all stocks items. The following check list is provided as a basis of comparison between working records and an ideal. It makes little difference whether the records are maintained manually or by computer.

1   *Stock reference number*   The basis of any good stock system is a good coding system which quickly identifies all like items in categories.
2   *Description*   This should be sufficiently detailed to ensure that the item can be promptly identified. The description does not have to be as full as one would expect to find on a detailed specification sheet.
3   *Using department*   This is essential for the purpose of checking usage quantities and subsequent management controls. It will also prove useful when cost centres are involved. In such cases the stock record can double check the requisition.
4   *Location reference*   If the item is permanently located in a particular place in the stores, the location reference must be recorded. The information will have to be continually updated if the stores is run on a random location principle.
5   *Units of issue*   The information will be obtained from production control or other requiring point. Consultation should take place to ensure that unnecessary splitting of standard packs is not occurring. The emphasis here should be on minimising administrative effort and associated labour.
6   *Running totals*   The basis of good stock records is the

accurate recording of all receipts in terms of quantity and dates. Issues should be equally noted. The resultant stock figures should equate to the stocks in the stores.

7 *Allocated stocks* There will be many companies who are purchasing items for specific contracts. It is vital that these items are recorded so that no one is deceived into thinking that they are 'free stock'. The information for allocating this stock will be from sales orders received.

8 *Quantities on order* The stock controller must have accurate information regarding all outstanding purchase orders. This should ensure that he does not duplicate the same demand leading to excess stocks when all items are received.

9 *Stock control levels* Good stock records will have details of the various levels for controlling stocks. This should include:

   a Maximum stock level — this represents the quantity above which the item stock should not rise. This will be partly linked to the financial controls in that all maximum stocks multiplied by a value per item give a theoretical maximum stockholding investment.
   b Minimum stock level — this represents the level below which stocks should not be permitted to fall. It will be fixed at such a level which takes safety stocks into account.
   c Re-order level — This is the quantity at which the item needs to be re-ordered.
   d Warning level — it may coincide with the minimum stock level but in any case it will represent the level at which stocks are at risk and urgent expediting action is necessary.

10 *Financial valuation* The stock records should be capable of providing a price per unit and an extention to a total valuation. In some companies this is treated as confidential information and is not permitted in the stores activity. Whilst this has something to commend it, there is also a point of view which states that the storekeepers should be made aware of individual prices. It is quite certain that the value of some items is not apparent by its physical appearance.

6.3 Economic order quantity

Every student of purchasing and stock control will encounter the Economic Order Quantity (EOQ) theory. It is widely used in industry and yet widely misunderstood. Figure 6.1 should help with the subsequent reading.

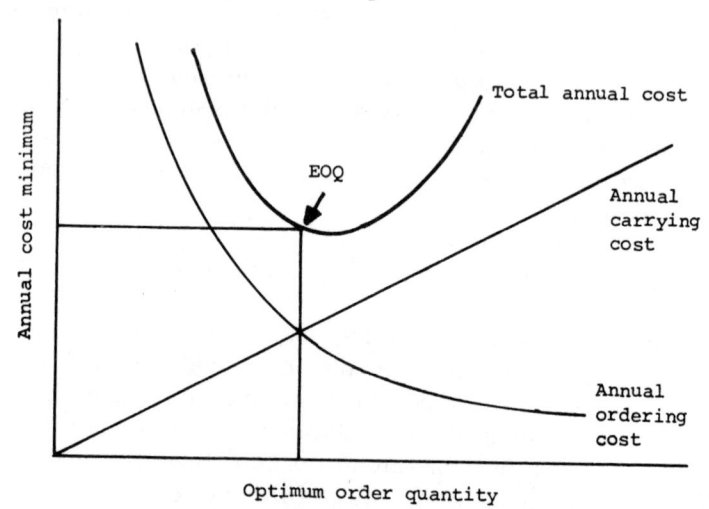

Figure 6.1 Diagrammatic view of EOQ

The EOQ is arrived at by using a formula. There are many variations on a basic theme. A classical formula is:

$$Q = \sqrt{(2AS/rv)}$$

where A is the ordering cost per order, S the annual usage, in pieces, R the inventory carrying charge (a decimal fraction) and V the cost per piece. If an assumed case is taken as an example where A is £5, S is 600, R is 25 per cent and V is £2, and substitute in the formula we get:

$$Q = \sqrt{(2 \times 5 \times 600/0.25 \times 2)} = \sqrt{12000} = 110 \text{ units}$$

This shows that this part should be ordered in lots of 110, about 5.4 times per year, i.e. every ten weeks.

There are a number of points which must be made regarding the use of the EOQ. The ordering cost per individual order, A, can be calculated by finding the total cost of operating a buying department per annum and dividing by the total number of purchase orders placed per annum. Caution needs to be applied here however because the figure can be reduced by placing more orders, e.g. rather than place one order with twenty items on it, place twenty single-item orders, which is more inefficient.

The annual usage rate, S, would seem innocuous and yet it should be known and should be reasonably constant otherwise the application of EOQ can be highly dangerous. If the item is, for example, a seasonal item, the use of EOQ is not to be recommended. Inventory carrying charges, R, can also be calculated and 25 per cent per annum is a reasonable average figure to use, if specific charges are unknown. The cost per piece, V, is a known fact and usually quite easy to obtain.

6.4 ABC inventory categories

It is reasonable to argue that stocks should be classified according to their importance. The ABC method is such a system. Figure 6.2 represents a graphic display of ABC production inventories. This shows that in this case 10 per cent

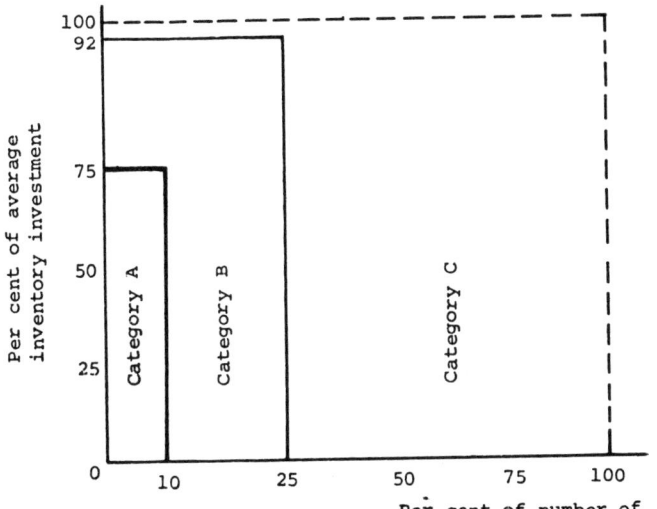

Figure 6.2 ABC analysis

of the inventory items account for 77 per cent of average inventory investment. One quarter of the inventory items account for 92 per cent of average inventory investment whilst the remaining 75 per cent of inventory items account for only 8 per cent of inventory investment. This distribution of items relative to investment is typical of that found by the authors in a number of studies. It offers considerable scope for the practice of management by exception. The analysis on the previous page shows that by concentrating efforts on one quarter of the items, control is achieved of 92 per cent of inventory investment. The policies for dealing with each category of stock may vary, for example:

> A category items — review policy every month
> B category items — review policy every three months
> C category items — review policy every year

In terms of cash flow, A and B category stocks should be concentrated on. A fundamental problem facing many buying departments is the sheer volume of C category items which require a disproportionate volume of administrative effort relative to their value. The simple fact must however be faced that an out-of-stock situation on one of the C items could stop production.

The management practice of categorising stocks will ultimately involve many departments — who will need to co-operate to ensure that the total inventory is optimised.

6.5 The review level system

This system of controlling inventory is time-based. Figure 6.3 is illustrative of the nature of the system.

The basic system consists of review dates at regular intervals of time, e.g. every month. At each of these dates a forecast, based on past demand is made of the anticipated future demand for the item over a period X. This period X is equal to the sum of the lead time (L in Figure 6.3) and the review period (P in Figure 6.3). The period X emerges from the fact that stocks are at risk over period ($L + P$). If no order is placed at review R1, the next opportunity for placing a purchase order is review R2, which means that the delivery would only be made at time N on the diagram, the review level may be expressed as follows:

Review level = $(L + P)X$ (Forecast usage period) + safety stock

At the time of each review a review level for the item is calculated and stock on hand, plus balances outstanding for delivery is compared with it. The quantity to be ordered is:

Q = Review level − Stocks − Balance due

The basic system is one of replenishment when the deficiency between the review level and total stocks is ordered. Many firms are concerned with average stocks. In this case these are a direct function of:
1   The frequency of review.
2   Variations in the usage pattern.
3   The average usage per month.
4   The magnitude of the safety factor.
5   The length of the lead time.

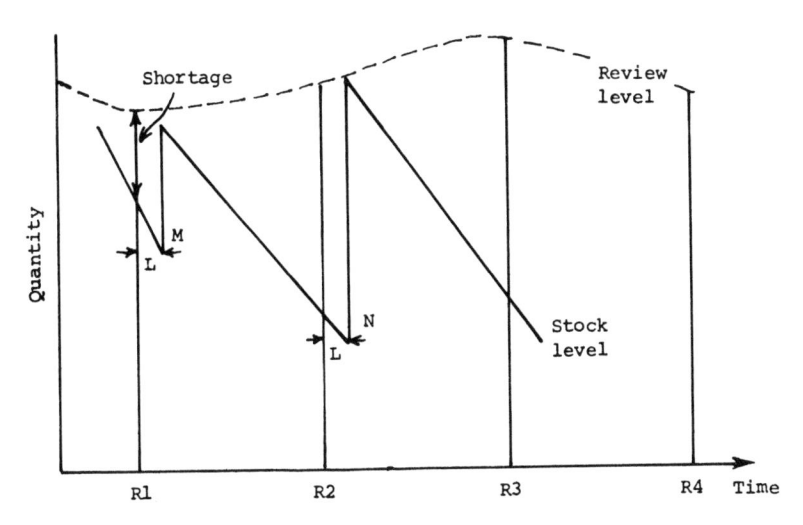

Figure 6.3 Review level system of stock control

118 THE BASIC ARTS OF BUYING

6.6 Exponential smoothing

Any stock control will have an element of forecasting within it. The use of moving averages is very common but has serious defficiencies, not the least of which is the considerable number of individual calculations.

Exponential smoothing is the simplest of a family of forecasting systems that have been applied to inventory control. The exponential smoothing forecasting system requires only one historical datum — the old forecast. When making a new forecast, it simply adjusts the old forecast by a fraction of the difference between the old forecast and the actual last period's demand. In formula form, the technique is:

New average forecast = Old average forecast + α (Actual — Old average forecast)

If the terms are rearranged the formulae becomes:

New average forecast = α (Actual demand) + $(1 - \alpha)$ (Old average forecast

The factor α represents the weighting factor to be used and is a fraction within the range 0 to 1. The higher the value of α, the greater the weight given to the most recent demand the more responsive the forecast will be to month-to-month changes. If we assume that $\alpha = 0.1$, that the forecast of average demand for May was 200 units and that the actual usage in May was 250 units, the computation of next months

TABLE 6.1

	J	F	M	A	M	J	J	A	S	O	N	D
Monthly demand	48	60	50	72	80	60	66	72	80	61	65	75
Exp. weighted average with $\alpha = 0.1$ and no initial estimate	0	5	10	14	20	26	30	33	37	41	44	46
Exp. weighted avarage with $\alpha = 0.1$ and an initial estimate of 50	50	50	51	51	53	56	57	57	57	61	61	62

forecast of average demand will be:

June's forecast = α(May's actual usage) + (1 − α) May's forecast)
= (0.1) (250) + (0.9) (220)
= 25 + 198
= 223

Forecasting using exponentially weighted averages we obtain the results shown in Table 6.1.

6.7 Determining the reorder level and safety stock

The Economic Order Quantity theory enables a company to calculate how many of an item to order within the fixed order quantity system. This however is only part of the story. Figure 6.4 shows an inventory pattens that would be ideal if achieved in practice. It makes a number of assumptions:
1. Constant usage.
2. Items always ordered at correct time.
3. Delivery always made on time.

This results in an inventory pattern in which stocks never rise above the maximum theoretical level nor do they fall below the minimum theoretical level.

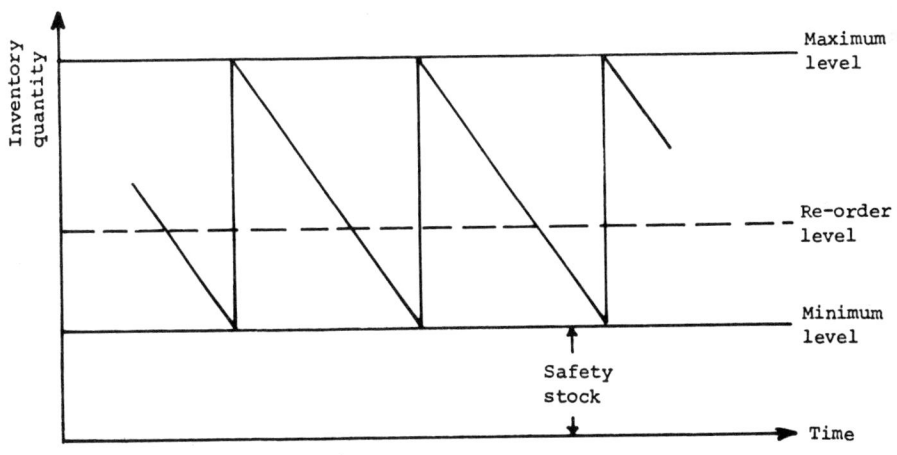

Figure 6.4 Inventory quantity

In practice the continual problem is that of deciding when to re-order and how much safety stock to carry. The major consideration is the desired service level that the particular company wishes to achieve. Put in everyday language a retail shop, selling shoes, could perhaps expect to satisfy 96 customers in every 100. Quite clearly in the latter instance the stocks would not need to be as great. This service factor is usually referred to as a K factor. To use this in stock control it is necessary to introduce the dispersion of values about the mean. It is a feature of all normal curves that the area enclosed by one standard deviation on either side of the average is 68 per cent, by two standard deviations 96 per cent, by three standard deviations 99.8 per cent, and so on. Statistical tables make it possible to interpolate for intermediate values of the number of standard deviations. We can select the value of K that will result in no stock outs for the desired percentage of the replenishment periods. Figure 6.5 shows the percentage protection against stock outs during each replenishment period for the selected number of standard deviations and Figure 6.6 the normal dispersion about the average.

The cover or safety stock will be a matter for management who must decide the extent to which it is prepared to invest capital in stocks. In the fixed re-order point system, the re-order point will be established as follows:

Reorder point, P = Average rate of usage during the maximum reasonable lead time plus safety stock

It may also be expressed as

$$P = B + \bar{S}_d L$$

When the average inventory level, I, is given by
$$I = B = Q/2$$
Where I is the average inventory level (in units), P the recorder point (in units), B the buffer stock (in units), $\bar{S}_d$ the average daily sales (in units) and L the lead time (in days). This can be shown diagrammatically as shown in Figure 6.7.

Check lists are an invaluable aid in every management function. Albert Battersby [1] has produced an excellent check list for questioning the very nature of all stocks.

Value of K	0.00	0.52	0.84	1.04	1.28	1.34	1.41	1.48
Protection, %	50	70	80	85	90	91	92	93

Value of K	1.56	1.65	1.75	1.88	2.05	2.33	2.57	2.88
Protection, %	94	95	96	97	98	99	99.5	99.8

Figure 6.5 Table showing values of K for stock-out protection

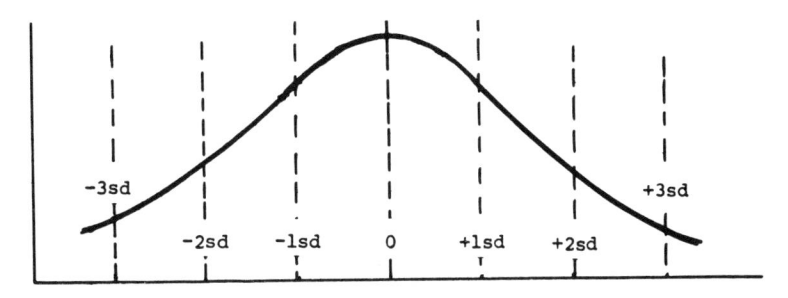

Figure 6.6 The normal dispersion about the average

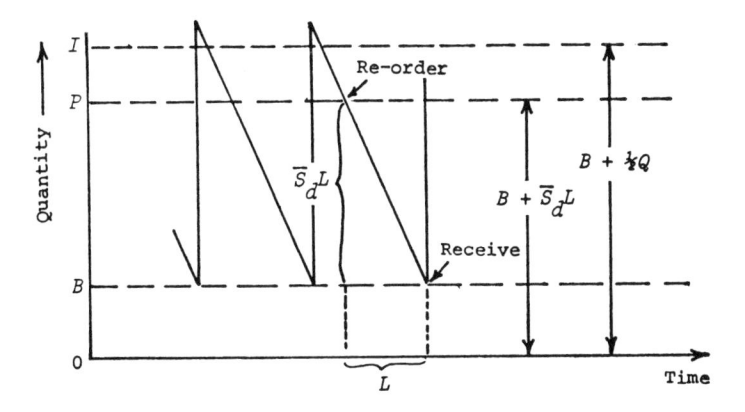

Order point = Expected lead time usage + SS

(Safety stocks, months + Lead time, months)

x (Average monthly usage units) = Order points, units

Item	Monthly usage	Lead time, months	SS, months
1	100	1.0	1.0
2	500	2.0	1.0
3	20	2.5	1.0

The re-order points are computed as follows:

	(SS + Lead time)	(Av.months usage)	= OP
1	(1.0 + 1.0)	100	= 200 pieces
2	(1.0 + 2.0)	500	= 1500 pieces
3	(1.0 + 2.5)	20	= 70 pieces

Safety stocks are often said to be one month's supply (used above)

Figure 6.7

What is this stock?

Description:
    Name of material
    Finished product
    Partly processed or intermediate product?
    Raw material
    Waste for disposal
    Special characteristics, e.g. bonded stock

Specification:
    Grade
    Limits of impurities, dimensions, etc
    Passed inspection or rejected for rectification
    Storage life
    Fashionable? Perishable? Obsolescent?

Identification:
    Batch number, etc.

Value:
    Standard or actual
    Material or works cost
    Selling price
    Cost of containers

Boundaries:
    Define exact points in the process at which material enters or leaves the stock.

Why is it held?

Absorbing fluctuations in:
    Sales: *(a)* random, short-term, *(b)* seasonal, *(c)* long-term
    Production: *(a)* cycle, *(b)* breakdowns, *(c)* workload — machines and men
    Raw materials: *(a)* delivery availability, *(b)* reliability, possibility of rejection, *(c)* strategic

When?

Date manufactured

Date ordered
Date received into stock
Date packed or prepared for dispatch
Date due for dispatch
Note any unusal delays

Who is responsible for it?

Responsible for: *(a)* adding to stocks, *(b)* taking from stock, *(c)* transferring from one stock to another, e.g. regarding, *(d)* storage and handling, *(e)* recording
Distinguish between: *(a)* day to day decisions (tactical), *(b)* policy (strategic)

How is it stored?

Bulk
Packages
Heated? Refrigerated? Air conditioned?
Protected against pilferage
Methods of handling

How much?

Is storage capacity: *(a)* freely available, *(b)* just adequate, or *(c)* inadequate?
Do we own it or rent it?

The concept of stockless buying

There have been many titles given to this technique, including stockless buying, contract buying and systems contracting. We believe that the most appropriate description is stockless buying. It indicates precisely what is intended, that for certain items in stock the physical stock will be held by a nominated supplier who agrees to supply all the needs within

24 hours of being notified that it is required. This method of controlling stock has given many companies advantages and there is no reason why anyone should not consider it as a negotiation tool.

It is obviously ideally suited to MRO (Maintenance, Repair and Operating items) which usually do not require the extent of sophisticated inventory control as that demanded by production items. With MRO items there is usually a tortuous route once a need has been identified. The steps may be traced as follows:

1   Identification of need.
2   Prepare a material requisition and submit for approval to nominated signatory.
3   Nominated signatory checks requisition and signs if he is convinced of the need. If not a delay will occur whilst this is done.
4   Requisition passed to appropriate stores.
5   Stores check the item and ensure all information is provided.
6   Stores make record of the transaction after issuing item.
7   If reorder point is reached stores reorder by preparing a purchase requisition which is passed to buying department the latter step will have to be made if an out-of-stock situation applies.
8   Buying department routine is applied, enquiries, evaluation, of sources, etc.
9   Purchase order placed.
10 Supplier selects item and dispatches. This assumes that he has the item in stock, if not he will go through stage (8) also, further adding to the delay.
11 Stores receive item and advise all interested departments.
12 Stores issue item.
13 Stores pass documentation to appropriate departments.
14 Supplier forwards invoice.
15 Supplier ultimately paid.

The time elapsed in such a transaction will vary but may take anything from seven to ten days depending on the location of the supplier.

The buyer should do all in his power to eliminate these hold-ups which do not improve the operational efficiency of the company. If he can contact a supplier who carries a wide range of stock concerned with maintenance items, e.g. bearings, gaskets, nuts and bolts, etc., he should negotiate a contract under which the supplier agrees to maintain a 24-hour service to the buyer. It is possible to have direct access communication equipment between buyer and seller if the volume is sufficiently large.

This system of stockless buying has many advantages for the buyer's company:

1. Continuity of a supply service is more assured when the seller has such a contract that guarantees him all the off-take on a wide range of items.
2. It is possible, indeed highly probable, that keener prices will ensue from such an arrangement. MRO items are usually lots of small quantity items, carrying small quantity extras. The fact that these are collected together makes it a more appealing proposition from the sellers' point of view.
3. A monthly invoice may be submitted rather than many individual ones which the old system invites. The savings here in administrative and clerical effort are substantial.
4. Valuable storage space will be released for other items or better still the space may be given over to production needs with the attendant saving on stores operational costs.

When negotiating a supply agreement involving stockless buying it is essential that the buyer makes contractual provision for the items concerned. To this extent the system is no different from any other purchase:

1. There should be written agreement on the range of items included.
2. Invoicing procedures should be agreed.
3. A time limit for the contract should be agreed, together with the respective rights to cancel.
4. Prices and method for reviewing increases to be agreed.
5. Supply period designated, e.g. 24 hours, 48 hours.
6. Insurance to be the supplier's responsibility.
7. Responsibility in the case of a stock out by a supplier occasioning delays in essential maintenance.

The paperwork used in a good stores system will be

Proof code			STOCK CONTROL CARD		Stores code				
	Code	Clear	Description				1		2
Unit of issue			Brief title		Bin location		Code		Clear
Check figure			Full spec.		Unit of purchase				
Re-order point					Card number				
Urge level					EOQ				
Date	Req.No. / Order No.	Allocation / Supplier code	Cost centre / Est. value	Week No.	Job No. / GRN No.	Orders	Receipts	Issues	Stock balance	On order balance	Verification

Figure 6.8 Example of stock control card

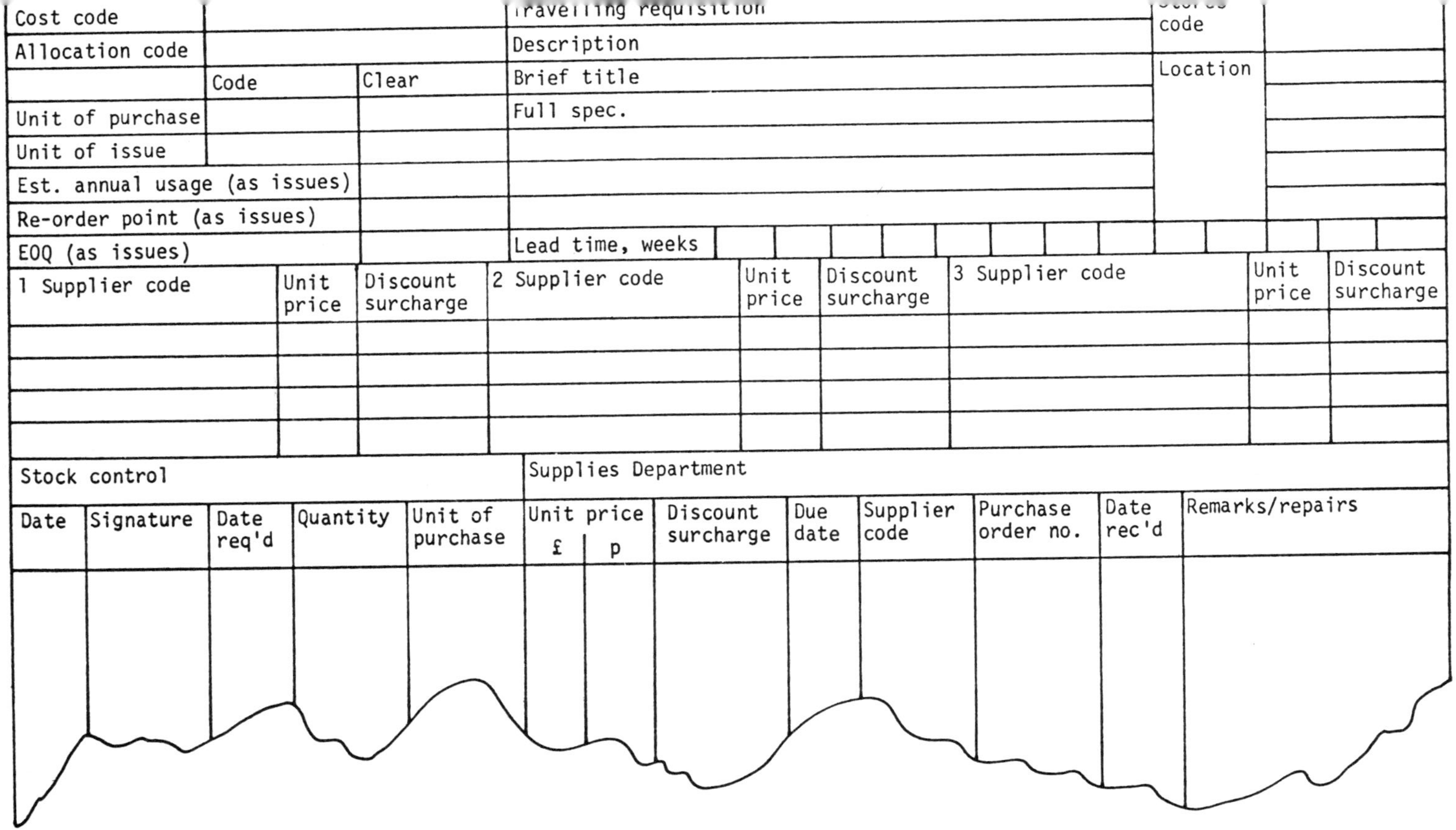

Figure 6.9 Example of a travelling requisition

```
                                    ABC Company Limited
                                    Any Street
                                    Any Town

    Supplier's address              Telephone:
                                    Telegrams:
                                    Telex:

                                    Date:


Dear Sirs,
                        DISCREPANCY ADVICE

We have received goods as shown below which, for the reasons
stated, are not in accordance with our Purchase Order. Please
advise us by return of the action you propose to take since,
in the circumstances, there will be a delay in passing your
invoice for payment.
```

Order details	Item No.	Description	Quantity

Receipt details	Item No.	Description (if different to above	Quantity

Further details

                                    Yours faithfully,

                                    for Supplies Controller

Figure 6.10   Example of Discrepancy Advice

Estimated bin quantity after receipt	Supplier						GRN No. 123579
	Description						Stores code
Units of quantity	Actual receipt quantity	Purchase order no.	Item no.	Supplier code	Order week no.	Delivery week no.
Code	Clear						
Purchase							
Issue							
Bin location	Terms	Allocation code	Cost code	Job no.	Advice note no.
Invoice no.	Invoice date	Unit price £ p	Total invoice price £ p	Price checked	Passed by

Figure 6.11 Example of Goods Received Note

(a)

Stores Issue Note				XY 3456	
Date	Stores code	Unit of issue	Issue code	Quantity	
Description					
Reason for return					
Present location					
Allocation code	Cost code	Issue week	Job no.	Bin location	
Received note	Authorised by	Issued by		Estimated bin qty after issue	

(b)

Stores Repair Note				735849	
Date	Stores code	Unit of issue	Issue code	Quantity for repair	
Description					
Reason for return					
Present location					
Allocation code	Cost code	Return week	Job no.	Serial nos. (if any)	
Returned by	Authorised by	Received by		Purchase enquiry/ order no	

(c)

Stores Credit Note				060607	
Date	Stores code	Unit of issue	Issue code	Quantity	
Description					
Reason for return					
Present location					
Allocation code	Cost code	Return week	Job no.	Bin location	
Returned by	Authorised by	Received by		Estimated bin qty after issue	

Figure 6.12

Job:	Stores Controller	Analyst:
Job Holder:		Date:
Report to:	Engineering Supplies Manager	

PURPOSE:
Provide and efficient service to the factory for the physical inspection, receipt, handling, location, storage, condition and issue of engineers' materials, together with all other bought-out requirements whether as initial, replacement or repaired stock.

DIMENSIONS:
Number of people:
Estimated annual salary bill:
Annual value of receipts for storage:

NATURE AND SCOPE OF THE POSITION:
The position, together with the two Tools Engineers (Continuous and Pilger Mills), the Senior Supply Planner and the Supplies Controller, reports to the Engineering Supplies Manager.

A Goods Received Foreman acts as the Stores Controller's deputy. He is assisted by two records clerks and two goods receivers. The remaining 10 day and shift workers report directly to the Stores Controller for handling, bin loading and issuing.

The stores operate within agreed budgetary limits established by the job holder and his superior. Activities central to the function are the control of receipts, satisfactory storage, and issuing of stock together with the maintenance of the associated records of goods received and outstanding for delivery. When a Purchase Requisition is raised the incumbent, together with the Supply Controller, assists the Senior Supply Planner in determining the estimated annual usage. This procedure only applys to initial or unique purchases, since recurrent items are re-ordered through the Stock Control System.

Advice notes of incoming goods are checked against the Purchase Order and suppliers immediately informed of any discrepancies. Reconditioned and new items are received into the Stores by a similar method and are treated in an identical manner. A four-part Goods Received note is raised, a copy of which is passed to Stock Control. All goods of whatever nature, excluding production steel, are initially received and inspected at Hope stores. For convenience, a few items may be re-directed to be stored elsewhere in the factory. It is essential that the systems adopted for storage and classification permit the speedy location of all items, to ensure that on receipt of authorised Stores Issue Notes, materials can be provided with a minimum of delay. To facilitate this process, the Issue Counter is permanently manned 24 hours a day, 7 days a week. When required, a fork lift truck and overhead crane are available to assist the movement of goods to and from the storage bins. Stock movements, amounting to about 1000 receipts and 6000 issues per month, are recorded at the time of the transaction. The maintenance of the stock in a satisfactory condition is at all times the responsibility of the Stores Controller, working in liaison with the Supplies Manager and the Senior Supply Planner.

The Auditors are permanently located in the Stores. They are responsible for verifying the accuracy of the Stock Control Record Cards and the Computer Stock Tabulations against the physical stock in the stores. At daily intervals they pass written progress reports to the Financial Accountant. Discrepancies between physical and recorded stock are shown in a Journal 4 Report to the Accounts Department and are investigated in conjunction with the incumbent and the supplies controller. The job holder is responsible for reporting breaches of the company rules by the Stores Auditors to the Financial Accountant, to whom they are responsible.

Control over the job holder's subordinates is maintained through personal daily contact. Weekly written reports on the Department's performance are sent by the incumbent to his superior. Annually the performance of the Department and its personnel are reviewed by the job holder in conjunction with the Engineering Supplies Manager.

The challenge of the job is to maintain and develop satisfactory storage and issuing procedures within the established cost limits, to meet the changing requirements of the Engineering and Production Departments. The attainment of this objective clearly entails the development and continued training of subordinate staff.

Continued overleaf

132 THE BASIC ARTS OF BUYING

> PRINCIPAL ACCOUNTABILITIES:
> 1 Ensure that the Stores personnel and systems of working are developed to continue to meet the increasingly diverse requirements of the Engineering and Production Departments for a prompt and efficient Stores service.
> 2 Assist the Senior Supply Planner and Supply Controller in establishing re-order levels to ensure that stock items are consistently available.
> 3 Provide Stock Control with detailed information of the movement of items in and out of the Stores area.
> 4 Ensure that the Stores Auditors are provided with the necessary facilities and receive the co-operation of the Stores personnel to enable them to fulfill their obligations of verifying Stock Control Cards and Computer Stock Tabulations against the physical stocks.
> 5 Ensure that the Engineering Supplies Manager is kept fully informed of the Department's progress towards acheiving budget and performance objectives.

Figure 6.13 Job description for a Stores Controller

designed to suit the purpose in mind. The selection included here are indicative of what is required.

Figure 6.8 shows a stock control card.

Figure 6.9 is a travelling requisition which 'shuttles' between the stores and buying department.

Figure 6.10 is a discrepancy advice sent to suppliers when there is a difference between the advised quantity and actual quantity received.

Figure 6.11 shows a typical goods received note.

Figure 6.12 is a family of stores notes: *(a)* represents a stores issues note, *(b)* a stores repair note and *(c)* a stores credit note.

If any stores management system is to be optimised it is essential that all the staff know what is expected of them. This will be done by the use of job descriptions. Reproduced in Fig. 6.13 is a job description for a stores controller (reproduced with permission of the Weldless Steel Tube Company Limited, a Tube Investments company).

7 Global Procurement

The majority of buyers do not source abroad. They are content to restrict enquiries to suppliers in the home market, mistakenly justifying to themselves and their managers that they are doing a good buying job. As most industrial countries depend to some extent on importing raw materials, manufactured and capital goods, some buyers have been involved, traditionally, in buying abroad. With the increasing development and changes in world trade, e.g. growth of the European Economic Community, pressures are being exerted on buyers to widen their sourcing across land and sea borders.

7.1 Why buy abroad?

As buyers experience problems of price, quality and delivery on goods bought in the home market, they will give more thought to buying abroad. Importing involves dealing with a customs barrier and possibly a sea barrier too; these present additional problems. Trading practices within foreign industries may be different from those of home-based suppliers. Nevertheless, buyers' horizons must be widened and the possible disadvantages assessed against the anticipated gains of buying abroad.

A buyer is presented with a particular type of evaluation exercise when he compares quotations submitted by foreign suppliers with those received from home-based suppliers.

There are a number of possible cost elements to consider in the total price build-up including freight, insurance, handling charges and customs duty. With experience, a buyer soon becomes familiar with the relevant aspects. The good buyer has to justify to himself and his purchasing manager that he has done an adequate sourcing and buying job. A buyer must source abroad but what prompts him to do so in the first instance? The day has gone when he could feel satisfied he was buying advantageously on price, quality and delivery from his home market. His reason for sourcing abroad could be one of many, such as:

1   *Goods not available from home market*   Home-based suppliers, previously able to supply particular goods may have discontinued manufacture. They may not now be able to meet the required delivery dates. Another reason could be that manufacturing licences granted by foreign companies have expired or have been withdrawn.

2   *Unsatisfactory quality of goods from home market*   The quality of goods now offered from the home market may have deteriorated compared with the quality previously supplied. Also, resulting from developments abroad, goods of a higher quality now required by the buyer may be available from pace-setting foreign suppliers but not from the home market.

3   *Home market prices too high*   The buyer may have to buy within a keen estimate, a task he finds impossible in the home market. He is thus compelled to source abroad. He may have received reasonably acceptable quotations from home-based suppliers but rightly considers he might obtain keener prices by sourcing abroad. Issuing enquiries abroad should increase his scope for reducing prices.

4   *Unsatisfactory after-sales service from home market*   The buyer may have been able to obtain goods of the required quality with deliveries to time at acceptable prices from home-based suppliers but has been dissatisfied with the after-sales service. Inadequate after-sales service may include unsatis-

factory guarantees or a supplier's refusal to supply working drawings, operating and maintenance manuals or instructions.

5 *Unsatisfactory conditions of sale imposed by home-based suppliers* A home-based supplier may refuse to give transfer of title before delivery. Terms of payment may be too stringent and be unacceptable to the buyer. The supplier may refuse to indemnify the buyer against all possible claims for infringement of patent rights.

6 *Customer choice* Plant, equipment or materials may be required by a buyer for a contract with a customer who has specified items of foreign supply either because of previous experience with similar goods or because he wishes to standardise in order to minimise spares inventories.

7 *Replacement of goods of foreign origin* The buyer may have no option but to buy the replacement items abroad as these are unobtainable from his home market.

8 *Reciprocity of trade* Occasionally, a buyer may be faced with seeking supplies abroad because his organisation has reciprocal trade agreements with foreign suppliers or with associated companies based abroad. Even trading intercompany, the buyer would still be involved with many aspects associated with buying abroad.

The reasons for buying abroad are, therefore, many and varied. The buyer's work load will increase when he widens his horizons and sources and buys abroad. The extent of this work will depend on whether he is buying across land or sea barriers and if there are tariff and language barriers too. Buyers should source abroad, but they should, at the same time ensure they have fully sources their home market.

7.2 Locating sources of foreign supply

To enable him to locate possible foreign sources of supply, the buyer has access to several aids to ease his task.

1 Trade directories   Perhaps the most useful aid to the buyer are the trade directories which are generally classified and cross-referenced alphabetically by commodity, supplier and country of supply. These directories include such well known international editions as Kellys, Kompass, and Jaeger and Waldman, the latter being a telex directory.

2 Trade literature   Most buyer will see the various trade magazines, brochures, leaflets and the advertisements displayed in other magazines and journals which circulate within their organisations. The keen buyer must set aside some time each week to scan through such publications to look for items of possible interest to himself or his buying and technical colleagues.

3 Trade fairs   Trade fairs fall into two categories: industry sponsored and government sponsored. Such fairs are usually well advertised in trade journals but the opportunities a busy buyer may have to visit them will largely depend on his work loads, where the fairs are being held, i.e. distance factor, the type of goods on display and the buyer's potential value of business to place.

4 Contacts   A buyer may have contacts who may be able to assist him to locate possible sources of supply. These contacts may be based abroad or in his home country. Perhaps one of the buyer's colleagues within his own organisation has dealt with particular foreign suppliers. Suppliers may have agents based in the buyer's country. The buyer may have contacts in other companies who can assist him. A foreign government's embassies and consulate staffs, particularly commercial attaches, may be able to advise buyers.

The buyer may have the services of his own organisation's sales staff or agents based abroad. He may have contacts in associated companies based abroad, who are geographically located to provide assistance. The buyer can also approach commercial attaches with his own country's embassies, consulates or high commissioners offices abroad. Ministries responsible for trade may provide assistance to buyers. Such trade ministries or departments may publish booklets of the

'Hints for Businessmen' type, which together with trade publications issued by the major banks, provide useful information on trading prospects with particular countries.

7.3 Preparing an adequate enquiry

There are a number of points the buyer must consider when he prepares his enquiry document. He has to cover the same sort of points applicable to enquiries issued to the home market. The difference is one of emphasis:

1 Defining requirements The main need is for clear, unambiguous specifications free from jargon, colloquial expressions and terminology or abbreviations that may not be understood (or be misunderstood) by foreign suppliers. For example, if a British buyer is enquiring from a German supplier for a quantity of '144 off', (the Imperial 'gross'), he should state '144 off' and not state 'gross' which has a rather different meaning in German. Buyers must ensure that the conditions of purchase to be applied to a possible order are clearly and precisely stated. There is need for close consultation between the buyer and his technical colleague at the enquiry stage to prepare an adequate enquiry.

2 Language Enquiries in English may be accepted by many foreign suppliers, particularly in Europe, but language difficulties may be experienced on some occasions and the buyer may need to seek assistance and have his enquiries translated into the languages of potential suppliers.

3 Delivery requirements The delivery date required must be related to the point at which the buyer wishes the goods to be available on that date. The buyer must, therefore, state clearly his requirements — 'Ex-works', 'FOB (Free on Board) named foreign port or airport', 'Free named border town', 'CIF (Cost, Insurance, Freight) named home port or airport' or other required destination.

4 Posting enquiry The buyer must appreciate that where

distance is significant, he must allow extra time for his enquiry to reach the foreign supplier. Postal charges for foreign mail are much higher than for internal mail and he should, therefore, restrict enclosures to the minimum to reduce package weights. For example, where a section of a drawing is adequate to specify requirements, a full drawing need not be sent.

5   *Evaluating quotations*   On receipt of a quotation the buyer would check, initially, to see if it was of possible interest, consulting as necessary with his technical colleagues where a check on specification was required. Close attention must be paid to wording because of possible misinterpretations of a particular meaning. A number of facilities are available to buyers and their technical colleagues to assist them with translations. Such facilities include language bureaux and freelance translators. Where an organisation is involved in developing trade with particular countries, there may be sufficient demand on translation work to justify employing a translator on its staff.

To evaluate the total cost of a quotation, a buyer must consider a number of elements of cost, where these are applicable:

>   Price of goods (ex-works).
>   Packing cost.
>   Cost of freight and insurance. The buyer must note, particularly, the sections of the journey covered by the supplier in his price. He must then arrange separately through his agents to cover the balance of journey if the supplier is not covering the whole journey.
>   Cost of port or airport handling charges.
>   Duty payable.
>   Import and insurance agents' fees.

Other aspects to be considered are firstly, the possible need to buy forward foreign currency (where payment is to be made in foreign currency) to avoid paying an increased price to the supplier for the goods should there be an adverse movement in currency rates of exchange. Secondly, a foreign supplier may demand more stringent terms of payment from the buyer than he has made to his home suppliers. This is understandable as the supplier is entering a new market with attendant risks. Where the buyer feels he may have to accept such terms, he must assess the resulting loss in investment earnings.

Only when the total cost of all these elements has been determined can the buyer make a realistic cost comparison between quotations received from foreign and home-based suppliers.

7.4 Supplier appraisal

The extent to which a buyer undertakes a supplier appraisal is not related directly to whether the potential supplier is foreign or domestic. The possible value of an order or the critical nature and complexity of the required goods are key aspects for determining the extent of appraisal. Nevertheless, there may be need for a deeper investigation of the foreign supplier. He may have a good reputation in an established home-market, but be a newcomer to the export trade, unknown internationally. Where the value of the business to be placed and high specification standards warrant an in-depth appraisal, the buyer must pose a number of questions to which satisfactory answers are required. Why does the foreign supplier want the buyer's business? Does he have a sound home-based market and if so why does he wish to export? Is the supplier subsidised by his own government and if so, to what extent? Is there a possibility of the withdrawal of such a subsidy and, if so, what would be the effect on price and delivery?

Obviously, much depends on the value of the possible order and its complexity and urgency as to what efforts a buyer must make to carry out a satisfactory appraisal. The supplier's financial status may be an aspect requiring particular attention. The buyer can utilise the services of financial specialists such as Dun and Bradstreet to carry out investigations. Such investigators operate in a number of countries. They can report on credit rating, possible mergers and take-overs, financial associations with other companies and company statements issued.

Does the foreign supplier have the production facilities and the spare capacity to undertake the work by the required delivery date? Does he have adequate engineering and design support? Who are his major suppliers? Are his quality-control facilities adequate? The buyer's sales staff or agents based abroad may be conveniently located, geographically, to inspect a potential suppliers facilities, to meet his staff to discuss matters of concern and finally, to decide if they can be recommended to the buyer as a satisfactory supplier.

Where time and circumstances demand, the buyer should carry out thorough preparatory work. He can make known his intentions to source abroad to his home-based suppliers to test their opinions. To avoid losing valuable business to an overseas supplier, they may make constructive suggestions, stressing possible pit-falls the buyer may have overlooked or has not fully appreciated.

In making his appraisal, the buyer must satisfy himself on the foreign supplier's ability to meet specification, quality standards and delivery requirements.

7.5   Price and currency

When a buyer places an order with a foreign supplier, he would normally wish to make payment in his own currency unless there were special reasons for not doing so. He would also seek a keen price, firmly fixed for the duration of the contract where this could be negotiated. The buyer would thus avoid paying an increased price should there be adverse fluctuations in the rates of currency exchange or increases in material and labour costs of manufacture.

The supplier may not agree to a fixed price being paid in the buyer's currency but require that payment be made in the supplier's currency. A foreign supplier may offer the alternatives of a price fixed firm for the duration of the contract or a datum price related to costs current at time of submission of quotation, subject to a price variation. The buyer may frequently have this choice when buying in the home market. Of particular importance, however, when buying abroad is determining what particular materials and labour indices are to be applied to calculate price variations. Such indices must be nationally recognised, the data being obtainable from official department of trade publications. The buyer must also check on the datum indices ruling at the date of quotation and the price variation formula to be applied to the order so that he can verify all possible claims for price increases which may be submitted.

7.6 Payment in foreign currency

Where the price is to be paid in a foreign currency, the buyer has two courses of action open to him. Firstly, he can take the risk that there will be no adverse fluctuations in currency exchange rates which would be to his organisation's disadvantage, and therefore not take precautionary measures. Secondly, he could take the wiser and more sensible action to buy forward foreign currency to meet his commitments on terms of payment, where there were sound reasons for so doing, i.e. the buyer's currency was in a weaker position relative to another currency agreed for the contract. What factors does a buyer consider when he decides on the action to take? He has to consider known facts against assumptions and probabilities. Facts may include known current economic, industrial and political climates at home and abroad or current devaluation or revaluation pressures being exerted on particular currencies.

Currencies tend to align with certain other currencies at particular points in time. Take as an example, a French or a British buyer wishing to place an order with a Dutch supplier for payment in guilders. There may be strong revaluation pressures on the German Deutschmark. The guilder and the Deutschmark may both be classified as 'hard' currencies. This could mean that if the Deutschmark was revalued relative to the buyer's currency (French franc or British pound sterling), then the guilder may be revalued similarly. On the other hand, the buyer may be dealing with a potential supplier whose currency tended to align more closely with his own currency. A third possibility is that the rate of exchange of the foreign supplier's currency may fluctuate to some intermediate position and not align with either the supplier's or the buyer's currencies.

The international currency market must be carefully studied before deciding on the course of action. Details of buying forward premiums are published at least weekly in financial newspapers. Foreign trading banks normally issue daily statements on currency, rates of exchange and buying forward premiums. Where the buyer is required to make a down payment with order he will be concerned only on the possible impact of fluctuations in rates of exchange on the balance to be paid. Another important point is the period over which the risk extends up to the date the last payment falls due.

The decision to buy or not to buy forward must be a speculative one and will depend on the amount involved and the current economic, industrial or political situation prevailing at home or abroad and the time scale of the contract. An organisation should have agreed procedures for buying forward currency. A buyer may have to consult with his purchasing manager who in turn may have to discuss with his financial colleagues or purchasing director when the order value exceeds a stated amount. Valuable as published details may be, it is advisable to seek advice from the trading bank where large sums are at risk. A buyer may wish to place an order valued at say, £100,000 or its equivalent in some other currency. The alternative courses of action are to incur a definite buying forward commitment of say, 3 per cent of the order price (£3000) or alternatively, face the possibility but not the certainty, of paying say an additional 10 per cent of the order price (£10,000) should his own currency devalue relatively during the period of the contract.

7.7 Terms of payment

A buyer may have to make more stringent terms of payment when he deals with a foreign supplier for the first time than he would normally make to his home-based suppliers. This is understandable. The supplier too faces a risk when he deals with a new customer abroad. He may make a customer appraisal which includes an investigation into the buyer's financial status. Later, when business relationships are established, payment terms may be eased to fall closer in line with terms normally agreed in the home market.

National banks take particular interest in terms of payment and they may limit the percentages of order prices which can be made as down payments or progress payments prior to submission of shipping documents. It is essential that buyers do not contravene the regulations laid down by their national banks. The foreign trading section of the buyer's bank will act on his behalf and keep him informed of national bank import regulations currently in force or due for revision. Problems may arise. Occasionally, a buyer may have to place a letter of authorisation with a foreign supplier to hold a stated price, to take up production capacity or to enable the supplier to place sub-orders for materials or equipment on long deliveries so that he in turn can meet the buyer's delivery requirements. There may not have been time to prepare and issue a purchase order by a deadline date. In placing the letter (or telex) of authoisation, the buyer may have agreed to make specified terms of payment including a down payment with order. In these circumstances, the buyer must avoid contravening the regulations laid down by his national bank before commiting his organisation to making specified payments to a foreign supplier. Failure to obtain such clearance could result in the national bank refusing to authorise payments with the result that the supplier does not proceed against the 'order' or he suspends work at a later stage pending release of progress payments.

The method of payment may take one or a combination of many forms which include:

1 A letter of credit for total value.
2 Payment with order, balance paid against a letter of credit.
3 Payment with order, balance paid on receipt of goods.
4 Cash with shipping documents.
5 Cash with order and interim payments.

The supplier may require a variation to one of these methods of payment.

Letters of credit are of many forms — irrevocable, revocable, divisible, transferable or assignable and can be a combination of two or more forms. A letter of credit is a generally accepted form of payment for goods bought abroad. The document is issued by the buyer's bank and is transferred to the supplier's bank, sometimes passing through an intermediary, or 'respondent' bank with whom both the buyer's and the supplier's banks have established contact. The cost of a letter of credit depends on the value of the buyer's account with his bank. Also, 'hard' currency countries tend to have low interest rates on letters of credit.

7.8 Customs and excise requirements

Customs and excise departments issue details of their tariffs which include classification of goods, prohibitions, restrictions, customs duties, excise duties, reliefs from duties, drawbacks and allowances. Normally, goods to be imported into a country may either require a licence or be imported against a quota. In certain special cases, goods may be imported licence or quota free.

1 Open licence   Such licences are generally issued by departments of trade and allow the import of goods (with certain specified exceptions) by type and source.

2 Individual licences   These licences allow holders to import the goods specified for a stated period. One form of individual licence allows goods of unlimited volume, weight or value to be imported from a specified source. Another form of individual licence may specify definite limits of volume, weight or value.

3 Quotas   These may be established from time to time and allow for the import of particular items or groups of items from specified countries.

4 Licences not required   Goods which can be imported without licences depend on the regulations in force in the importing country concerned. The schedule lists of such goods may vary from time to time because of changing circumstances. Some departments of trade may allow such items as trade samples, returned goods, personal or household effects, printed trade material and gifts to individuals to be imported without licences.

5 *Import licencing areas* Customs and excise departments apply different rates of duty on goods being imported, dependent on the nature of the goods and the country of origin. Countries of origin may be classified within specified import licencing areas including:

>The Dollar area
>The Eastern area
>The GATT area
>The Specified Territories
>The CEFTA areas
>The Mediterranean area
>The European Economic Community area

6 *Compliance with regulations* A buyer, or his agent, must not make arrangements to import goods or to send goods abroad for repair or further processing without first ensuring that, when required, the necessary licence has been granted or an assurance received that one will be granted.

Those concerned in buying goods abroad must note that:
1. Licences are not normally transferable.
2. Heavy penalties may be imposed for evasions, smuggling or for making false declarations.
3. The issue of a licence does not relieve the importer from payment of customs duties (where applicable) or from compliance with any other regulations or restrictions to which the goods are subject.
4. Goods must be imported before the licence expires. As soon as an importer receives information that goods cannot be consigned within the stipulated period, he must apply immediately for an extension to the licencing period.

7.9 Customs clearance

Importing is a specialist field where it is normal practice to engage an agent to act on the buyer's behalf to clear goods through customs, normally at the port, airport or other point of entry of the goods into the country. The agent has to present certain documents to Customs and Excise which may include:

> Supplier's original invoice in duplicate or triplicate
> Packing lists
> Bill of Lading
> Import licence
> Evidence of country of origin
> The appropriate Customs entry form
> Freight account
> Insurance account

The Bill of Lading is issued when goods are being imported by sea. This document is essentially a contract for the conveyance of the goods, a receipt for the goods and evidence of ownership.

On receipt of these documents, and if in order, Customs will assess any duty payable and then release the goods for despatch to their destination on payment of the duty. Customs entry forms are many in number and are used in connection with such requirements as goods from free preference areas, goods liable for specific rates of duty by weight, measurement or volume and goods liable for *ad valorem* duty, i.e. duty to be paid related as a stated percentage of the 'landed value' of the goods. The landed value is the sum of the cost elements incurred by the buyer up to the point the goods are presented to Customs, including order price, freight and insurance and dock or airport handling charges.

7.10 Import agents

Thorough preparatory work must be done to speed the movement of goods through Customs. To achieve this objective, the buyer must select a good agent to deal with all the various aspects related to importing. To select a good agent, the buyer can seek the advice of shipping companies, chambers of commerce and Customs and Excise. He can consider advertisements placed by import agents in the various shipping and freight journals. He can interview short-listed agents to determine the length of time they have been in business, the particular commodities in which they specialise and the exporting countries with whom they have dealt. The buyer can check on satisfied customers. It is important that just as a buyer does a supplier appraisal so he should do an agent appraisal when the situation demands.

Once the buyer has selected his agent, he needs to develop a good working relationship with him and to learn as much as he can about his work. He needs to understand and appreciate the agent's problems. The keen buyer will also learn about trading areas such as the EEC and participate with the agent to seek solutions to import problems. The agent may need a copy of the purchase order. He will certainly require such information as description of the goods, invoiced value of the goods, anticipated date and place of despatch, border point or airport or port of arrival and name of the buyer's insurance company. To determine the tariff heading under which the goods are to be imported, the buyer may need to consult with his agent, particularly where the goods are not readily identifiable with a tariff heading.

The agent will also require the supplier's name, address and where available, telephone and telex numbers. The supplier should be instructed to telex the agent as soon as he has details of the actual consigning arrangements such as the approximate weights, sizes and numbers of pieces making up the consignment, name of ship, and ports of despatch and arrival (if importing by sea), the names of the air-freight company and airports of despatch and arrival (if the goods are being airfreighted). The agent will also require routing instructions from the points of entry by sea or air to the buyer's specified destination. The buyer must instruct the supplier to send the following documents to the agent to facilitate clearance of the goods through Customs: original Bill of Lading, the stipulated number of copies of invoices, specifications and packing lists. Certificates of origin of manufacture may also be required. Where goods of 'home' manufacture are included in the consignment, copies of invoices for these goods will also be required so that a claim can be made for exemption from duty, as applicable.

Once he has received the necessary documents, the agent can present these to Customs and pay any duty assessed on the landed value. He will also pay applicable port or airport handling charges and arrange for the goods to be consigned to their destination, dealing also with transport charges incurred. On completion of his assignment, the agent will submit his invoice to the buyer giving a breakdown of the various charges incurred in the import transaction, including his own fee.

The buyer's choice of agents may depend very largely on the method of import; by sea or air, the ports or airports of entry, whether the goods are being transported across a land border by rail or road vehicles, or being transported across the sea by ferried vehicle.

7.11 Insurance

Goods being imported from abroad must be insured for the whole of the journey from the supplier's works to the stated final destination. The buyer must decide what the most advantageous and economical method of insurance is: 'Ex-works', 'FOB', 'CIF., etc. In the case of 'Ex-works' insurance, the buyer has to arrange insurance cover for the whole of the journey. In the case of 'FOB', the supplier takes out insurance and takes the risk from despatch from his works to when the goods pass over the ships rails at the port of shipment. The buyer then takes the risk for the remaining portion of the journey to the stated destination. With 'CIF' insurance, whilst the seller has insured the goods up to the time they pass over the ship's rail at the home port of arrival, the buyer takes the risk from the point the goods pass over the ship's rail at the port of shipment. There are, however, many other forms of insurance cover the buyer could consider. He could, for example, instruct the supplier to arrange freight and to insure

TABLE 7.1 Selected price basing points: place of delivery and passing of the risk

Terms	Charges paid by the buyer (cumulative)	Delivery takes place (at/on)	Property and risks pass (on)
1 Warehouse to warehouse - all risks whatsoever	Nil	Buyer's premises	Delivery to buyer's premises
2 CIF named home port	Home port dues. Dock handling charges. Transport to warehouse. Duty, clearance and delivery to buyer's premises	On tender of Bill of Lading to buyer	Over the ship's rail at port of shipment
3 CIF	Marine insurance	On tender of Bill of Lading to buyer	Over the ship's rail at port of shipment
4 FOB	Shipping expenses, documentation and freight	When safely loaded	Over the ship's rail at port of shipment
5 FAS	Dock and port expenses, and outward customs facilities	Under the ship's hook	When the ship is able and ready to load
6 Ex-works	Loading on to road or rail vehicle	Seller's premises or other notified warehouse	Notification that the goods are at the buyer's disposal

for the whole journey and to consign the goods on a 'Warehouse to Warehouse — All Risks Whatsoever' basis. In this case the buyer pays for these charges within his order price. (See Table 7.1.)

Insurance of the goods is an element of cost that the buyer has ultimately to pay. He must satisfy himself, before goods are despatched, that they have been adequately insured by one or both parties to the contract for the entire journey. No stages or sections of the journey must be left uncovered. To reduce freight and insurance charges to a minimum, the buyer can consider alternative proposals. He can ask the supplier to quote 'FOB', 'CIF', 'Warehouse to Warehouse', etc., and at the same time obtain quotations from his own insurance agent to decide on what arrangements to make. The buyer arranges for the full insurance when he imports on an 'Ex-works' basis. The supplier arranges the full insurance when the order is placed on a 'Warehouse to Warehouse' basis. With other forms of insurance cover such as 'FOB' or 'CIF' this is 'split insurance'. The main problem facing the buyer importing on these bases is the difficulty of determining where damage, sustained during the journey, actually occurred, and therefore, whose insurer is liable. There may be delays in settling a claim. The claim may not necessarily be settled in the buyer's favour. However, many buyers import on a 'split insurance basis', and obtain satisfactory results.

7.12 Instructions to the buyer's insurance agent

When the buyer places an order and has to arrange insurance cover or takes the insurance risk for part of the journey, he requires the services of an insurance agent who must be given full details of the import, including, possibly, a copy of the purchase order. The agent would be instructed to arrange provisional cover from the point the buyer takes the insurance risk. Naturally, when dealing with equipment, components or materials, one thinks in terms of arranging for insurance to the point of receipt of the goods at the buyer's premises or other stated destination. However, occasionally, when capital equipment is being imported, the buyer may arrange for the supplier to deliver, install and commission the plant. The buyer must then ensure that the plant is adequately insured up to the point of 'take-over' of the commissioned plant.

Once the buyer has received shipping details including anticipated date of despatch and other necessary consignment details he can notify the insurance agent of the anticipated date of shipment, approximate weights, sizes and numbers of pieces forming the consignment, expected date and place of arrival at the named port, airport or border point, the sum to be insured and the period of insurance cover required. The amount to be insured normally would include the order value plus any additional freight and handling charges plus a nominal 10 per cent to cater for possible increases in charges. To assist the insurance agent, the buyer should instruct the supplier to telex the agent as soon as final shipping arrangements are known so that he will be aware of the actual dates, names of ships and port of shipment (transport by sea) and in the case of transport by air, the airline, airway bill number and where known, the flight number. Finally, the agent requires details of the actual consignment, the final value, and place and expected date of arrival.

7.13 Payment for imports

Regulations vary from country to country but normally, some form of government or national bank currency exchange regulation control act will be in force. Such regulations may prohibit or restrict the transfer of currency or gold to persons or organisations residing or doing business in any country abroad, particularly outside a defined trading area of which the buyer's country is a member, without a permit issued by his national bank or some other authorised bank. The necessary permit would normally be obtained through the applicant's bank depending on circumstances, the following forms may be required:

    Foreign currency application form
    Home currency transfer form

Import licence (where applicable)
Evidence of purchase of goods and value
Evidence that the goods have been despatched or will be despatched on receipt of payment
Copy of settlement invoice
Special copy of the Customs entry form (for goods above a specified value)

A national bank may restrict levels of payment to be made in advance for imports except in special circumstances with prior permission. There is usually a stated validity period for currency transfer forms. Enquiries relating to currency control can be made to the importer's bank or direct to the department of the national bank which is responsible for import and export currency exchange control.

7.14 Progress and inspection

For most buyers, inspection and progress present them with particular difficulties when suppliers are located in foreign countries, perhaps several hundreds or thousands of miles away across land or sea borders. A buyer may have done a good sourcing and supplier appraisal job. He may wish to arrange inspection and progress visits to the supplier's work to ensure that quality standards are being maintained and work is proceeding to schedule. The need for him or his technical colleagues to visit the supplier will depend very much on the value of the order, its complexity, the order time scale related to the work content of the order, i.e. the urgency factor, and the assessed supplier reliability particularly on anticipated quality control or delivery problems. Where it is deemed essential that visits must be made because of special circumstances, then significant cost might be incurred in sending an expediting engineer or a quality control inspector. One man might be briefed to deal with both progress and inspection. Obviously this approach might have to be restricted to special circumstances. Where the buyer's organisation has sales staff or agents operating abroad such people may be able to assist, particularly if they are close to the supplier's works and qualified to undertake the assignment.

The bulk of progress work can normally be handled by telex. This is a most useful means of communication with a supplier because the buyer can state his requirements clearly and precisely and the message can be transmitted promptly to the supplier. This method of progressing is much less expensive than using the telephone where difficulties might be experienced contacting the person required. A requirement may be fairly comprehensive and it may not be readily explained by telephone, particularly if there is a language problem. The telex message enables the recipient to study what is actually required and also provides the buyer with a record of action taken, and when. In an emergency, efforts would obviously be made to contact the supplier by telephone, following up as necessary by telex to confirm the details of the discussion and the agreed action.

On the question of quality, the buyer may require samples of goods to be submitted for checking before authorising release of order batches, where the nature of the order demands. He may arrange for visits by quality control inspectors. The buyer may also instruct the supplier to produce the appropriate material assurance and test certificates. The buyer should negotiate with the supplier that, in the event of goods found on receipt to be defective, these would be replaced promptly at the supplier's expense. In very urgent circumstances, the buyer may need to obtain replacements locally from the home market. He should, therefore reach agreement with the supplier on liability for such cost incurred, where the supplier is unable to supply replacements promptly.

Buyers should demand that goods supplied shall be to the required standards of quality. They may also require suppliers to submit certificates of quality when the goods are due for shipment.

7.15 Terms and conditions of purchase

With the increasing development of world trade and the forming of larger trading communities, efforts are being directed to the preparation of acceptable conditions of contract which attempt to reconcile major differences between conditions of sale and purchase. It must be accepted, however, that there may be significant differences between a buyer's proposed special conditions of purchase and the foreign supplier's conditions of sale. Many suppliers state in their quotations to foreign customers that in the event of an order being received, should any dispute arise between the two parties to the contract which they cannot resolve, and has to be settled in court, then the law of the supplier's country shall apply. This clause is included in the conditions of contract document, 'Incoterms', prepared in 1953 by the International Chamber of Commerce. In the same document, a transfer of title clause is included which states that transfer of title shall not pass to the buyer until he has made final payments against an order. These are two particular aspects on which the keen buyer will use his purchasing power to negotiate modifications. Where the buyer makes substantial progress payments prior to delivery of goods, he must protect his interests in case of the supplier's possible bankruptcy. Where he makes a significant down payment with order, he should obtain a guarantee from the supplier's bank that the contract will be executed or monies paid, refunded.

Where complex or prototype plant or equipment is ordered, there is a greater risk of possible infringements of patent rights, especially when buying abroad. The buyer must, therefore, obtain the foreign supplier's agreement in writing to indemnify the buyer against all possible claims from third parties for infringements of patents.

Where transfer of title to the goods has been agreed for the contract, materials and equipment obtained by the supplier for the contract should be identified with the buyer's order number. The supplier must also be instructed to insure the goods in the joint names of the buyer and himself for the requisite period and produce evidence to the buyer of such insurance.

7.16 Summary

Some buying decisions are more difficult to make than others, involving the possible weighting of many factors to be considered. The buyer who has restricted sourcing to his home market has to consider many aspects and be prepared to deal with increased documentation when he buys abroad. In deciding whether or not to place an order with a foreign supplier, he must, initially, determine that the required goods can be imported, if a licence is required and what duty has to be paid. He must check also that there will be no problems on payments. The buyer has to define his requirements more clearly and precisely. For a major or vital order, a thorough supplier appraisal must be undertaken. Once an order has been placed, special efforts may be necessary on progressing and quality control.

Perhaps the main difference a buyer must note when he buys abroad is the need to work closely with such people as import and insurance agents and foreign trading bank staff (see Figure 7.1). It is vital to the success of a contract placed with a foreign supplier, that he does work closely with such people to ensure that necessary documents are raised and submitted, particularly to customs and excise and the national bank to facilitate processing of the order and the subsequent prompt clearance of the goods through custome.

There is a challenge to the buyer buying abroad for the first time. It also presents a continuing challenge to the buyer with wide experience in foreign markets. Both have to consider many if not all, of the following points before making a decision on the selection of a foreign supplier:

1 Consequences of breach of contract.
2 Assessment of the true total cost of the import.
3 Ability of the supplier to meet specification and quality standards.
4 Possible language problems.
5 Vulnerability of supply lines due to weather, port or airport delays.
6 Possible effect on a contract resulting from changing government trading policies.
7 Domestic Factories Acts and equipment insurance requirements.
8 Subsequent spares and servicing requirements.
9 Rejection of sub-standard goods received, time factor to replace and determination of liability for cost.

10 Possible loss of goodwill from established home-based suppliers.

Yes, we agree that the list of the above points looks formidable. It is important that buyers consider all applicable aspects when they source abroad. They must know precisely how to tackle the task. Obviously, a buyer may not source abroad for goods of low annual expenditure unless he has a quality, delivery or some other particular problem. On receipt of quotations from foreign suppliers he must evaluate them and assess if there will be a definite advantage in placing his order abroad. A buyer may have been dissatisfied with price, quality or delivery of goods received from his home market but even when he has not been dissatisfied, he cannot consider himself to be a good buyer unless he effectively demonstrates to himself and his manager that he has done an adequate sourcing job. He cannot claim to have done so unless he has sources abroad.

A buyer's aim must be to buy commodities at prices that are at least as low as the prices paid by his competitors. This objective is difficult to measure but, basically, the buyer's task is to buy at the lowest possible prices compatible with obtaining quality, delivery and other necessary safeguards. Bought-out goods and services generally account for more than 50 per cent of an organisation's total operating costs. A buyer must aim, therefore, to buy at prices lower or equal to those paid by his competitors, even though he works for a non-profit making organisation.

The buyer can at least demonstrate the extent to which he has sought lower prices by the extent to which he sources abroad. Such sourcing must then be followed up by effective supplier appraisal. The buyer must then evaluate the possible impact or effect of all relevant factors and negotiate with the maximum skill his bargaining position allows him to make the best buy. He must resist the temptation to source only in his home market because he believes that steel, rubber, plastics or some other required materials or components are more expensive abroad. A buyer must appreciate that material prices can change rapidly. Also, possible higher material costs abroad may be offset by a foreign supplier's lower labour costs, higher productivity or higher efficiency. There is also the possibility

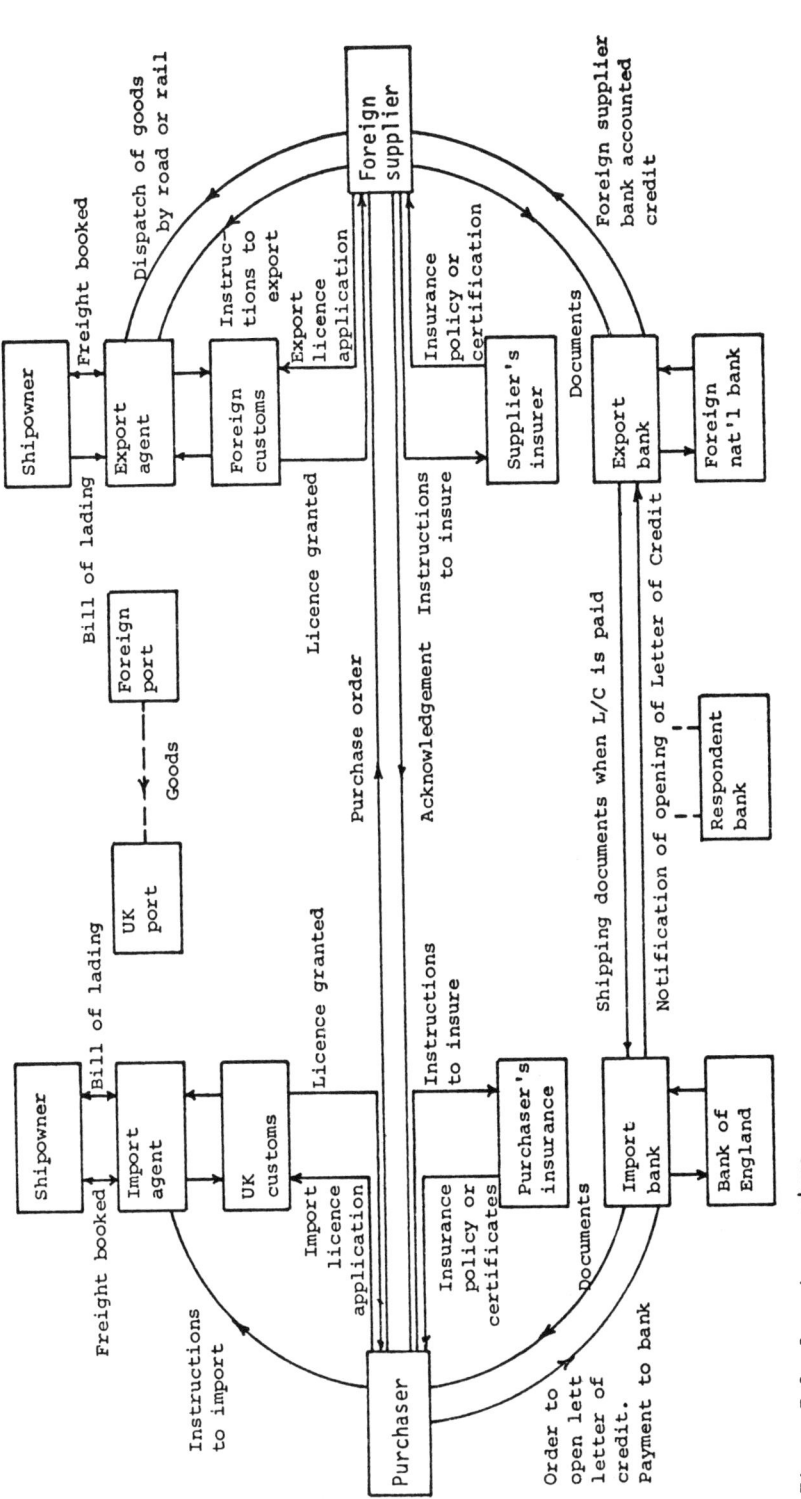

Figure 7.1 Import procedure

that a particular foreign supplier may be prepared to reduce his price to fill spare capacity.

There are a number of factors that will make foreign buying more important. Traditional reliance on home suppliers has become unacceptable when international trading profit margins are slender. The buyer must accept that dynamic, senior management will expect him to trade on an international basis. Equally, he will be held accountable for all his decisions. We believe that the advice and guidance contained in this chapter will lead to more effective decision-making.

8 A Review of Purchasing Techniques

8.1 Introduction

Imagine that a person has been taken into hospital for a very serious operation. He does not know the surgeon but he begins to imagine the event. The surgeon will have a team who are supported by the latest equipment and instruments. The patient rightly expects everyone to be highly trained and know when to use the appropriate surgical techniques.

This is analagous to a buying activity. A company has the right to expect each buyer to be highly trained and know when to use the appropriate buying technique to deal with a specific buying problem.

There are many techniques available to the buyer. Some will be used exclusively in the buying department whilst others will be used in collaboration with colleagues in other departments.

8.2 Value engineering and value analysis

Value engineering is the application of value analysis techniques to new products in the development or prototype stage.

Value analysis is an analytical technique designed to examine all the elements of cost and function of an existing product to determine whether or not any item of cost can be reduced or eliminated whilst retaining all functional and quality requirements.

The perceptive reader will distinguish the essential difference between the two approaches. Value engineering is applied before a product goes into production. This is the correct time to investigate costs since any changes are minimal in cost. For example, no tooling will have been ordered at this time and design changes will not be associated with prohibitive cost changes. Having said this it must be recognised that once a product enters the manufacturing phases there will be continuing opportunities for cost investigation and likely reduction. This will require the application of value analysis techniques. A warning needs to be made however. Any design changes at this stage may involve additional expenditure on tooling changes. This will require very accurate and detailed cost investigations aimed at ensuring that any additional expenditure can be recovered during the life of the product.

These techniques are not the sole province of the buyer. He will be only one of a team who co-operate to reduce costs. They will need to adopt an inquiring attitude associated with a discipline of not leaving any stone unturned.

Value engineering and value analysis are generally attributed to Harry Erlicher and L. D. Miles of the General Electric Company (USA) at the time of the close of the Second World War. They found that many materials were in short supply or were simply not available. Necessity has often proved to be the mother of invention and this was no exception.

A typical value analysis study will consist of a job plan. It could follow the lines shown below.

8.2.1 Stage one: information

This is an essential feature of the study when many facts must be gathered. The functions must be determined, specifications listed and costs must be allocated to specific functional areas. Questions will be asked concerning the product's use and performance and its cost. The buyer should expect to play a vital part here because he has access to existing cost records for purchased materials and components.

8.2.2 Stage two: speculation

This is a critical phase when the creative effort is expended and brainstorming sessions take place. No idea is dismissed nor criticism passed. Every functional specialist will play his part and in this regard the buyer has an excellent opportunity for demonstrating his creative talents. Miles developed his ten tests for value. These have stood the test of time and are worth recording.

1. Does its use contribute value? This is not primarily the buyer's concern, rather that of marketing. Something may have esteem value rather than use value. The best example is a car bumper which is chrome plated for appearance. The fact that it is decorative does not help its main use, i.e. that of protecting the car.
2. Is its cost proportionate to its usefulness? Here again the buyer is not primarily concerned. Other functional specialists are in a better position to answer this one.
3. Does it need all its features? The buyer has a potential involvement here by making sure that all suppliers have an opportunity for making suggestions aimed at reducing costs. It is necessary to realise that most sellers have highly specialised knowledge and may well have investigated similar items before. A buyer's problem is not always unique.
4. Is there anything better for the intended use? The buyer with his continual market investigations is in a unique position to advise his colleagues on the team. New products may replace older designs. These may afford opportunities previously not anticipated. The buyer must ensure that all such ideas are investigated which means no pre-judgement on his part.
5. Can a usable part be made by a method that costs less? Again the buyer will be in a strong position to investigate this aspect of the study. It will require specialist knowledge of manufacturing techniques and a constant appraisal of the technical press. Also, visits to suppliers premises will assist with creative searching.
6. Can a standard product be found which will be usable? There have been many situations where specials have

been bought because of ignorance that a standard part exists. This aspect of cost investigation should be considered by the buyer.

7   Is it made on proper tooling — considering the quantities used? This applies to castings, forgings and pressings and requires the application of specialised knowledge. The buyer is responsible for expenditure on bought-out goods and services and he should co-operate with his technical colleagues to seek adequate information on this feature.

8   Does the sum of material, labour, overhead and profits equal its cost? This is purchase price analysis in its purest form and essential to any well run buying department. The technique will be covered later in the chapter. Naturally the buyer is expected to play a leading role in the application of this technique.

9   Will another dependable supplier provide it for less? Comment on this aspect would be superfluous for any self-respecting buyer.

10   Is anyone buying it for less? This question was posed in the context of a large corporation where there was a chance that buyers in two or more locations might be buying the same part for different prices. It is therefore essential that these facts are known and investigated. It obviously requires good inventory cataloging for it to become possible.

The buyer who has gained credibility in this organisation will find that he can become a respected member of the value engineering/analysis team.

8.2.3 Stage three: evaluation

At this juncture the team will note all the advantages and disadvantages of the various ideas. They will have to assess likely costs of the many options and will probably have discussions with all suppliers who have shown an interest in the work concerned. The difficult part is to determine the improved worth of a new idea. The buyer will play a leading part in discussions with outside sources.

8.2.4 Stage four: report

Good management practice demands that a team such as that being discussed accounts for its actions. The culmination of an investigation will be the issuing of a report which records the discussions and summarises the potential savings, together with the likely effect of changes.

8.2.5 Stage five: implementation

This will obviously be at the option of the management of the company. Once cleared for action there must be a pre-determined change procedure and a monitoring system that records actual achievements against those predicted.

8.3 Learning curve analysis

Continual repetition of a task leads to an increase in the speed at which the task is carried out — perhaps because of increasing dexterity on the part of the person doing the job. This basic fact has led to the adoption of the Learning Curve as a technique for measuring and predicting the change in production cost output. Increased dexterity is not the sole factor of improvement. There are a broad group of innovations that may also assist, e.g. work simplifications, engineering changes, flow process changes and improved tooling.

It would be quite wrong to assume that this technique can be universally applied. It requires particular product circumstances. The aircraft industry has contributed a great deal of knowledge to the application of learning curve analysis. The basic reasons for this are that the use of direct labour is heavy and assembly operations predominate and are non-mechanised and repetitive in nature.

The characteristics of the learning curve can be illustrated as shown in Table 8.1. The important relationship here is that between labour hours required per unit and the units produced, but taken at each doubled quantity. Reference to the table will show that as the quantity doubles from 2 to 4 there

TABLE 8.1

Units produced	Labour hours required for each unit at indicated unit number	Difference in labour hours per unit	Difference, per cent
1	60,000	–	–
2	48,000	12,000	20
4	38,400	9,600	20
8	30,720	7,680	20
16	24,576	6,144	20
32	19,661	4,915	20

is a 20 per cent reduction in the labour hours required. There is a similar percentage reduction when the quantity doubles from 4 to 8. This establishes, for a theoretical example, a learning curve of 80 per cent. If this relationship is plotted on ordinary graph paper a hyperbolic curve will result. If however, log-log paper is used a straight line will ensue.

It is only in an ideal world that the reduction in labour hours would be exactly the same percentage each time the quantity produced doubled. If the buyer is using the learning curve as a negotiation tool he must be realistic and expect that there will be variations in the percentage reduction.

If he is buying a product that has some of the elements inherent to opportunities for learning he must ensure that the price he pays takes account of this fact. The application of the technique should not be underestimated. Many manufacturers are suspicious of its use and will resist discussions centred on the divulgence of cost data.

8.4 Supplier appraisal

When the buyer is faced with a potential supplier with whom he has no previous trading experience it is essential that information is gathered on which the buying decision will be based. This detailed information will be in addition to that contained on the quotation.

The classic definition of a good supplier is that coined by Professor Wilbur B. England:

'A good supplier is one who is at all times honest and fair in his dealings with the customers, his own employees and himself; who has adequate plant facilities and know-how so as to be able to provide materials which meet the purchaser's specifications, in the quantities required, and at the time promised, whose financial position is sound; whose prices are reasonable both to the buyer and to himself, whose management policies are progressive; who is alert to the need for continued improvement in both his products and his manufacturing processes; and who realises that, in the last analysis, his own interests are best served when he best serves his customers.'

Supplier appraisal is a technique that the buyer can use to gather essential data on the potential supplier's operations. Research in the United Kingdom has shown a lack of systematised approach; the buyers who have co-operated with the research listed eleven ways in which they conducted supplier appraisal. These are shown below as an indication of a fragmented approach.

1. Visit by purchasing representative.
2. Visit by liaison engineer.
3. Visit by supplier quality assurance survey engineer.
4. Plant lists and questionnaires completed by supplier to determine flexibility and financial stability.
5. Details of industrial relations history.
6. Details of machine tool maintenance programme.
7. Details of purchasing records kept.
8. Conditions of buildings and whether leased.
9. Date founded.
10. Trade association membership.
11. Balance sheets for previous three years.

None of these factors or ways of investigating is useless. The good buying activity will devise a co-ordinated methodology of investigating suppliers facilities. The approach will involve a two-pronged analysis, quality and commercial. These factors are in the appropriate sequence. A quality assurance visit is essential prior to further examination. If the potential supplier is unable to meet the desired quality standards a serious assessment of the whole situation will have to be made. The buyer's company may decide to assist the seller with expertise to improve his capabilities. One major United Kingdom car manufacturer has a relatively simple grading system for all supplier investigations:

    'A' category supplier — unlimited sourcing possible
    'B' category supplier — limited sourcing
    'C' category supplier — no sourcing until quality assurance give indication that standards have improved

When major purchases are being considered it is useful for the buyer to co-operate with quality assurance personnel to devise a check list that can be used on supplier visits. The following extracts are provided for guidance.

8.5 Quality appraisal

Does the company practice quality control or is control exercised by inspection?

To whom is the senior member of the above control organisation responsible?

Does the senior member of the above control organisation have adequate authority?

Does the company audit the performance and procedures of the above control organisation?

Does the company possess laboratory facilities applicable to the control of all materials and processes used?

Who decides action to be taken on items rejected by laboratory?

Are there adequate inspection media, measuring media and measuring instruments available for product control?

Does the firm work shifts or normal day work?

If there is shift work, is there adequate control operating at all times?

Are stored, in-process and finished materials or components adequately identified to prevent misuse? (State the method used.)

Are rejected materials, part-finished and finished components adequately identified and suitably segregated to prevent use, shipment or intermixing with conforming goods? (State method used.)

Is stock rotation practiced on stored, in-process and finished materials or components, to facilitate identification and segregation of defectives, at suppliers works, at customers works or in service?

Is there a system for controlling and recording authorised deviations from specification?

The above points are indicative of the detail required if buying decisions are to be totally effective in reducing the risk involved in introducing new suppliers. Having undertaken such a study it is then necessary to investigate the commercial aspects. Extracts are produced from the commercial appraisal system used by the Military Aircraft Division of British Aircraft Corporation.

> Supplier's name and address.
> Factory address if different.
> Division or subsidiary.
> Officers and Executive.
> Company organisation.
> Licence facilities.
> BAC conditions of purchase accepted?
> Do you permit the customer to have access to
>> Operations?
>> Facilities?

Records?
Do you have established overhead rates?
Are these approved by any Government Agency.
Do you apply learning curve techniques for calculating direct labour?
What is the curve?
Can you provide audited financial statements for previous years and current (unaudited) statements appropriate to the company or divisions of concern?
What is the current value of the order book?
What is the monthly output?
List supplies and/or services which can be provided.
Do you have recent contracts involving engineering design for:
1   Aircraft industry?
2   Government?
3   Others?
Are you able to produce drawings and engineering data to MIL specifications and aeronautical standards?
Describe your configuration, design data and change control procedure.
Facility security clearance held (level).
Show employee hours spent last year on
a   Engineering
b   Manufacturing
c   Quality assurance
d   All other departments
e   Total of above
Do you furnish product support for your products?
Do you manufacture test equipment and special tooling in support of your products?

These questions have been devised by a highly specialised buying activity dealing with sophisticated equipment. This accounts for the range of questions and their obvious bias. It must be stressed that the above list is only a random sample from a very detailed check list. It serves to demonstrate that the buyer should be innovatory and sufficiently motivated to develop his own list to deal with his particular situation. It is not suggested that such a detailed investigation is made for every supplier. However, where a part is deemed to be essential to production or service functions, the supplier must be shown to be capable of handling the requirement.

8.6 Supplier rating

Suppliers appraisal is a technique aimed at providing vital facts regarding a potential supplier before any business is conducted. The technique of supplier rating is intended to provide continuous facts regarding the actual performance of a supplier. Aljian [2] has stated:

> 'Modern progress in procurement methods has seen increasing emphasis placed upon the meaningful evaluation of seller performance. In simple fairness to one's suppliers and oneself this must be reduced to a quantitative basis. An adequate and effective system for measuring the merit of suppliers can thus become the unassailable proof of a purchasing operation's honesty and efficiency. It is the final answer to every charge of bias and favouritism.'

This comment amply justifies the efforts that must be expanded on supplier rating systems. These will vary in complexity, depending on the range of factors being monitored.

Buyers in the United Kingdom were asked to co-operate with an investigation [3] into this aspect of their work. The question asked was 'What factors would cause you to change a source of supply?', and the buyers were asked to Tick the appropriate row:

PRICE/COST BENEFIT _____
POOR DELIVERY PERFORMANCE _____
POOR QUALITY PERFORMANCE _____
OTHER _____

The responses are detailed below:
- 68.6% ticked all factors.
- 13.7% ticked price/cost benefit as the sole influence for changing a source of supply.
- 5.8% ticked poor delivery performance as their sole criteria for changing a source of supply.
- 0.0% mentioned poor quality performance.

TABLE 8.2 Quality performance

Month	Total deliveries	Rejects	Rejects as % of deliveries
January	390	Nil	00.0
February	760	30	3.9
March	890	65	7.3
April	600	50	8.3
May	750	80	10.6
June	900	100	11.1

    6.1%   did not respond to this question.
    5.8%   ticked 'other' and a summary of their responses is detailed below.

1 Design change to level outside capabilities of a current source of supply.
2 Dual source for high volumes.
3 Rationalisation of parts to one supplier.
4 Abolish monopoly factor.
5 Bad communication.
6 Lack of service.

These responses are worth noting because they give an indication that there are some elements of a supplier's performance that must be watched on a continued basis. These are (1) price, (2) quality, (3) delivery. Each of these offers the considerable advantage that they can be quantified and therefore not open to the criticism that bias or prejudice has entered someone's judgement. The way in which such a system could operate may be illustrated as shown in Table 8.2. If this were a real situation it would show a deteriorating situation which becomes obvious when the figures are shown in comparative form. If they were taken in isolation, along with many other figures it would not be so obvious. Producing figures is one thing but using them is quite another. In the example given it would be necessary to involve quality control personnel to discuss the rejection rate in an attempt to isolate the supplier's problem. This approach would be common sense and should help to improve relationships between buyer and seller.

    Price, quality and delivery performance are capable of a numerical quantification whereas other elements in a supplier's

performance are not. Examples of others that should be monitored are:
- Continuing financial viability
- Technical assistance provided
- After-sales service
- Labour relations
- Supplier's ability to heed special instructions
- Handling of complaints
- Prompt provision of quotations
- Salesman's knowledge of his products
- Prompt provision of catalogues and other product information

This list of additional factors serves to demonstrate that the buyer's opinion will have to be made on some matters. If this view is supported it leads to the area of controversy currently voiced by many senior buyers who see supplier rating as an unnecessary evil. Louis De Rose [4] has commented:

> 'Once sources have been qualified, however, it then becomes important that buyers evaluate them in the light of actual experience. This means the setting up of performance rating standards so that distinctions can be validly made between good and marginal suppliers. Obviously, the purpose of such standards is to supply the buyer with objective information which will prove his judgement in all areas of source selection. Unfortunately too many rating systems are designed to minimise or eliminate buyer judgement, looking at some index as a mechanical means of source selection. However, the fact that such indices are statistical . . . hence give the appearance of being scientific . . . make them no more objective than the assumptions upon which they are based, and these are often faulty or irrelevant.'

Ultimately, the buyer is accountable for the selection of his suppliers. Their continuing involvement in supplying critical items must be based on sound business reasoning. This demands of the buyer a methodology that provides factual evidence on the suppliers' performances. This should be the basis for action aimed at ensuring satisfactory performance.

The buyer who can say with conviction that the performance falls short in a specific area, and quantity, is in a more powerful position that the buyer who merely casts an opinion.

8.7 Purchasing research

The adoption of purchasing research as a technique for improving buyer performance has led to a significant growth area in the buying function. Purchasing research has been defined as 'the development and maintaining of a total awareness of the company's business environment relative to the purchasing activity; identifying and examining those aspects which could be of significance to the company through their impact on purchasing; formulating policy proposals, to optimise the buying contribution to company profitability'.

In very large buying departments the purchasing research group will be a separate part of the department who undertake a wide range of duties which are intended to improve the quality of the buyer's job. The position has been admirably summarised in a study by Fearon and Hoagland [5]:

'Purchasing in this company is an analytical job. We do not believe in haggling with vendors, but we want to be able to negotiate realistically. Arriving at realistic prices requires knowing the types and quantities of raw materials and purchased components that go into a product, the methods a vendor uses to manufacture components, the labour rates and time required to produce components, and the profit and burden allocation. Our philosophy of purchasing research is that if its time and training permitted, the buying group would be doing much of a research job. However, buyers are normally not able to conduct the studies necessary to improve buying efficiencies. Purchasing research is fulfilling a function that otherwise would not get done. We have found that it is profitable to apply staff specialisation and research concepts to purchasing.'

The potential scope of purchasing research is virtually unlimited but the following list of typical project areas

is indicative of the potential:
1. Price trends of major purchased commodities and interpretation for future forecasts.
2. Changes in the economic environment as they influence home and foreign purchases.
3. Research with technological improvements which may have a bearing on the company's range of manufactured components.
4. Active search for and investigation of substitute materials.
5. Investigation of standard items with a view to rationalising inventory range and classifications.
6. Assessment of potential suppliers' capabilities.
7. Continual appraisal of suppliers' financial viability and profitability. This is essential information when conducting negotiations on price changes.
8. Involvement in value engineering and value analysis studies.
9. Investigation of the possible use of computers in the total procurement activity.
10. Development of reporting facilities within the buying department and with colleagues in other functional areas.
11. Continual appraisal of working methods, forms design and control procedures.
12. Interpretation of political events world wide and their likely impact on major purchased commodities.
13. Analysing of the reasons behind price changes.
14. Analysis of supplier cost information and hence profit margins.
15. Examination of alternative transport methods.
16. Investigation of packaging design, use and ultimate cost.
17. Assessment of materials handling techniques to ensure that this aspect is optimised.
18. Assessment of methods used in stock control procedures.
19. Conducting internal audits of the buying department.
20. Development of information bank on trade, tariff and other legislation as they effect purchased materials, components and services.

This is not a comprehensive list but offers considerable scope for original thinking and innovation in the buying activity.

Opportunities will always exist provided there is the

necessary resolve and expertise within the buying department. One company has stated that significant cost savings can be made in almost any purchased item, if that item is subjected to intensive, systematic, fact-based study. The same company provided seven guide-lines for the purchasing research and analysis function. These are excellent thought provokers:

1   That purchasing research is a permanent function and not a one-shot arbitrary cost-cutting method.
2   A significant improvement goal must be established.
3   Research must focus on how, not whether, to make savings.
4   The approach calls for a disciplined thoroughness that challenges every aspect of the cost associated with a component.
5   Improvement ideas must be thoroughly supported by facts and specific evidence.
6   Major improvements frequently require significant changes in the way an item is purchased.
7   Well planned, aggressive follow-up is needed to ensure that savings are realised and maintained.

The opportunities are no less obvious in the smaller company but here the buyer will have to undertake purchase research as an integral part of his everyday duties. He will need the resolve to continue major investigations despite all the pressures to which he is subjected. Achievements will be made and those are good for morale in addition to the obvious benefit of furthering the interests of buying in the company's heirarchy.

8.8   Line of balance technology

The technique is not widely used in buying, but has much to offer. Line of balance is a technique for assembling, selecting, interpreting and presenting in graphic form the essential factors involved in a production process from raw materials to completion of the end product, against a background of time. It is essentially a management-type tool, utilising the principle of exception to show only the most important facts. It is a means of integrating the flow of materials and com-

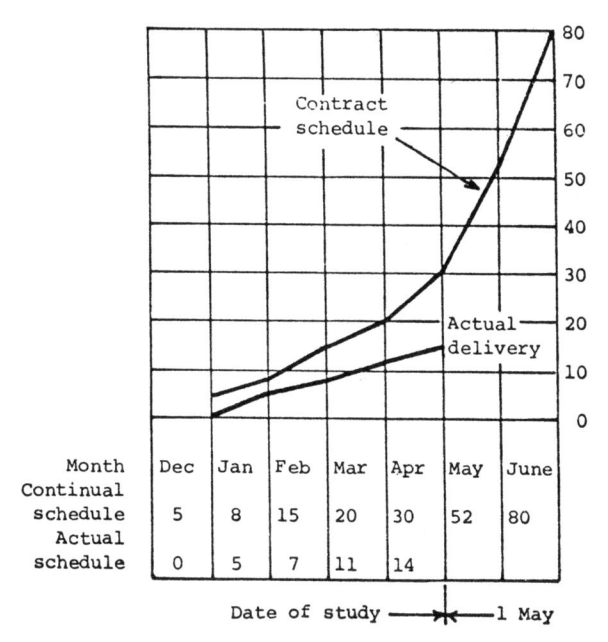

Figure 8.1

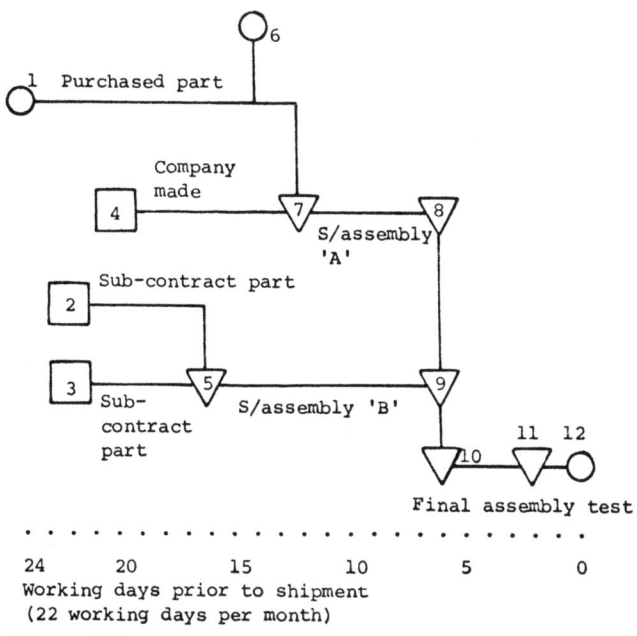

Month	Dec	Jan	Feb	Mar	Apr	May	June
Continual schedule	5	8	15	20	30	52	80
Actual schedule	0	5	7	11	14		

Date of study ⟶ ⟵ 1 May

Figure 8.2

Working days prior to shipment
(22 working days per month)

ponents into the manufacture of items in accordance with phased delivery requirements.

The technique is applied graphically through the use of various charts. Figure 8.1 is a chart of cumulative delivery requirements, and will show cumulative scheduled requirements against actual delivery performance. Figure 8.2 is the second of those charts and shows the lead times required between selected 'key stages' in a manufacturing sequence. Such a diagram is particularly useful since it shows a schematic lay-out of the whole manufacturing process. The key stages may be analysed in terms of inputs, e.g. raw materials received, or outputs, e.g. sub-assemblies completed, or both. The buyer would be involved in providing information on the receipts of principal raw materials, other key purchased parts and sub-contracted sub-assemblies.

Figure 8.3, the third stage, is a bar chart showing progress achieved. It shows the cumulative quantities of materials received and production of items at each of the key points selected for analysis. The identification numbers on the bar chart (horizontal axis) correspond to the identification numbers on Figure 8.2.

For the purposes of illustration the line of balance has been superimposed on Figure 8.3. It represents the cumulative quantities of parts, materials or assemblies that would be required at the date of the study to fulfill the cumulative delivery schedule for end items up to the specific date. It is usual to plot the key points from left to right in descending order of length of lead time required.

The key advantage of this technique is its summary which immediately focuses attention on procurement and production imbalances. Not only does it highlight the shortages but also the excess availability of parts. The latter can be a most useful aid to inventory control.

(We acknowledge the use here of the US Navy NAVMAT P1851 (REV 4-62) *Line of Balance Technology*.)

8.9 Critical path analysis

Many industrial projects are highly complex, demanding a

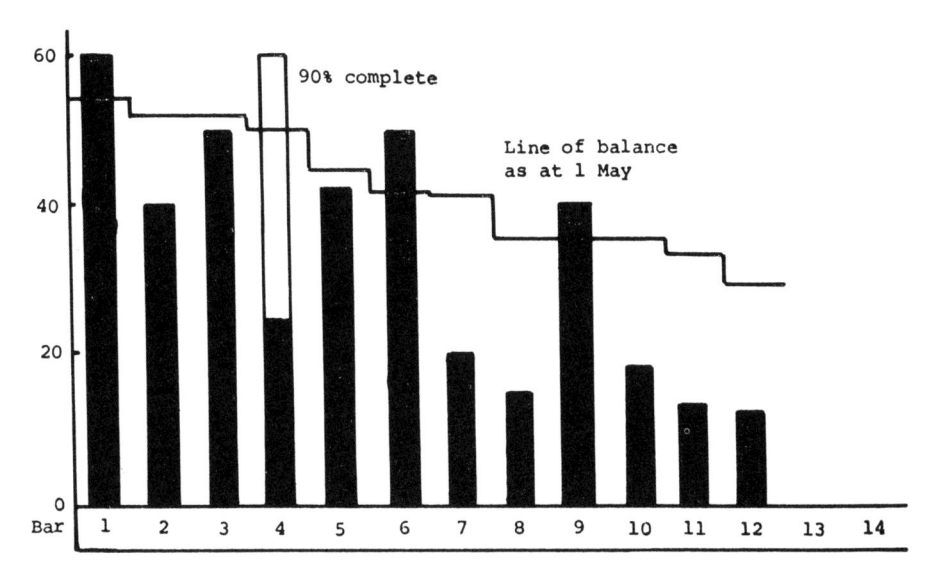

Figure 8.3

precise phasing of materials, labour and services. If costs are to be optimised it is essential that all these inter-related factors are scheduled effectively. In the 1950s new techniques were developed and have become known as Network Analysis. This generic description covers two basic systems: PERT — Programme Evaluation and Review Technique, and CPA — Critical Path Analysis. The latter will be dealt with in this section.

The *critical path* is defined at that series of inter-related activities, the delay of any one of which would necessarily delay the projects completion by an equal amount of time.

A simple illustration is provided by Perrigo which adequately introduces the topic. It concerns five people who leave place x and who subsequently meet at place y. Their routes are varied as shown in Figure 8.4. In a network chart it would be simplified to that shown in Figure 8.5.

The language of CPA refers to events and activities. In Figure 8.5 these would be as follows:

Event	1	represents	'leave place X'
	2	represents	'leave place A'
	3	represents	'leave place B'
	4	represents	'leave place C'
	5	represents	arrive at Y

178   THE BASIC ARTS OF BUYING

>   *Activity* 1-2   represents   walk from X to A
>   1-3   represents   walk from X to B
>   1-5   represents   walk from X to Y
>   2-4   represents   walk from A to C
>   2-5   represents   walk from A to Y
>   3-4   represents   walk from B to C
>   4-5   represents   walk from C to Y

It is now possible to allocate estimates times for travelling each distance:

>   Walk from   X to A   = 2 hours
>   X to B   = 4 hours
>   X to Y   = 3 hours
>   A to C   = 1 hour
>   A to Y   = 3 hours
>   B to C   = 2 hours
>   C to Y   = 3 hours

These are the figures superimposed between the events in Figure 8.5. If we wish to find the shortest time for all the men who leave X to arrive at Y, it is necessary to find that series of activities which takes the longest time. The answer is 9 hours and represents a sequence 1-3-4-5. This represents the critical path. It is a significant message because it now shows that the man who walks from X to A to Y could take another 4 hours without delaying the total time. When this type of logic is applied to industrial projects it identifies the critical points which will include the raw materials and purchased components. It will also indicate those materials which may be delayed without necessarily casuing a hold up in the final completion date for the contract.

8.10   Supplier development

This is one of the main techniques that needs to be used increasingly in the buying function. Supply difficulties are frequently encountered where the buyer finds himself in a situation where he has only two sources available. Both of these may be very large companies who are not particularly interested in the buyer's individual problem. To the buyer this is a restrictive situation calling for original thinking if he

Figure 8.4

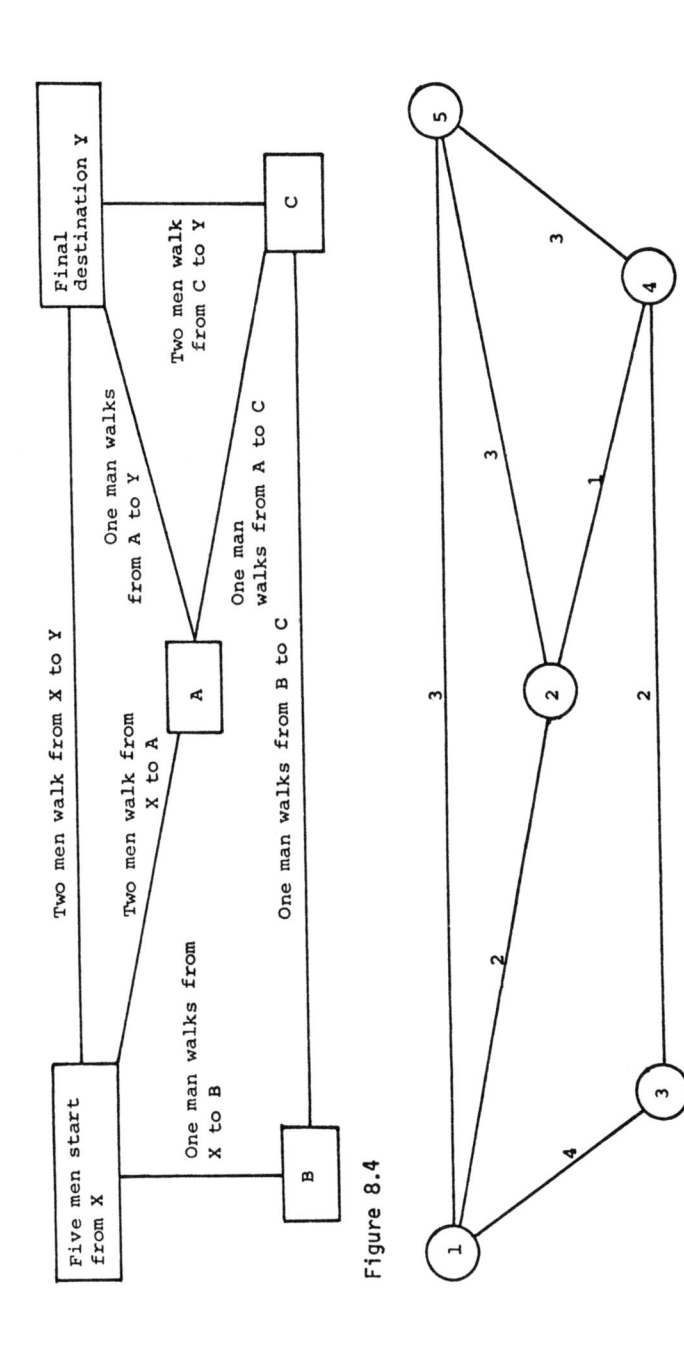

Five men start from X
Two men walk from X to Y
Two men walk from X to A
One man walks from X to B
One man walks from A to Y
One man walks from A to C
One man walks from B to C
Two men walk from C to Y
Final destination Y

Figure 8.5 (Source: A.E.B.Perrigo, *Modern managerial techniques*, Van Nostrand)

is to 'break out of the noose.'

The technique of supplier development should help considerably here. It consists of the buyer, who has a particular need, searching the market place to find a supplier who is interested in meeting that need, but who, for one reason or another, does not possess the necessary capability. Let us assume that the buyer requires a complex plastic moulding as part of a wine cask. His existing contacts are not very interested in fulfilling his rapidly increasing orders. A thorough search of the market reveals a small company that is interested in entering the field of plastic mouldings. Their basic problem is that of inadequate finance (working capital) and specific knowledge on quality control. Subsequent discussions between the potential supplier and the buyer reveal that a short term loan of £30,000 and advice from his quality control personnel would enable production to commence. Discussions with the Finance Director reveal that the buyer's company has no problem with liquid cash and is prepared to make the loan providing it is linked to asset security. The quality control personnel are quite happy to give any assistance necessary, free of charge.

This rather simple example, based on real life, demonstrates how the buyer's initiative opened up a third source of supply previously denied his company. Many would consider it a small price to pay for the added security of supply. In one sense the buyer is in a selling situation with supplier development. He is trying to convince the potential supplier that there is continuing business which affords a good chance of possible diversification and increased profits. There are few sellers who would not be interested in such a proposition.

9 Measuring Buying Performance

Increasing attention is now being directed to measuring buying performance. Despite this interest, progress has been slow in determining and applying realistic standards against which to measure such performance. Reference is made in buying literature to quantitative and qualitative aspects of measuring performance and also to the three distinct areas of measurement, classified as conceptual, behavioural and resultant. These aim not only to analyse end results but to show how improvements to performance can be made.

Why should directors of organisations wish to measure buying performance? What would be their objective? An organisation, whether it be a profit-making industrial concern or a non-profit-making public undertaking, must aim at financial viability. Consequently all departments within an organisation must work together to harness their concerted efforts, making effective contributions towards maximising financial viability. As at least 50 per cent of most organisations' total expenditure is incurred in buying raw materials, bought-out goods and services, buying has a particularly vital role to play. The buying department has to provide an efficient and effective service and to minimise the total expenditure it incurs in a number of areas:

1   Over-expenditure on bought-out goods and services.
2   Cost of failure to meet production requirements.
3   Cost of failure to negotiate and apply adequate terms and conditions.

4   Cost of failure to provide information to Management and internal departments.
5   Cost of making additional efforts on expediting, transport and quality control.
6   Cost of not satisfying outside customers.
7   Cost of excessive stockholding.
8   Cost of failure to dispose of surplus plant, equipment or materials at maximum prices.
9   Cost of operating the buying department.
10 Cost of measuring the buying department's performance

All these elements of cost must be considered within the total expenditure evaluation.

These are ten separate but related areas where cost is incurred and where the buying department is at the centre of activities. A buying department cannot be assessed as having made a maximum contribution to an organisation's financial viability unless the sum total of these separate elements of cost is minimised. In measuring, or attempting to measure, buying performance, consideration must be given to all factors which may influence performance such as market supply conditions, requisitioning, using and other department restrictions and, of course, the organisation's own policies. (See Figure 9.1.)

Buying staff must accept the need for realistic measurement and they should co-operate to develop valid schemes. Having listed the areas of activity and cost where measurement should be applied, we should consider how this can be achieved. In our opinion there is little point in measuring performance unless the buying function is first properly staffed and organised so that it can operate within the framework of a sound buying policy. The department's work load has to be determined and analysed. Job descriptions for buying staff must be prepared. Efforts must be directed towards building a sound foundation from which to measure performance realistically and gainfully. Communications and departmental relationships too, are important aspects on which initial action is vital. Whatever corrective action is deemed necessary, this has to be applied sensibly with the co-operation of staff concerned so that desired end results can be achieved in minimum time at minimum cost.

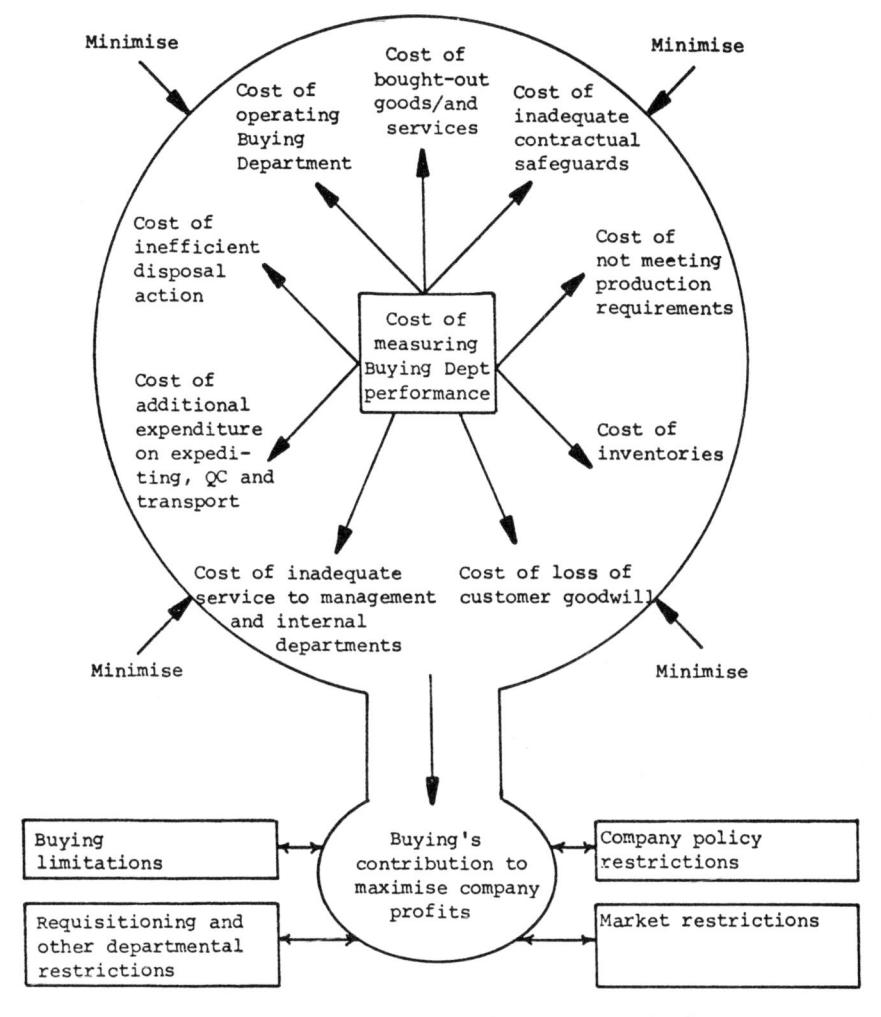

Figure 9.1 Buying's main role - maximising its contribution to company profitability

It is impossible for a buyer to work effectively if his scope is restricted by technical or other requisitioning staff who give him insufficient time to source for competitive quotations. Similarly, an expeditor's scope is restricted when the buyer places an order with a supplier who has a poor delivery performance record. He would be faced with having to apply increased efforts to avoid or minimise possible delays, reducing the time he has available to deal with other urgent or important orders.

Let us consider the main areas of cost for which the buying department has responsibility or is very much involved, and on which purchasing managers, buyers, expeditors and purchasing research staff must work in co-operation with other staff to maximise their contributions to the organisation's financial viability.

9.1 Over-expenditure on bought-out goods and services

The efficient buyer seeks to pay the keenest prices possible for the goods and services he buys in a given market situation with the time at his disposal. He will be concerned that technical or other requisitioning staff give him reasonable notice of requirements, do not erode his negotiating position with suppliers or contractors and prepare specifications which give him opportunities to source in the widest possible market. He will be concerned also with possible reciprocal trading policies and the restrictions they may have on his buying strategy.

To measure the extent of over-expenditure on bought-out goods and services, datum or target prices must be established. Theoretically, the keenest prices a buyer seeks to pay should be at least as low as his competitors would pay under similar market conditions, contract time scale and value of business to place. Establishing such price targets on this basis is not easy but it is a primary area where efforts must be made to find acceptable bases for realistic measurement not only for individual buyers, but for the buying function as a whole. However, prices cannot be measured in isolation from other equally important aspects such as quality, delivery, after-sales service and contractual safeguards.

9.2 Cost of failure to meet production requirements

An important aspect affecting production is quality. Goods may be delivered to time but found to be sub-standard and thus have to be rejected and repaired or replaced, thus incurring delays to programs. Materials may be delivered which appear to be sound and acceptable on receipt but subsequently during processing, defects are found, e.g. castings where porosity is disclosed during machining. The foundry who, in such circumstances, may accept liability to replace defective castings free of charge, may not normally agree to stand the cost of the abortive machining. Sub-standard plant, equipment, or materials disclosed during assembly, installation or erection could also cause delays to programs with consequent financial loss whilst rectification work was carried out.

To meet commitments, production departments require materials or components to be available in sufficient quantities. They are concerned, therefore, that items on order should be delivered by stated dates to avoid disruption of programmes. Whem deliveries extend beyond programmed dates, an organisation may incur additional costs through replanning work on higher-rated machines, overtime working, under-utilisation of machines or sub-letting work. Production should be considered in its widest sense. A department needing the goods or services may be installing capital equipment or it may be working on a customer contract on site. In each case, a hold-up in the installation programme may delay plant or equipment being put into operation and may thus delay a return on capital outlay or the receipt of progress payments from a customer.

To minimise the incidence of delays and subsequent costs incurred resulting from a supplier's inadequate delivery or quality performance, the buyer and expeditor have significant parts to play. Their tasks cannot, however, be tackled or measured in isolation. Quality control staff must provide effective assistance, initially at the supplier appraisal stage. Requisitioning staff must provide realistic, achievable specifications and try to give reasonable notice of requirements.

9.3 Cost of failure to negotiate and apply adequate terms and conditions

This is an area where little measurement is attempted because of obvious difficulties. There are many aspects to consider.

A buyer seeks the best terms of payment possible but at the same time he has to ensure that a supplier does not offset any concessions he makes by increasing his price equivalently or by making compensatory adjustments elsewhere. Terms of payment is a tangible aspect where a single achievement can be measured financially at the time an order is placed. However, if considered in isolation from other aspects, total achievement is not assessed.

The extent to which a buyer negotiates satisfactory special conditions of contract and reconciles conditions of sale and purchase can be investigated and assessed. What may not be assessed readily is the objective measurement of potential loss resulting from a buyer's failure to negotiate adequate safeguards for his organisation. Financial loss may well arise should a buyer not negotiate adequate contractual safeguards. Material and plant performance guarantees are particular aspects which demand careful attention because failure to tie up these adequately could result in heavy additional expenses later.

Insurance is another area where a buyer must be thorough in determining his requirements and must follow up by ensuring that the supplier or contractor takes out adequate insurances. Accidents may or may not arise. The buyer must seek protection, however, against all possible risks. He may have to check on public liability, employer liability and contract works all-risks insurances where site work is involved. Depending on the nature of the work being carried out and the complexities or the hazards on site and the type of insurance required, the insurance cover required may vary from a few hundred pounds to several million pounds.

Transfer of title, patent infringement, storage, handling charges and liquidated damages (delivery and plant performance) are some of the many aspects where a buyer is required to safeguard his organisation's interests and where, therefore, his efforts should be measured. Effective, efficient buying performance is not just a matter of avoiding or minimising actual loss in the short term but of avoiding or minimising potential loss in the long term too.

9.4 Cost of failure to provide information to management and internal departments

Buyers and expeditors have to provide adequate information promptly for use by management and internal departments to enable them to make decisions and to plan work. It is particularly important that management is kept informed of forecasted long-term material prices and availability on significant items. With information received from the buyer on manufacturing lead times, requisitioners can themselves aim to provide the buyer with a better service by giving more notice. Efforts can then be co-ordinated in planning the release of requisitions and enquiries so that orders can be placed giving suppliers reasonable time to meet delivery target dates. Buyers should also keep technical staff informed on new materials, processes or new sources of supply of possible interest, such information being used ultimately to reduce costs.

Expeditors have the important task of notifying production staff promptly of known or anticipated material delivery delays. This action may facilitate the planned revision of programmes to avoid or minimise additional costs. Part deliveries or changes in delivery sequences might also be helpful to production and the expeditor should explore possibilities with all parties concerned.

Buyers and expeditors should, therefore, provide an effective service to management and to their colleagues in the works. This they are better able to do when they acquire knowledge of key commodities and their end uses. They can then put constructive suggestions to overcome or to minimise supply problems to the using and requisitioning departments. This is a qualitative aspect of buying work that should be developed and assessed.

9.5 Cost of applying additional efforts on expediting transport and quality control

When a buyer places an order with a supplier, he rightly expects an adequate service for the price paid. The expeditor or himself should not need to be 'nursemaids' constantly chasing the supplier, assisting him to avoid mistakes or to resolve his problems affecting quality or delivery. Some degree of effort on the part of the buyer or expeditor is to be expected. It is a question of how much effort. However thorough has been the buyer's sourcing and supplier appraisal, special efforts may have to be made subsequently, after the order has been placed, to safeguard his organisation's interests.

To obtain deliveries to time, or to minimise delays, expeditors may have to make regular visits to suppliers' works even though the need for such visits was not envisaged when suppliers were selected. Goods and services must be provided to required quality standards. There may be increasing need for quality control staff to undertake inspection and testing work, additional to that provided within contract prices.

What has to be assessed is the cost and effort incurred undertaking this additional work and the extent to which such work resulted from buying's shortcomings on sourcing, supplier appraisal, negotiating and expediting.

Additional transport charges may also be incurred necessitating the use of the organisation's transport or hiring vehicles to collect goods which the supplier had, initially, undertaken to deliver within the order price.

9.6 Cost of not satisfying outside customers

In addition to direct costs incurred by the failure of suppliers to deliver goods of the specified quality to time, the buyer's organisation may be liable to pay a customer liquidated damages for late completion of contract or for failure to meet specified plant performance. Loss of customer goodwill may also result. This could mean that the customer does not place further business or he is able to negotiate more onerous terms and conditions on future contracts. Achieving customer satisfaction is a fundamental objective and buyers and expeditors have major roles to play in co-operation with production control to meet customer requirements. Any system of measuring buying performance must, therefore, assess the extent to which buyers and expeditors attain this objective.

9.7 Cost of excessive stockholding

Irrespective of the effects of inflation on prices or material scarcity, economic stocks need to be maintained. Stock levels are related to supply and demand and prices (or anticipated prices) and consequently they must be flexible and not static. Buyers, expeditors and purchasing research staff each have some responsibility for achieving economic stockholding. They cannot, however, take full responsibility as they depend to a great extent on the efforts of material control and stores staffs (and other requisitioning staffs) to assess requirements related to demand. Production control is also much involved, particularly when it defers, extends or modifies programs or reduces or accelerates the rate of usage of materials and components.

This is a particularly difficult area in which to measure the buying activity, but nevertheless, capital tied up in stocks is of major concern to most organisations and consequently managements need to set standard or budget forecasts against which actual stock levels can be measured and liability for excesses established. Corrective action can then be taken.

9.8 Cost of failure to dispose of surplus plant, equipment or materials at maximum prices

Buying may be responsible for disposing of a wide range of surplus items or materials such as:
- Capital plant and equipment
- Ferrous and non-ferrous metals
- General materials: rubber, plastics, timber
- General stores items
- Commercial vehicles and motor cars

Office equipment

When called upon to dispose of these items, buyers become sellers and they must, therefore, seek the highest prices possible for their sale. In the case of ferrous and non-ferrous metals, established market rates can be used to measure the buyer's selling performance. Where capital plant is for disposal, the buyer may seek prices in line with current market value prices which may have been evaluated by technical staff.

Much depends on the scale and nature of disposals as to whether or not buying should be responsible for this function. In a large organisation with a large scrap through-put, a separate material disposals department may have responsibility for this activity. However, when buying is responsible for disposals the buyer's performance in this area should be measured.

9.9 Cost of operating the buying department

An organisation may spend under £50,000 per annum on buying goods and services, or it may spend upwards of £300 million. How does one determine how a particular buying department should be organised and staffed? How many buyers are required and of what calibre? How many office-based expeditors are needed to progress orders on a routine basis by telephone, telex, letter, or urging card? Should there be a complementaty field expediting service provided by experienced, more highly paid, expediting engineers, under buying control, who are able to make regular visits to suppliers' works on a planned basis, as well as in emergencies, to actively progress orders placed. Should such staff combine inspection duties with their expediting duties or should inspection remain under a separate quality control department?

Consider too, buying involvement in corporate planning. How much time and effort should be devoted by buying, working in close co-operation with marketing and sales, to considering future supply requirements and to estimating probable price movements and material availability within the time-scale of the organisation's corporate plans? Purchasing research may need to look particularly at key materials which are required to meet sales budget targets.

The departmental work load must be assessed and the calibre and numbers of staff required to handle it determined. Hence the buying salaries budget can be calculated. Overheads must be determined. What accommodation, facilities, equipment heating and lighting are required to enable buying staff to carry out their duties satisfactorily? What allowance should be made for expenses incurred on supplier visits for the purpose of sourcing, appraising, negotiating and expediting?

Are the activities of the buying department to be restricted to buying, expediting and purchasing research or will the department embrace other functions such as stores and material control? All these aspects have to be considered to determine the total cost of operating the buying department.

9.10 Cost of measuring buying performance

Whatever methods are used to measure buying activities, cost is incurred. This cost must be offset by the benefits derived from the application of such measurement. Measurement for its own sake is valueless. Departmental and individual performances must not only be measured, but they must be significantly improved to achieve greater effectiveness and hence, greater contributions to maximise an organisation's financial viability. This must be the primary aim for introducing measurement.

Measurement of performance is then a further element of cost which has to be considered within the total picture of buying performance and cost.

9.11 Measurement — what does this involve?

Measurement is the art of comparing an object or an activity against a standard. What is a standard? How can a person, section or department be said to have performed well or badly unless those responsible for judging have a clear objective basis for determining what is an acceptable level of performance? Assessments can and do vary significantly depending on who sets the standard and the person's subjectiveness or objectiveness, rigidity or flexibility. What may be considered to be an acceptable performance to one director or purchasing manager may not be acceptable to others. Let us therefore, consider some aspects of standards for measurement applicable to the buying function. (See Figure 9.2.)

9.12 Standards of performance

Standards for buying performance must be set realistically and fairly so that targets are achievable and the results obtained meaningful. Corrective action can then be applied to obtain desired improvements. When setting standards, the following aspects should be considered:

1 Relevance to the purpose The aspect to be measured must have relevancy. For example, measuring the total number and value of purchase orders placed weekly or monthly by various buyers would have little relevance where orders have been placed for many commodities which differed greatly in type, value and frequency of issue. Some organisations may regard the value of orders placed per buyer as an aspect to be measured irrespective of significant differences in the nature of the work carried out by the buyers. We support the view that there must be similarity and regularity of work pattern to warrant measurement of one buyer with another or against their past performances.

2 Influencing factors Perhaps the main problem facing the person setting a standard is how he can take full account of all the factors that affect the basis for measurement? A buyer's or an expeditor's performances will be affected by restrictions imposed on them by the organisations' policies, market conditions or by requisitioners. In assessing a buyer's performance on price, for example, certain questions should be posed. 'Did he have reasonable time to source and negotiate?' 'Did his colleagues erode his bargaining power?' 'Have there been any significant changes in market conditions?'

An expeditor may have successfully progressed orders placed on a single existing supplier for a particular company.

KEY AREAS

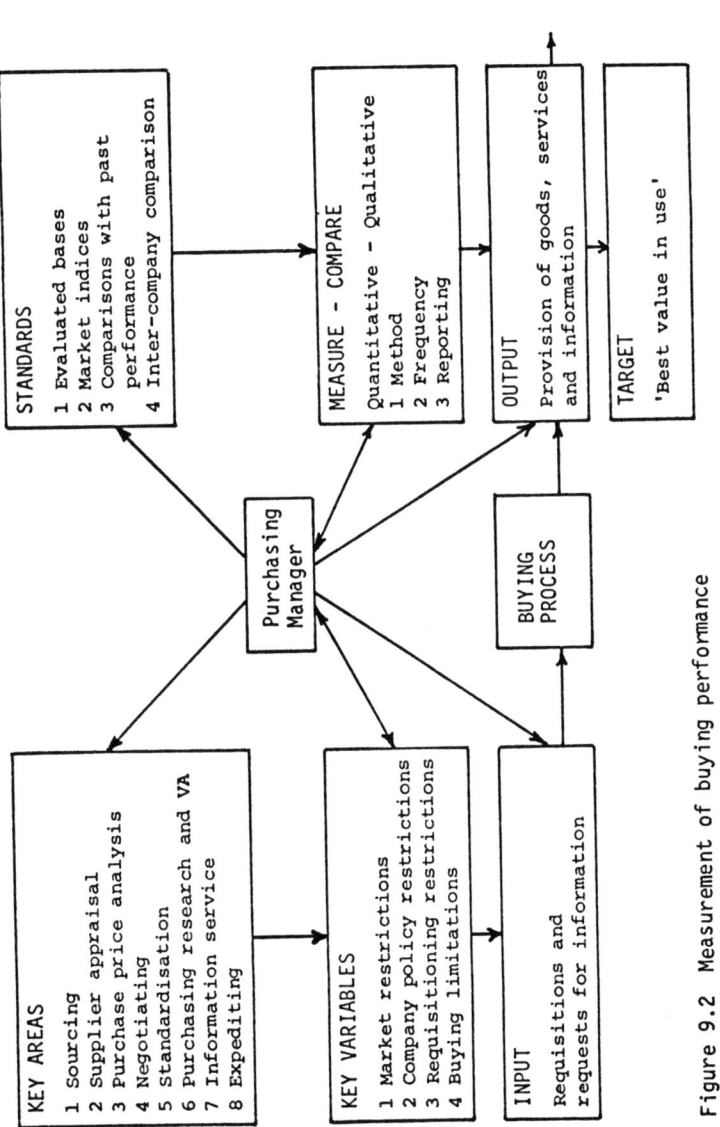

1 Sourcing
2 Supplier appraisal
3 Purchase price analysis
4 Negotiating
5 Standardisation
6 Purchasing research and VA
7 Information service
8 Expediting

KEY VARIABLES

1 Market restrictions
2 Company policy restrictions
3 Requisitioning restrictions
4 Buying limitations

INPUT

Requisitions and requests for information

BUYING PROCESS

Purchasing Manager

STANDARDS

1 Evaluated bases
2 Market indices
3 Comparisons with past performance
4 Inter-company comparison

MEASURE – COMPARE

Quantitative – Qualitative

1 Method
2 Frequency
3 Reporting

OUTPUT

Provision of goods, services and information

TARGET

'Best value in use'

Figure 9.2 Measurement of buying performance

Because of changes in buying policy, it may have been decided to share future business between two suppliers. Consequently, the expeditor is faced with an entirely new situation and he may fail to secure deliveries to time in spite of any efforts he makes. Similarly, there may be reorganisation in his department which may affect his scope to perform, adversely or otherwise. His section may be depleted because of illness. Such changing circumstances must be taken into account.

3 *Flexibility*   Standards set must be flexible so that they can be modified to meet changing circumstances such as those given in the 'expeditor' example above.

4 *Achievability*   Where standards or targets set are not reasonably achievable, staff will not be motivated or stimulated to strive to achieve them. There will be no incentive. Excuses for failure to achieve them will readily be found. Obviously, differences of opinion may arise between a purchasing manager and his staff on what are reasonable and realistic standards. A purchasing manager must be objective when he sets individual targets so that he obtains the maximum effort, support and co-operation from his staff, essential ingredients for success.

5 *Period of application*   Standards should be used which can be applied continuously, not spasmodically, over a reasonable period of time. There is little point in introducing a scheme of measurement using data that will be unobtainable within a short time of its inception.

6 *Understandability*   Methods of assessing performance should be understood by staff whose performance is to be measured. The use of unnecessarily lengthy or complicated formulae should be avoided.

7 *Organisation approved*   Any performance standards introduced should have the full support of directors. Measurement of performance should be applied throughout an organisation and not restricted to one department.

Efforts should be made to demonstrate a fair, impartial approach, pressures to improve performances being applied equally across all departments.

9.13 Organisational foundation

We have discussed a number of related aspects to be considered when measuring buying performance. One can examine the bases for setting standards and also decide which activities should be measured. Measurement can be of two separate forms: quantitative which is tangible and qualitative which is intangible. We have considered too, the activities carried out in a buying department and the elements of cost which in total must be minimised so that buying maximises its contribution to an organisation's financial viability.

However, buying must be consolidated on sound foundations. We reiterate that there must be a clearly defined buying policy which has the full support of directors. Buying procedures must be issued. The work of the buying department must be evaluated, each member of the department having his duties and responsibilities clearly defined by a job description showing the extent of his activities, to whom he reports and where applicable, the staff for whom he is responsible and the details of their duties. These are essential prerequisites. It is one thing to set a standard against which a person's performance will be measured. It is quite another matter to ensure that the person has the capabilities, facilities, assistance, guidance and reasonable time to enable him to achieve his targets. It is particularly important, therefore, that the purchasing manager plays a major role in developing his department and encouraging staff to work as a team in a common purpose. Buyers, expeditors and purchasing research staff must be well selected, initially, and then trained and developed to tackle work loads which are within their capabilities; to meet targets set.

9.14 Quantitative measurement

The main aspects which lend themselves to quantitative measurement are price, quality, delivery, sourcing, competitive quotations and value, number and complexity of orders placed.

9.14.1 Measuring price performance

A buyer's achieved performance on prices paid for goods and services can be measured in a number of ways depending on the type of commodity and prevailing circumstances. These bases include measuring against an evaluated cost estimate, measuring historically, i.e. against a previously achieved performance, and measuring inter-company or inter-division, where realistic comparison can be made between departments operating under similar conditions. Finally, price measurement can be made against market prices given for metals and raw materials, quoted daily or weekly in recognised national publications and bulletins.

1 Measuring against an evaluated cost estimate This method of measurement depends wholly on the skill of the evaluator who is required to set target prices for commodities against which the buyer's performance will be measured. An objective approach is essential, which considers all influencing and relevant factors. The evaluator has to determine the method of manufacture and to look at such elements of cost as materials, tools, labour, overheads and profit. He will consider packing, transport and handling charges to determine the price the buyer should pay. He must also look at possible aggragation of order quantities for which he will make due allowance for appropriate discounts. The greater the quantity of items produced, the greater is the supplier's scope to improve his manufacturing methods, to better organise his work flow, to reduce material waste and to reduce material costs by buying in quantity. The supplier's operators too find ways to simplify and speed up their work through repetition. This applies, particularly, in electronics, instrument and electrical component work which calls for a high degree of manual dexterity which is not restricted by machine packing (re learning curve).

2 *Measurement against past performance* This method is frequently and universally used and although it does not facilitate measurement against an evaluated standard, nevertheless it is a method that has much to commend it. The extent to which individuals, sections or departments improve on previous performance can be demonstrated if adequate allowances are made for changing circumstances. A buyer's success, or lack of success, can be related to market supply conditions and the extent of assistance he obtains from others, as well as by his own efforts. A buyer may in one year have placed an order for a particular commodity for delivery to time at a very keen price. In the following year, because of a rapid deterioration in the market supply position, he may devote ten times as much effort and pay an increased price significantly greater than that represented by the movements in price indices, to obtain a delivery which is less than satisfactory. Is this buyer less efficient on the second occasion? A market situation can deteriorate rapidly and therefore all relevant factors must be considered when past and present performances are being compared.

Another important point to be considered when measuring against past performances is that the degree of improvement tends to reduce year by year as the scope for improvement reduces. The largest savings should be achieved in the initial years of measurement.

3 *Measuring inter-company or inter-division* Where a large organisation comprises a number of divisions or separate companies, the performance of the buying function in one division or company may be compared with that of another. For a comparison to be valid, the nature of work and size of work load must be similar. Many aspects of buying can be compared in this way such as the numbers of orders placed per buyer, the total value of orders placed per buyer, the percentage of orders running late, the extent to which they run late and the percentages and cost of defects reported by production or quality control.

As in the case of measuring past performance, which can also be used for inter-company or inter-division comparisons, measurement is not made against an evaluated standard. This method, may, however, disclose significant variations in results achieved and thus can prompt investigation into abnormally high, or low figures returned. Corrective action can then be taken to improve sub-standard performances to raise them to achieve the higher levels of performance.

4 *Measurement against market indices* This method facilitates comparison of prices paid by buyers for raw materials and metals against published market prices. This comparison of prices gives some indication of how successful a buyer has been in his purchases, but obviously, the quantity bought has to be taken into account when assessing performance. Such publications as metal bulletins, print weekly or daily details of current market prices. This method does, therefore, enable measurement to be made against a realistic standard.

These then are four different bases for quantitative measurement, two of which compare a buyer's, a section's or a department's performance with those of others, made in one case at different locations and in the second case, at different points in time. The other two methods compare performance with existing standards either evaluated by the buyer's specialist colleagues or set by market published prices.

9.14.2 Unpriced orders

The numbers of unpriced orders placed can be measured and related as a percentage of total orders placed. This would give an immediate indication of the extent to which a buyer had failed to agree prices with suppliers before placing orders. There is much greater scope to obtain the keenest prices when a buyer uses his full bargaining power before placing an order. Efforts must always be directed to negotiate and establish the keenest prices before placing orders. A zero level of unpriced orders does not mean that a buyer has bought at the keenest prices. Conversely, a high percentage of unpriced orders does not mean that a buyer has necessarily been lax. There may be good reasons why prices could not be established before orders were placed. However, the number of unpriced orders must be contained within specified limits, and results achieved measured.

9.14.3 *Quality*

Quality performance can be measured readily in terms of percentage rejects, number of complaints received from production, cost of rectification work and the cost of lost production which results from deliveries of sub-standard materials, equipment or plant.

9.14.4 *Delivery*

Delivery performance can be measured in two ways. Firstly, to the extent to which deliveries run beyond specified dates can be measured. A check can be made on the number of orders running one, two, three, four weeks late and assessing such unsatisfactory performance as percentages of total orders placed. Secondly, the cost incurred by production resulting from overdue orders can be valued and reported on weekly or monthly, a final assessment being made at the end of each year.

9.14.5 *Sourcing*

The efforts a buyer makes to widen his sourcing can be checked. The number of enquiries issued and competitive quotations received can be related to the number of purchase orders placed. The extent to which a buyer sources and locates new suppliers and the frequency he issues new enquiries for repeat orders would also be noted.

A buyer must apply the principle of Pareto's Law to his thinking and be selective and concentrate his main efforts to deal with commodities which incur the highest annual expenditure, present major delivery or availability problems, or create major problems after receipt for using departments, e.g. defects. Measurement of sourcing should take account of this selectivity.

9.14.6 *Value, number and complexity of orders placed*

Total departmental or individual performances can be measured to some extent by the numbers and value of purchase orders placed if full consideration is given to their complexity and the time required to process. For example, a simple one line order which requires a minimum of sourcing or negotiating effort could be given a datum rating of 'one' i.e. unity, depending on the size, nature and complexity of an order, and consequently the time a buyer needs to devote to its preparation, a weighting factor can be applied to two, three, four . . . ten times unity. The buyer's productive output in terms of numbers of orders placed can then be measured more realistically.

His performance can be measured against previous performance, a colleague's performance or an evaluated standard. Output measured in this way is strictly a numerical assessment of volume handled. Quality of performance in terms of prices paid, quality of goods and delivery achieved has to be evaluated and related to purchase order work output. The following formula shows how this method of measurement could be applied. (See Figures 9.3 and 9.4).

The most difficult aspect is to apply a satisfactory weighting factor for each order placed to cater for changes in market supply conditions. An order placed in say, January of a particular year may be given a weighting factor of 'three'. In six months time a similar order may require a weighting factor of 'six' because of greatly changed circumstances. The problem is who should and can adjudicate and evaluate? The person best able to report knowledgeably on the supply position is the buyer himself. Obviously, he cannot set his own standards as he has a vested interest in giving favourable weightings.

The average time required to convert requisitions into purchase orders too can be calculated and compared against agreed standards.

Category	Type of order	Assessed work content, min	Weighting factor	Number off orders placed
A	Simple, one-line repeat orders with price established - not due for re-sourcing	Under 5	1	201
B	} Orders differing in increasing work content	6-12	3	122
C		13-23	6	51
D		24-36	10	22
E		37-59	16	7
F	Complicated multi-page orders involving negotiations	Over 60	*	2

*Time spent on this type of order may vary considerably and include visits to suppliers' works. The total time for such orders must therefore be carefully assessed.

Assume weighting factors for F of 31. Then the total work content

$$= A + B + C + D + E + F$$
$$= (1 \times 201) + (3 \times 122) + (6 \times 51) + (10 \times 22) + (16 \times 7) + 31 \times 3)$$
$$= 201 + 366 + 306 + 222 + 112 + 62$$
$$= 1269 \text{ work units}$$

Figure 9.3 Measuring work output of purchase orders placed (excluding correction factors for performance on price, quality and delivery)

Price (assessed on major items representing over 80 per cent of amount spent		Correction factor
A Above budget price - 5% or more		0.5*
3-4%		0.7
1-2%		0.8
Up to 1%		0.9
B Budget price		1.0
C Below budget price - Up to 1%		1.1
1-2%		1.2
3-4%		1.3
More than 5%		1.4*
*Further correction where percentages are significantly different. Corrections for quality, delivery and contractual safeguards would also need to be made.		

Figure 9.4 Measuring work output of purchase orders placed: correction factors

9.15 Qualitative measurement

As qualitative measurement is less tangible than quantitative measurement it thus presents greater difficulty when applied to buying. Objective judgement is required on such aspects as supplier selection and performance in a total sense, which includes supplier reliability at all stages up to and including after-sales service. Buying's standing within an organisation must be related to the quality of service which management and departmental staffs receive from buying compared with the standard of service they need. The quality of such service includes not only the quality of the buyer's efforts to place orders with reliable suppliers, obtain the keenest prices within estimate, obtain deliveries of specified qualities of goods to time but includes also the value of information and the promptness by which he provides it to management and staff. Useful information must flow regularly from buying to management, requisitioning, using and other departments.

By successfully applying a planned, logical, organised approach to supply problems and by demonstrating the quality of the service it provides, buying can win the confidence of management and staff, achieve credibility and obtain a high rating, qualitatively.

Purchasing research plays a vital part in the total buying activity dealing with such aspects on major commodities as sourcing, commodity price analysis, forecasting price and availability, value analysis and other cost reduction techniques. Both qualitative and quantitative measurements are required to demonstrate the success of the buying effort to investigate alternative supply sources, supplier facilities and methods, item simplification, quantity aggregation, standarisation, transport and handling charges, market statistics and cost of storage.

9.16 Programmes for measuring buying performance

Organisations need to develop programmes for measuring buying performance which set realistic targets to be achieved within agreed time scales by buyers, expeditors and purchasing research staff, in the various areas of the total buying activity. Objectives must be determined. Initial consideration must be given to aspects that can be measured readily but, at the same time, have sufficient work content and be of sufficient importance to warrant the application of measurement. There are too many examples in industry where undue efforts are concentrated into looking into the work of junior staff. An example is the clerical work measurement of young female staff. What should be measured also, is the productive output of senior more highly paid staff, commercial and technical, whose contributions to a department or an organisation are the more important.

10 Conclusions

The theme of this book has been the increasing need for professionalism in buying. The need for this is manyfold but includes the significant fact that the buyer has to deal with other professionals who will be well trained and experts in their own right.

We have stressed the need to challenge all aspects of the buying job. To illustrate the difficulties facing the buyer we include in full an article on Price Variation Formulae (Section 10.1) which is reprinted with kind permission of *Modern Purchasing*. The article deals with the many aspects of PVF — a technique likely to be found in increasing use in future contract dealing.

10.1 Who gets the best from price variation?

> Price variation formulae — the means by which sellers take into account rising labour and material costs — are rarely challenged by the buyer. Based on indices which are rarely explained and may be adversely weighted in relation to the contract, they could result in too high a price. Brian Farrington, Senior Lecturer in Purchasing Management at St Helens Management Centre, has been investigating.

The inflationary background to buyers' negotiations in the past year has focused attention on the many possibilities of increased prices from suppliers during the run of a contract. Price variation formulae — the means by which a seller gets a buyer to agree to an uplift in final contract price as a result of increased materials and labour costs — have long been used in the electrical contracting industry where contract periods can extend over several years. But now there is an increasing awareness of sellers to the principle of getting a buyer to agree to some form of price escalation over much shorter periods. Many such attempts are vague, stating only that the seller reserves the right to pass on extra costs. But others are more complicated and these are the subject of this article.

Buyers who agree to such formulae should establish what they really mean. For often there is a total lack of investigative practices on the part of the buyer's organisation.

Based on indices that are rarely explained and may be adversely weighted in relation to the contract, price variation formulae could result in too high a price.

Whether government intervention in the prices field is desirable or otherwise matters not in this context. What is important, is that phase one, two and potentially three, have shed considerable light on price variations by intensifying the need for cost information to be provided by suppliers.

Purchase price analysis techniques — long used in the motor industry as a means of accurately estimating constituent costs of a product to determine the correct price — have now been adopted by the Price Commission which insists that a company pleading its case for a price rise shows the various elements of its price. At the very least this will involve materials, labour, overheads and profits. The traditional reluctance of many sellers to discuss such fundamentals has now to a certain extent been changed and buyers should now take the opportunity to create a pressure of their own making for this type of information; a pressure hopefully more permanent than the Price Commission. Suppliers should be forced to realise that a more open discussion of costs is what the buyers should have as a right.

If the buying profession is to be realistic it must accept that cost will change in the duration of a contract and obviously, the longer the duration the more the change is likely to be. With exceptionally good fortune costs may even decrease. But that's unlikely.

Price variation seems inevitably to mean upping the price at the conclusion of a contract. This investigation has been conducted to ascertain the use made of such formulae, and at whose initiative. Approaches were made to trade association, suppliers and many professional buyers.

If there was a prize for the trade association most actively involved in PVF practice it would be awarded to the British Electrical and Allied Manufacturers' Association (BEAMA). Their reply to my enquiry stated: 'The type of formulae produced by BEAMA and very widely used in industry is invariably used on contracts for custom-built equipment with contract periods ranging from six months up to seven or eight years for power station contracts. These formulae are not used to calculate price increases as such, but are written into the contract as an agreed method of establishing the final price. BEAMA issued the original contract price adjustment (CPA) formulae in 1940 and the principle of operation had remained virtually unchanged since that time. This method of calculation has been adopted internationally and practically all CPA formulae in common use are based on BEAMA principles.'

It is this last comment that requires a response. Obviously all formulae will be based on these principles since they break a price into its constituent parts. Is there any other way of dealing with price variation? There is no doubt that the BEAMA principles have acquired wide accord since their 'method' has been adopted by many companies and public organisations. The following example is applied to electrical machinery in home contracts:

Variations in the cost of materials and labour shall be calculated in accordance with the following formulae;

Labour The contract price shall be adjusted at the rate of 0.45 per cent of the contract price per 1.0 per cent difference between the BEAMA labour cost index last published before the date of tender and the average of the index figures published for the last two-thirds of the contract period, this difference being expressed as a percentage of the former index figure.

Materials The contract price shall be adjusted at the rate of 0.45 per cent of the contract price per 1.0 per cent difference between the price index of materials used in the electrical machinery industry last published in the *Trade and Industry Journal* before the date of tender and that index figure last published before the end of the first three-fifths of the contract period, this difference being expressed as a percentage of the former index figure.

There are additional comments which refer to contracts with or without erection. A worked example follows.

Basis of claim for contract price adjustment

Customer . . . .
Customer's order number . . . .
a Contract price: £10,000
b Date of tender: 10 January 1970
c Labour cost index at date of tender: 100
d Date of order: 2 February 1970
e Date when ready for despatch/taking over: 10 October 1970
f Contract period between d and e days: 250 days
g Date at one third of contract period: 26 April 1970
h Date at three-fifths of contract period: 2 July 1970
i Average of labour cost indices for period g to e: 107.7
j DTI index figure of materials used in electrical engineering machinery/mechanical engineering industries last published before date of tender: 141.7
k DTI index figure last published before date at h: 150.9
l Percentage adjustment for labour

$$= 45 \times \frac{l-c}{c} = \frac{7.7}{100} \times 45 = 3.465$$

m Percentage adjustment for materials

$$= 45 \times \frac{k-j}{j} = \frac{9.2}{141.7} \times 45 = 2.922$$

n Total percentage adjustment for labour and materials = 6.387

Total price adjustment

$$= \frac{a}{100} \times n = \frac{£10{,}000}{100} \times 6.387 = £638.70$$

BEAMA also advise variations to the basic formulae application for turbogenerating and allied plant, distribution transformers, electroheating equipment and industrial electronic equipment.

The discerning buyer will observe that basically the BEAMA method deals with labour price movements over the last two-thirds of the contract which many would argue to be fair, because it is during this period that labour is concentrated on a contract. The index is calculated by BEAMA and is based on information supplied by the DTI. Precisely what information was not mentioned and one can only hope that regional disparities are taken into consideration.

Materials prices are fluctuated over the first three-fifths of a contract, which again is usually the period when materials are purchased and received on a contract. The problem arises in both cases where labour and materials are assumed to be in equal proportions (45 per cent). This, it seems, needs challenging as a basic piece of logic.

It is also pertinent to question the basis of indices using the DTI material indices. Copies of these were obtained for the purpose of this research and highlight the urgent need for buyers to actively challenge all information supplied by the seller. The DTI material indices are prepared after taking into account a number of constituent elements which are subsequently weighted (by the DTI) to a total base weight of 100.

This naturally assumes that the buyer's contract possesses precisely the same weightings of materials, which is highly unlikely. Some extracts are given in Figure 10.1 for illustrative purposes and these show clearly how an index is weighted and can be unduly influenced by a minority of items. It should serve as a timely warning that any index proposed to the buyer should first be challenged by requesting a detailed explanation of its base and its constituent elements. Having obtained these they must then be related to the specific contract. Clearly this should all be a base for competent negotiations.

652000 Basic materials and fuel purchased by manufacturing industry		
Code number	Specification	Base weight (1968)
322110	Copper wirebars	6.3
6040000	Fuel purchased by all manufacturing industries	10.5
6600000	Food and drink materials	28.2
8101000	Crude oil	11.8
		56.8

The remainder of this index is made up from a further 70 items.

6840,000 Materials and fuel purchased by the timber industries		
Code number	Specification	Base weight (1968)
8106,100	Imported softwood	36.5
8106,200	Imported plywood	10.2
8106,700	Imported hardwood	8.9
		55.6

The remainder of this index is made up from a further 57 items.

6860000 Construction materials - all work		
Code number	Specification	Base weight (1968)
339400	Space-heating, ventilating and air-conditioning equipment	7.6
4692050	Ready-mixed concrete	7.1
4692550	Asphalt (mixed)	3.8
8106100	Imported softwood	10.0
		28.5

The remainder of this index is made up from a further 44 items.

Figure 10.1

Another price variation formula in common use is that of the British Metalworking Plant Makers Association. The price is amended in accordance with the following formula:

$$P = P_0 \left(0.1 + a\frac{M}{M_0} + \frac{S}{S_0}\right) - P_0$$

where
- a = proportion of materials in contract price
- b = proportion of wages in contract price
- P = price increase or decrease
- P_0 = contract price
- M = average index of materials cost
- M_0 = index of materials cost for month preceding base date
- S = revised wage index
- S_0 = wage index at base date

This formula assumes a fixed element of 10 per cent, expressed as 0.1 in the formula. It has the added attraction that the material and wages elements are varied according to the specific nature of the contract. The index of materials costs is that notified to the BMPMA by the DTI.

The average index of materials cost (M in the formula above) is the average of the price indices for each month (or part of month) from the point in time two-fifths through the manufacturing period to the point in time four-fifths through the manufacturing period. (The manufacturing period is defined as the period measured in calendar days from the date of order or instructions to proceed, whichever is the earlier to the date when the equipment, the subject of the claim, is ready for delivery.)

The wage index is the BEAMA engineering labour cost index. The revised wage index is the average of the index figures published during the last two-thirds of the manufacturing period.

Price adjustment has received considerable attention in the building industry. In January 1968 the Economic Development Committee for building appointed a steering group on price fluctuations formula which reported in January 1969 [6]. Interesting comments were made in its findings. For

example:
> 'Where fluctuations are adjusted by the conventional methods there is a considerable "shortfall" between the total fluctuations and those which are adjustable under the standard conditions of contract. The items which are not subject to adjustment include:
> 1. Incentive payments when these are adjusted as a result of changes in the rates of wages.
> 2. Salaries or wages not governed by a recognised wage-fixing body.
> 3. The levy under the industrial-training scheme.
> 4. Plant charges or hire rates.
> 5. Consumable stores and the like.
> 6. Materials not specifically included in the basic list.
> 7. Overhead charges and profit.
>
> We have every reason to believe that many contractors and sub-contractors are not as well informed as they should be of the full extent of this "shortfall", which we estimate may range from 25 to 45 per cent of the total fluctuations.'

This report was followed in May 1971 by another dealing with civil engineering contracts [7]. It made recommendations for a formula based upon indices related to the costs of labour (LA), plant (PL), aggregate (AG), bricks (BR), cement (CE), cast iron (CI), coated roadstone (CR), fuel (FU), imported softwood (IS), reinforcement (RE), and structural steelwork (SS). Indices were generally available for these items and were used as follows:

Factor for price variation

$$= [\, 0.15 + A\frac{LA_c}{LA_0} + B\frac{PL_c}{PL_0} + C\frac{AG_c}{AG_0}$$
$$+ D\frac{BR_c}{BR_0} + E\frac{CE_c}{CE_0} + F\frac{CI_c}{CI_0}$$
$$+ G\frac{CR_c}{CR_0} + H\frac{FU_c}{FU_0} + J\frac{IS_c}{IS_0}$$
$$+ K\frac{RE_c}{RE_0} + L\frac{SS_c}{SS_0} \,] - 1$$

where LA_0 is the basic labour index six weeks prior to the date for the return of tenders, and LA_c is the labour index applicable to the certificate being the value current six weeks before the last day of the period covered by the certificate (the document generally used for monthly and final payments in the civil engineering and building industries). The coefficients designated A, B, C, D, E, F, G, H, J, K, and L are applied respectively to items *LA, PL* and so on, to determine the proportionate effect which each index is to have on the total. The values of these coefficients for each project will be stated in the enquiry document. Some coefficients may be zero. The recommendation was that the value stated for the co-efficients total 0.85 (which leaves 15 per cent of the contract price as a fixed element), and that the total amount due to be paid under the contract for fluctuation of price shall be the aggregate of the amounts calculated in accordance with the above.

The formula would operate as follows. Assuming that the value of the contract was made up of 35 per cent labour, 20 per cent plant and 45 per cent materials and that the materials may be sub-divided into:

	Percentage
Aggregate (for use in concrete)	6
Bricks (including tiles and salt glazed ware)	1
Cement (including lime)	2
Cast iron	Nil
Coated roadstone (including all material containing bitumen in addition to roadstone as such)	17
Fuel	8
Imported softwood (for shuttering and false work)	4
Reinforcements	5
Structural steelwork (temporary works)	2
	45

CONCLUSIONS

The coefficients to be applied to the indices related to the above items (A, B, C, etc., respectively) which are included in the formula to give the proportionate effect of each index are required to total 0.85. It follows that each percentage quoted must be multiplied by 0.85/100 to give the corresponding coefficient. Thus the coefficient becomes:

A — relating to labour   35 × 0.85/100 = 0.2975
B — relating to plant   20 × 0.85/100 = 0.1700

By similar calculations C = 0.0510, D = 0.0085, E = 0.0170, F = zero, G = 0.1445, H = 0.0680, J = 0.0350, K = 0.0425, L = 0.0170

If it is assumed that the values of the basic indices in the example are:

$LA_0 = 120, PL_0 = 100, AG_0 = 170, BR_0 = 150,$
$CE_0 = 130, CR_0 = 145, FU_0 = 110, IS_0 = 210,$
$RE_0 = 125, SS_0 = 130$

The values of the indices for a particular certificate are assumed to be:

$LA_c = 148, PL_c = 109, AG_c = 220, BR_c = 170,$
$CE_c = 152, CR_c = 190, FU_c = 127, IS_c = 275,$
$RE_c = 150, SS_c = 160$

Applying these values in the formula the factor for the certificate concerned becomes:

$[\ 0.1500 + 0.2975 \dfrac{190}{145} + 0.1700 \dfrac{127}{110} + 0.1445 \dfrac{275}{210} +$
$0.068 \dfrac{127}{110} + 0.0340 \dfrac{275}{210} + 0.0425 \dfrac{150}{125} + 0.0170 \dfrac{160}{120}\ ] - 1$
$= 0.1500 + 0.3669 + 0.1853 + 0.0660 + 0.0096 + 0.0199 + 0.1893 + 0.0785 + 0.0445 + 0.0510 + 0.0209 - 1 =$
$0.1819.$

The contract price must now be upped by 18.19 per cent. The British Constructional Steelwork Association has also prepared a report on a formula for structural steel which, although it has not yet been implemented, has the basic support of the association. The report was prepared principally because material is purchased a long time before it appears in a certificate; because the use of only one material eliminates the averaging which is effective in contracts involving several materials; and because the labour used to fabricate and erect steelwork is subject to separate wage agreement machinery outside the working rule agreement of the Federation of Civil Engineering Contractors.

The formula calculation proposed for those civil engineering contracts where separate consideration of structural steelwork is required is as set out in the following recommendations:

a   That the calculations be based upon indices related to the cost of labour and materials only.
b   That the index for labour be based on that prepared by the Department of Employment for average earnings in mechanical engineering: Table 127: Mechanical Engineering, *Department of Employment Gazette*, HMSO monthly.
c   That the index for materials be that produced by the DTI for structural steel (code no. 3112.920).
d   That owing to the difficulties in timing of various operations the calculations of a single factor applicable to the valuation is not appropriate and the total structural steelwork price should be divided into three parts.
   1   Materials supplied to works.
   2   Fabrication and delivery of steelwork.
   3   Erection of steelwork.
e   That separate calculations be made in respect of each of parts (1) – (3) above and calculations applied as follows:
   1   The amount for material to be multiplied by
$$\frac{0.85\,(MS_c - MS_0)}{MS_0}$$
   2   the amount for fabrication and delivery to be multiplied by
$$\frac{0.85\,(FD_c - FD_0)}{FD_0}$$
   3   The amount for erection to be multiplied by
$$\frac{0.85\,(ER_c - ER_0)}{ER_0}$$

where MS_c is the index for structural steelwork materials applicable at the date on which the materials are delivered to the fabricator's works (the report goes on to discuss a basis which basically states that 'FIFO' will operate), FD_c and ER_c are the indices for labour applicable eight weeks and two weeks, respectively, before the end of the month to which the certificate relates, and MS_0, FD_0 and ER_0 are the indices applicable six weeks before the tender due date.

f   That the total due to be paid under the contract for adjustment of price be the algebraic sum of the monthly amounts calculated in accordance with the foregoing.

It is interesting to note that existing indices were considered unsatisfactory and that the DTI has agreed to the setting up of a new index. This will cover commonly occurring sections and plate thicknesses weighted in accordance with the following details:

Type	*Size*	*Weighting, %*
Plate	3/8 in × 4 ft × 30 ft	12.0
	½ in × 4 ft × 40 ft	11.0
	9/16 in × 34 in × 30 ft	5.0
	1 in × 4 ft × 55 ft	11.0
	2 in × 4 ft × 60 ft	8.5
Beams	36 in × 16½ in × 60 ft	19.0
	24 in × 9 in × 43 ft	8.0
Columns	8 in × 8 in × 40 ft	6.0
Plate	3 in × ½ in × 20 ft	6.0
Channels	8 in × 3½ in × 30 ft	4.0
Angles	2½ in × 2½ in × 30 ft	8.0
Tees	5 in × 3 in × 3/8 in × 40 ft	1.5
		100.0

The following example is typical of those emanating from the EEC countries:

> '*Price revision clause*
> Our prices have been estimated on the basis of the basic material cost factors. We therefore reserve the right of revising them, at the final settlement of accounts, with due consideration to any increases and/or decreases which may have occurred after the date of our quotation

in certain cost factors, e.g. in the prices of materials and/or in wages.

The value of partial payments will be determined on the basis of said formulae. Each partial payment will cover the corresponding proportional part of the total order value. The instalments paid will, therefore, not be subject to any further price revision.

$$P = P_0 \left(0.10 + 0.20 \frac{E}{E_0} + 0.70 \frac{L}{L_0}\right)$$

where P_0 is the price as quoted, E_0 the price of foundry pig iron No. 1 (excluding value-added tax) applied on the date of our quotation by the German steelworks, as notified by them to the High Authority (of the European Coal and Steel Community) in Luxembourg, E_0 = 296.80 DM/t, L_0 the minimum wage rate, including allowance for piecework pay, for a skilled workman of more than 21 years of age, as per the wage agreement for the iron, metal and electrical engineering industries of North-Rhine Westphalia on which the price of our quotation has been based (L_0 = 5.04 DM/hr), P the price as determined when the respective partial payment is due, E the price of foundry pig iron No. 1 (excluding value-added tax) when the respective partial payment is due and L the minimum wage rate, including allowance for piecework pay, for a skilled workman according to the wage agreement in force when the respective partial payment is due'.

These examples of prices variation formulae are just a few of those in use — although most follow the same pattern. If a buyer should decide to turn down a request for a price variation clause he is likely to be asked for a firm price which could eventually turn out to be more than would be payable under a variation clause; at least the seller will reckon so. It depends on the buyer's confidence of his own purchasing research capabilities and those of his department.

The common argument put forward in favour of price variation is that it provides an unequivocal means of determining price related to cost by the use of independently compiled indices and reduces the gambling element in long-term contractings. But for buyers to get the best end of the deal they must know how the index is compiled. Find out how the index is made up and relate it to the contract. You may wish to write your own formulae based more closely on the specific contract; or you may wish to keep very quiet!

However, one thing is sure, more and more use of such formulae will be made in the future, putting pressure on buyers who are not yet skilled in the practice of purchase price analysis.

Note: PVFs change from time to time, and the reader should check the 'current' mix of elements.

10.2 Case studies

A keen enquiring mind is a major attribute of the buyer. The comments in the book represent the views of the authors and in no way represent the sole way of dealing with all buying problems. Flexibility of approach is vital and the willingness to tackle major problems is the hallmark of the true professional.

We therefore include five case studies, typical of the problems which may be met in industry. The reader is invited to study the problems and make decisions on his likely action faced with that problem. This type of problem-solving is that used in more advanced purchasing courses and it is a refreshing, thought-provoking medium.

In an attempt to bring author and reader together, we are prepared to receive scripts for comment in response to the five case studies. These should be sent, stating name, address and company together with payment of £10.00 (applies to United Kingdom only) to Brian Farrington, 43 Lawrence Road, Windle, nr St Helens, Merseyside WA10 6HY.

Companies wishing to use the case studies in in-company training courses should also contact the author at the above address.

10.2.1 Purchasing case study: 'A fitting start to any job'

The Gyro Engineering Company had experienced difficulties with the supply and design characteristics of a range of compression fittings. These were used on a range of products being very successfully sold in the home and export markets. Basically, the difficulties led to the change to flared fittings.

It fell upon John Chewton, a newly appointed buyer with the Gyro Engineering Company, to fully investigate the total supply situation on this range of components which totalled some 200 items. He decided that the ideal starting point would be to obtain all available background information. He began by asking to see the Engineer responsible for 'signing off' the change. This was a short lived hope because Chewton discovered that he had retired many months ago. Significantly the engineering department could find no documentation of the detailed reasoning behind the design change.

His next call was to the experimental department who were very helpful. They had tested the new products and discovered that flared fittings were 100 per cent effective in sealing pipe joints. This was apparently a vital point because it made savings in fitting time, inspection and ultimate customer servicing. Chewton asked for, but could not obtain, any qualification of these alleged savings.

Chewton decided that his next step should be a simple investigation of the comparative market places. To achieve this he selected items and invited tenders. Seven potential suppliers were selected and the results are shown in Table 10.1.

When Chewton originally examined the drawings he was horrified to find that alongside the Gyro part number were the specific part numbers of suppliers B and D. There were many implications in this but his major concern was that supplier B informed him that their range was continually changing and they could not guarantee that any part number would be available when required by Gyro. When asked about their pricing policy, they gave an indication that when a part became 'a special' their prices usually carried a premium of 125 per cent. When Chewton pressed the point, the supplier said that they preferred not to put this in writing but that a gentleman's agreement would be more appropriate and that they would attempt to minimise any problems. They further explained that very few problems had arisen to date. Chewton decided that the attitude was that of a reasonable supplier. He

TABLE 10.1

A is the old part number - compression fitting
B is existing supplier - flared fitting
C - G are potential new sources (more information later)

Gyro part number	Price per 100 delivered to Gyro works, £						
	A	B	C	D	E	F	G
XY 58735	0.90	1.75	4.462	17.5	2.913	5.00	1.137
XY 58736	6.32	13.50	7.50	15.5	19.6	16.2	7.65
XY 58742	9.53	6.137	17.958	No quote	37.5	20.0	8.708
ZK 63425	8.15	8.703	9.458	27.00	30.00	20.0	25.5
ZK 63427	27.68	35.451	30.120	No quote	75.00	30.0	No quote

The annual quantities are as follows:

XY 58735	36,000
XY 58736	15,000
XY 58742	45,000
ZK 63425	10,000
ZK 63427	30,000

TABLE 10.2

Gyro part no.	Price per 100, £								Annualised volumes
	A	B	C	D	E	F	G	H	
XY 58735/10	1.10	3.23	2.58	-	3.30	3.31	-	1.75	72,000
XY 58736/11	1.50	2.76	1.97	-	2.30	2.17	-	1.87	45,000
XY 58742/12	-	2.52	-	-	-	3.50	-	2.12	90,000
ZK 63425/10	3.25	3.12	-	-	-	-	-	3.75	30,000
ZK 63427/11	0.87	1.45	-	-	2.75	2.42	-	1.12	90,000

left it at that.

Like any good buyer, Chewton decided that he would talk to the suppliers who had quoted and invited them to see him. He had never done this before. His previous *modus operandi* was to invite a selected number of suppliers. This was based on the simple expedient of excluding the highest and lowest quotations from any further consideration.

A brief summary of the discussions are included for your information.

Supplier A   The sales manager of this company forcibly expressed his regret that they had been eliminated as a supplier. He was of the opinion that their products were extremely competitive and were in fact still being used by Gyro's competitors. He felt that the design problems had not been satisfactorily investigated and invited Chewton to initiate a review of the technical difficulties. The sales manager said that his company would be prepared to support the investigation with both technical and financial support. In return he would require an undertaking that should Gyro revert to the use of compression fittings, Supplier A would be the sole source of supply. Chewton was unsure how to react to this suggestion and avoided any commitment.

Supplier B   Comments previously included in this brief.

Supplier C   It soon became apparent that this supplier was using antiquated manufacturing equipment and methods of production. Chewton asked them outright if they had considered the methods being used by their rivals, only to be told that they were a successful company and despite ancient methods they made good profits.

Supplier D   Their initial reaction to being told that the prices were too high was one of surprise. The technical sales representative investigated and said it was due to them having quoted for items not comparable with competitors. When he was asked to do this he stated that their 'Kon Tiki' range would fit the bill. He then quoted, from a standard price list, as follows:

XY 58735	£5.50
XY 58736	£11.00
XY 58742	£14.00
ZK 63425	£12.00
ZK 63427	£29.50

Chewton decided that frustration amply summed up his reaction. He was inclined to drop this supplier from his thoughts.

Supplier E This supplier was quite bland when faced with the fact that they were quoting extremely high. They explained that their items were made under licence to an American company. Chewton called this meeting to an abrupt halt because he could see no possibility of reducing these prices, nor was he inclined to try.

Supplier F Chewton had done his research on this supplier and had found them to be small (relative to all others who had quoted) but efficient. By prior arrangement, Gyro's quality control manager had visited them and given them a clean sheet. He was however, dubious whether they could produce a sufficient volume to meet Gyro's requirements. He added a rider that he felt the situation was a classic negotiation situation.

Supplier G This supplier was considered to offer excellent possibilities. Their production facilities were advanced and inspection facilities highly satisfactory. Chewton checked with other buyers in his sphere of operations and was told that the only problem was that of spasmodic deliveries. During Chewton's talks with this supplier he discovered that Supplier G had developed a revolutionary way of producing these parts and that it hadn't been patented. The more he thought about this the more he felt he should alert the other suppliers, in the hope that it would reduce their costs.

The situation had an added dimension because the fittings required nuts to provide the final finished part. Chewton conducted a further exercise to investigate this area. The outline findings are given in Table 10.2. In this instance all suppliers, other than H, had been involved with Chewton in his decisions.

When he contacted H he quickly discovered that they could not produce fittings but were anxious to supply the nuts which were their speciality. Equally, Chewton was left in no doubt that the fittings' suppliers were anxious to supply the nuts.

Chewton now decided that the time for reflection had arrived. There was no absence of facts but he wasn't sure whether he had enough, nor was he sure what his strategy and tactics should be from this point.

TASK

1. Analyse the information provided and make a detailed action plan for Chewton.
2. Discuss fully all the purchasing issues involved in this case.

10.2.2 'Lock, stock and barrel!'

George Wallace was a senior buyer with the Baroque Engineering Company who specialised in the manufacture of high quality motor vehicle accessories.

One of the key items in his budgeted spending was a highly specialised door lock. This was engineered with the specific intention of preventing unlawful entry into a motor vehicle. The lock comprised many individual items including pressings, rivets, springs, etc. It was the customary practice of Baroque Engineering Company to prepare their own specifications and to invite tenders from contractors who could supply the complete part.

Wallace had traditionally placed this contract with the Locprufe Company who had rarely caused any supply difficulties. Lately this situation had changed and Locprufe's deliveries began to deteriorate until the time arrived when their adverse performance began to threaten Baroque's supply position to their market. Wallace had been closely monitoring deliveries but had decided not to confront the management of Locprufe. His reasoning was that this action could damage the close relationships he had established with Mr Cushing the Sales Director.

The supply position finally became critical and Wallace was called into the Purchasing Director's office. He was faced by Mr Hardline who had been recently appointed and was rapidly gaining a reputation for an uncompromising attitude to recalcitrant suppliers.

'I've heard about Locprufe's difficulties, George. It is essential to our wellbeing that you resource this item. I suggest that you contact Quikmake Limited who have previously met my urgent requirements.'

Wallace left the office grateful for the advice. He thought that he was on a safe horse with a recommendation from his Director of Purchasing. That evening he sent an enquiry to Quikmake for the next twelve months requirements. In financial terms this represented £75,000 at current prices and based on current volumes.

Three days later the quotation was received with a price marginally below that of the existing supplier. Wallace knew that the company's procedure on quality control meant that a new supplier should be both commercially and technically competent to make a part which they had never previously supplied.

Wallace was of the firm intention that a new supplier would be an advantage and he subsequently cancelled his contract with Locprufe. He used non-performance on delivery as his reason. The new contract was sent to Quikmake who assured Wallace that the item presented no problem. When questioned on quality control the sales director stated that they had never had any problems with other customers. This assurance satisfied Wallace and he gave a verbal commitment on the telephone to Quikmake to begin production.

It was part of purchasing procedure to send a copy of the purchase order to quality control. When they received the order for the special door lock they queried Wallace's decision to authorise manufacture without the necessary quality approval. The quality control manager insisted on a visit to Quikmake and requested that Wallace accompany him. The visit was made and got off to a bad start when the premises were located in a dingy backstreet of Walsport. After a wait of ten minutes the sales director arrived with the comment, 'Blasted suppliers causing us problems again.'

After the pleasantries had been exchanged Wallace began to discuss the contract for the supply of the special door locks.

'Ah yes. We have placed all the orders for the parts but the main spring is causing a problem. The special steel and heat treatment means that there are few makers in our area. Still, we are doing our best, but there is likely to be a serious delay of at least two months.'

Wallace began to feel downcast and this got worse when the sales director revealed that they didn't employ a buyer.

'We manage to get by without one' was his comment.

Wallace decided to visit the sub-contractor to whom the spring had been given. With reluctance he was informed that the supplier was a Mr Keytone of 125A Crompton Street, Longworth.

When Wallace and the quality control manager were driving the four miles to Longworth, they expressed doubts about the sourcing policy of Quikmake. Wallace said, 'Fancy them not telling me that they couldn't make all the parts!'

They duly arrived in Crompton Street and were amazed when the premises consisted of a row of terraced houses. Wallace led the way to number 125A, knocked and were greeted by an elderly lady who said that they would want Mr Keytone. She led them through the house and into a back yard. They progressed down the back yard to a shed at the bottom. Mr Keytone stepped outside and explained that he had the contract for the springs but was having great difficulty meeting the production schedules issued by Quikmake. The fact that he had recently retired and only had one spring coiling machine didn't help matters. The quality control manager asked where the heat treatment was carried out. Mr Keytone explained that he did this in the gas oven in the house but that production stopped when his wife wanted to cook a meal! Even Wallace blanched at this and asked for a sample. With this they decided to leave and return to Baroque.

The drive back was very unpleasant, the quality control manager muttering threats about sorting out slap-happy purchasing systems that permitted such a situation.

On his return he tested the spring and was amazed when it passed all quality control tests. This information he passed on to Wallace who had been doing some hard thinking. He felt the situation was getting out of hand and that the solution lay with Locprufe. He telephoned them and spoke to Mr Cushing. 'I would like to talk to you about the door locks that I had to cancel', he began, 'perhaps we should get together and discuss a new arrangement'. Cushing replied, 'Thanks a lot George. Quite frankly, I wouldn't thank you for that contract. It caused us no end of trouble and we have now allocated the capacity to a more profitable contract. It may sound silly but the main spring was the major problem.'

Wallace was appalled at this reaction but decided to bluff. 'Never mind I have another source up my sleeve and I don't anticipate any problems.'

He had no sooner put the telephone down when Mr Hardline came into his office.

'How is the contract going for the door locks?' he asked.

QUESTIONS FOR CONSIDERATION

1 What do you think of Wallace's sourcing of the door locks?
2 What would you have done in the circumstances?
3 Was Mr Hardline's intervention 'good management'?
4 Should Quikmake have sub-contracted without the approval of Baroque Engineering Company?
5 What do you consider Wallace should have done to appraise Quikmake?
6 Did he make a correct decision to visit Mr Keytone?
7 What would you say to Mr Hardline faced with this situation?
8 How did Wallace handle the original contract with Locprufe?
9 Are there any other purchasing problems raised in this case?

10.2.3 A casting problem at the National Engineering Company

Dick Turpin, Purchasing Manager of the National Engineering Company, had been with the company for fifteen years. During this time he had devoted a lot of his undoubted energies and purchasing expertise to maintaining an equitable supply position on a range of castings. These were essential key materials, which, if not available, would cause a major stoppage of production at his company. This was a prime consideration in his purchasing policy.

The castings fell conveniently in two commodity groups, which for the purpose of this case will be called Range A and Range B. The expenditure on these items accounted for 28 per cent of the total spent on production materials, this latter figure being approximately £40 million in the current fiscal year. Dick Turpin, as he reflected on the situation, concluded that despite his attention, a series of unforseen events over the years had occurred and the overall position was becoming increasingly vulnerable.

Basically, the supply situation on castings took its first twist in the early 1960's when Stonely Castings declared their intention to make a serious inroad in the manufacture of castings which included Range A and Range B of National Engineering. These castings presented specific manufacturing problems, particularly from a quality control point of view. Stonely Castings made a formal approach to Turpin and asked for his support in their new venture. Indeed, they made it obvious that without a high proportion of his spending being committed to them they could not enter the field. Many discussions took place between senior representatives of each company and culminated with Turpin declaring his company's willingness to place a considerable amount of business with Stonely Castings. He was asked, by their sales director to enter into a gentleman's agreement that he would continue to commit a high proportion of his expenditure over the ensuing years. This assurance he readily gave, principally because he now felt he had materially helped to create a new source of supply, thereby increasing competition into what had previously been a restricted supply situation. His knowledge of the law convinced him the gentleman's agreement was reasonable, no party being contractually responsible for future events.

Turpin decided at this time that his sourcing strategy would be as follows:

Stonely Castings	—	Significant amount spent
ARB Group	—	Significant amount spent
Jackson Engineering Services	—	Negligible amount spent

The effect of this strategy on the supplying companies output presented an interesting pattern. Stonely Castings had committed 40 per cent of their total output to National Engineering. They made no secret of this fact and stressed the point in a letter to Turpin when confirming the initial 'agreement'. The offtake of castings by National Engineering from ARB Group and Jackson Engineering Services was far less significant.

In the ensuing two/three year period a number of significant events took place. Turpin became disturbed at the very poor quality performance of Stonely Castings. This situation was tolerated for a time because it was accepted in the industry that Range A and Range B castings were complex in character and demanded considerable expertise in manufacturing control. The situation became gradually worse when the Quality Control department of National Engineering decided to make a determined effort to impose their pre-established quality standards. The effect of this policy was to increase the rejection rate to Stonely Castings. It may be said that their reaction was typically negative although their management seemed to change with alarming regularity. During this time all three suppliers began to request price increases. These were eventually settled by Turpin who was satisfied that the price increase requests were within reasonable limits and, more importantly, were very similar from all three companies.

Turpin, during this period, was constantly monitoring the total supply situation. Two specific factors were worthy of note. The ARB Group were frequent visitors of his. They 'led the field' from time to time in submitting tenders for all items being produced by Stonely Castings. In the majority of instances the ARB Group offered lower prices than Stonely Castings but Turpin continued to place business with the latter company. His main reasons for doing so were that the ARB Group were believed to be exploiting their monopolistic position in the castings field, prior to the entry of Stonely Castings. Equally, in Turpin's view, the rather sorry state of labour relations at ARB Group were a major reason for not being over committed with them.

Sourcing considerations continued to occupy Turpin's time and in due course he located a potential source in Western Europe which if approved would provide a new overseas source. Engineering studies were undertaken and after commercial and technical approval had been received the Eurocast Company were given a share of castings in Ranges A and B. Turpin felt this was a master stroke on his part. National boundaries had been crossed and he made sure that the information was given to the representatives of his established suppliers. He believed that these companies would see his action as the 'warning light' should they ever be inclined to take advantage of him.

Coincidental it may be, but shortly after this, there was a significant improvement in the quality performance of Stonely Castings. Turpin began to feel more relaxed because there had also been a period of price stability. All good things have to come to an end! Stonely Castings began to adopt an aggressive policy and price increases were requested that could not be supported by normal market price trend movements. Naturally, all price requests were challenged, but hardly had settlements been reached than another was submitted. During the negotiations, the senior management of Stonely Castings kept making reference to the agreement they had with Turpin and insisted that if he took any business from they could be forced into a crisis. They advanced many reasons, technical in essence, namely to the effect that a minimum melt of metal was necessary and National Engineering business was essential to the economies of manufacture. Turpin was unimpressed, after all he had heard wild claims before when firms were justifying excessive price increases. Stonely Castings executives maintained that Range A and B castings were unprofitable and the only solution lay in further price increases. Turpin continued to take a firm line and evaluated all claims on a commercial basis and settled them accordingly. He was conscious however, of a growing antipathy from Stonely Castings' management.

The matter came to a head when Stonely Castings submitted a further large price claim. Turpin again resisted strongly and in fact refused to consider what was in his language 'an exhorbitant claim, wholly unjustified on commercial grounds'. This was not said lightly, it was supported by a price analysis study by his purchasing research section.

Almost immediately National Engineering were affected by a decline in the market for their finished products. This meant a cut back in schedules on all supplies. Naturally, this involved the schedules placed with Stonely Castings who were informed of the reduced off-take by the normal line of communications. In the case of Turpin, he merely forwarded a revised delivery schedule and asked that it be acknowledged. The schedules were accepted without comment by Stonely Castings.

At this time Turpin had the following supply situation.

2 items single-sourced with Stonely Castings
1 item dual-sourced with Stonely Castings and ARB Group
1 item triple-sourced with Stonely Castings, Jackson Engineering Services and Eurocast

Several weeks later the whole situation changed dramatically when Turpin received a telephone call from the chairman of Stonely Castings to the effect that they would be closing their foundry in three months time. He said that the decision was final and had been caused by the pricing policies of Turpin together with the reduced demand for their castings. Had he been prepared to pay a premium in the past he could have maintained Stonelys as a source of supply. The chairman rang off saying that they would of course assist Turpin in any way possible in the period prior to the closure.

Turpin received this news with considerable foreboding, realising fully the implications of Stonely Castings' actions. His cup was soon to be filled to overflowing. Some of the castings in Range A and B were being received from a subsidiary company of Stonely Castings. He was almost transfixed when their managing director informed him that following secret discussions they would be taken over immediately by the ARB Group. Turpin rapidly became alarmed. He was now faced with a major supply problem. Almost 'at a stroke' the supply situation had been transformed in the UK.

He was faced by one major group (the almost classic monopolistic situation) who were the only independent manufacturing group, in the UK. Turpin still suspected that they would take advantage of their monopolistic position and he was also apprehensive about their labour relations. He saw limited prospects with Jackson Engineering Services who were owned by a manufacturing group and would clearly give them first consideration for capacity. There was of course the possibility of increasing business with Eurocast Company.

Assume you are in the position of Turpin. You have three months in which to take decisive action to ensure the supply of key components. Range A and B are maintained both during the immediate months and the ensuing period.

What is: (*a*) your analysis of the complete situation, and (*b*) your recommendations for dealing with it? You are expected to comment in detail on all the management and purchasing considerations involved.

10.2.4 A further purchasing problem of the National Engineering Company

Dick Turpin is the Purchasing Manager of the National Engineering Company. For many years he has put a great deal of energy and time into the procurement arrangements for a key commodity bought by his company.

This commodity is semi-proprietary and is a critical item in the quality and performance of products made by his company. It also represents a significant amount in his total buying budget. The commodity concerned comes in many different versions but conforms to a basic concept of design. In fact there are some 30 different versions used in his company's products and since each costs approximately £2.00 it was obvious that a great deal of technology, research and development, investment and experience went into their manufacture. His company uses over one-and-a-half million of these items each year.

Dick Turpin has traditionally bought these items from two suppliers: General Engineering and Proprietary Components. There has been no particular policy with regard to the split of business between the two suppliers, each tending to gain business at the expense of the other as a new version of the component is required and each individual decision becoming based on the particular commercial merits at the time. Each company has maintained roughly the same share for many years, General Engineering enjoying some 60 per cent of the total and Proprietary Components the balance. In fact these two suppliers were really the only manufacturers of these components in the UK and whilst there are many other companies able to supply these items overseas none had really made any inroads into the UK in general or with National Engineering in particular. Almost invariably these overseas companies had been excluded by price.

Dick Turpin considered that National Engineering had received a pretty fair deal out of both suppliers over the years and although each remained coldly distant from National Engineering on commercial matters they did work extraordinarily well with the design engineers of National Engineering during development and were always able to offer a fairly clear cut case at the time Dick Turpin's buyers became faced with the need to make a sourcing decision. Very often the two suppliers were so close to 'Engineering' that they knew of a new version of this commodity many months before the Purchase Department of National Engineering but Dick Turpin was not too concerned about this because he was satisfied that at the end of the day his company did enjoy a fair deal.

Naitonal Engineering decided about a year ago to develop a powerful cost control area within the company to ensure that all products made by National Engineering were competitive within the world market place. Needless to say their Cost Control Department became significantly involved with purchased materials and one of the first studies they undertook was to examine the prices being paid for this range of semi-proprietary items to both supplying organisations. After many months of work the Cost Control Department advised Dick Turpin that, first, the prices being paid for many individual components bore no relationship with reality or with the prices paid for other similar components, and secondly, the total amount spent on this commodity range was some 20 per cent more than justifiable costs could support. Because of the potential savings involved, Dick Turpin came under increasing pressure from his company at large to make immediate improvements in the prices of these items and to gain considerable savings for his company.

Negotiations proceeded for many months but failed to achieve any conclusion. Each time Dick Turpin tried to get into close discussion on costs the suppliers' traditionally distant policy prevented him getting sufficient information from them to prove his case. Both suppliers 'slipped through his fingers' every time and in fact there were always many reasons put forward by his suppliers as to why prices should increases rather than decrease.

At about this time National Engineering decided to investigate manufacture of these items 'in works' and this study showed profound cost advantages by internal manufacture. The reaction by both suppliers was very non-commital to this, each saying that the trend with most manufacturers like National Engineering was to go away from 'in works' manufacture of these items to a policy of bought-out and in addition they were convinced that National Engineering really did not know the first thing about the manufacture of these items and as a result completely misjudged the true costs involved. Dick Turpin had to reluctantly admit that there was far more to the manufacture of these items than just buying the appropriate machine tools in question. Turpin was also very much aware of the fact that he was still unable to find any viable overseas source of manufacturer despite many determined attempts in this respect. He was also aware that certainly General Engineering, if not Proprietary Components, were actively filling all space capacity with orders from overseas competitors to National Engineering.

Whilst he had suspected some degree of collusion between both suppliers for some years he nevertheless could not understand how his suppliers could remain so completely unimpressed by National Engineering's cost attack and 'in works' study and still continued to insist that prices generally being paid for these components by National Engineering were too low rather than too high. Whilst the very competitiveness of both of his suppliers in the market place persuaded him that there was some truth in their views he had nevertheless agreed, understood and believed in the case presented by the Cost Control Department which illustrated an entirely opposite situation.

The Managing Director of National Engineering called Dick Turpin into his office one day and told Turpin that he had had long enough to implement the considerable savings identified by Cost Control and that he had one more month to agree a policy with his suppliers which firstly gave National Engineering some immediate price benefit and which also set National Engineering and its suppliers on a committed course towards increasing longer term savings.

TASK

If you were Dick Turpin, how would you meet the challenge from your Managing Director? What policy would you follow with both suppliers and Cost Control with the objective of meeting your mandate? What sequence of events would you follow and how would you co-ordinate action to resolve this problem?

'Stop Press'

General Engineering have just submitted a price claim request for a 9 per cent general uplift in prices to be effective as quickly as possible. With this claim they have also implied that this is not all in the forseeable future and that further adjustments may be necessary.

10.2.5 Purchasing case study: 'Dan Bright fired by Humperdinkum'

For the past seven years Dan Bright had been the buyer responsible for dealing with the Works Maintenance items required for the Broxburn Steel Works. His responsibilities included a section of general stores stock which represented approximately 10,000 items. In moments of solitude Dan admitted to himself that most of his energies were devoted to problems of stock replenishment. For other items he had found that he could rely upon the Works Engineer for a specification. Usually the latter could also recommend a source of supply.

The relining of No. 2 Furnace in the North End Annealing section provides an example of the relationships and methods of operation at Broxburn. It really didn't seem very long since Bill Hardhead, a project engineer, walked into Dan's office, handed him a requisition and said, 'Order that lot', Dan. 'We need them urgently for the shutdown period in eight weeks time. I know that the delivery time is tight but I have spoken to Gettem Limited who say they can obtain them for us. I've just had lunch with their representative who said that they specialise in quick jobs. If I were you I wouldn't waste time messing around with routine.'

When Hardhead left the office Dan decided to get on with the job in hand. He had never heard of Gettem Limited but he couldn't admit that to an engineer! His only source of reference was Paddys Directory which listed their name under the general heading of Furnace Supplies. The address was shown as 132 Crown Court, Coscot, London XY1 WAA. This was good enough for Dan, they must be OK if they can afford expensive advertisements like that.

The requisition was very helpful and it gave a lot of detail, including total prices:

285	Supporting Bricks	Ref. 505	£681.50
6	Recessed Bricks	Ref. 102	£ 33.40
24	Carbide Plates	Ref. 806	£ 46.20
2	Refractory Rings	Ref. 703	£ 69.60
3	Refractory Rings	Ref. 704	£117.20
1	Set Con. Assemblies	Ref. 83	£171.80

The delivery was quoted as 'required in 8 weeks'. Without any delay Dan took the requisition to Mrs Pledge, the order typist and told her 'Get this away tonight, it's urgent. Make sure you put a delivery of 6 weeks on the order. If I am not in sign it to avoid any delay.'

Ten days later Dan was walking through the Steelworks when he bumped into Hardhead who asked 'How's the order going with Gettem, Dan?' 'No problems!' was the confident reply by Dan. The further he walked, the less confident he became because he really couldn't remember seeing any correspondence regarding this item. In any case it wasn't his practice to examine every acknowledgement and indeed it was the departmental practice to retain only those for orders in excess of £50. The rest were destroyed after due note had been made of any delivery quoted by the supplier.

Eventually Mrs Pledge located the acknowledgement for Dan. She said, 'It isn't often you ask for these Dan!' 'What's the point anyway', Dan retorted, 'you can't do anything once the supplier sends his acknowledgement. He is the one in the driver's seat, not the buyer!'

When he examined the acknowledgement he found that each item was exactly the same as his order and the price was unchanged. There was however a rider at the bottom. This stated:

'Please note that the above prices do not include Duty and Importation charges and they are based on the present rate of exchange, subject to fluctuations. The goods will be despatched in seaworthy packaging from Germany. Despatch can be carried out approximately 6 weeks from receipt of order in Germany.'

Dan's reaction to this was perhaps typical of the average. 'You never know where supplies are coming from nowadays.' If he had turned over the acknowledgement and read the 'small print' he would have seen the following:

1 Goods are exhaustively inspected before leaving the works and any goods that the buyer may wish to have rejected because of failure to comply with this Company's specification must be the subject of written notice within six days of their receipt.
2 This company accepts no liability for consequential

claims or damage of any description.
3. We only accept liability for goods being of the capacity and performance required by customers or as being fit for any particular purpose if we have been given full and accurate particulars of the customer's requirements and of the conditions under which the goods are required to be operated.
4. Delivery commitments are entered into in good faith but the seller shall not be liable for failure to deliver on the specified dates, nor shall such failure be deemed to be a breach of contract, or any of its conditions, or part thereof.

NB: These are not all of the conditions of sale, merely a representative sample thereof.

In the ensuing weeks Dan took no further action. 'No news is good news', that was his motto! Bill Hardhead hadn't bothered him either — if he had Dan would probably have sent a routine chasing letter asking if the delivery would be maintained.

These relatively calm seas remained until three days before the order was due for delivery. On this day a letter arrived from Gettem which read as follows:

Dear Sirs,

DR BRUNNER, HUMPERDINKUM, PHALIA, WEST GERMANY

It is with great regret that we have to advise you that the building housing the administrative offices at the Humperdinkum Works caught fire and was largely destroyed. At the time of writing they cannot even be reached by members of our company who deal with Sales and Technical Service on behalf of Humperdinkum, either by telephone or telex. This will inevitably mean a delay because we cannot find duplicate records in UK. If your company has any orders outstanding will you please provide us with photocopies of the necessary paperwork.

Signed ED SCALER
TECHNICAL DIRECTOR

An examination of the letter showed that it had taken five days to reach him. Dan didn't lose any time and sent the

CONCLUSIONS

copies in the next post that day and waited for developments.

He got them! Bill Hardhead rang and asked, 'Got the bricks, lad?' 'No. I'm having some trouble with your supplier', replied Dan. 'There's been a fire in Germany and nobody knows what the hell is happening.'

'Then you had better find out. Why don't you get up off your backside and what the hell has Germany got to do with the bricks? Your head will roll if any delay occurs!'

The outcome of this outburst was that he telephoned Ed Scaler and asked for the items to be sent airfreight. Dan had no experience of materials coming by air but he felt that it should be straightforward. When he told Hardhead what he had done the reply was to the effect that he couldn't care less providing the goods arrived within two days.

For once things went right for Dan when a gigantic packing case was delivered on time and the goods were found to be 'as ordered'. The ecstasy was short lived. An invoice duly arrived which in addition to the cost of the items also stated:

Duty	£112.46
Carriage	£464.12
Exchange	£ 89.53

QUESTIONS FOR DISCUSSION

1. What is your opinion of Dan Bright as a Buyer?
2. What factors have led you to your conclusion?
3. Was the selection of Gettem Limited effectively carried out?
4. Could you suggest a selection procedure to prevent such occurrences?
5. Is the order chasing system a good one?
6. Do you agree with the method of dealing with acknowledgements at Broxburn Steel Works?
7. What would you have done when the original acknowledgement was received?
8. Did Gettem Limited do all within their power to help Dan Bright?
9. What would you have done when advised about the fire?
10. Who should pay the additional charges? Why?

11 If you were the Manager of the Purchasing Department what would you do next?
12 What would you now do if you were Dan Bright?

References

1 A. Battersby, *A guide to stock control,* Pitman.

2 G. W. Aljian, *Purchasing handbook,* McGraw-Hill.

3 B. Farrington, *Industrial source management,* unpublished MSc Thesis (1975).

4 L. De Rose, *Analytical purchasing,* Materials Management Institute (1962).

5 Fearon and Hoagland, *Purchasing research in American Industry,* Study 58, American Management Association, New York (1963).

6 *Formulae methods of price adjustment on building contracts,* NEDO (40p).

7 *Report on price adjustment formulae for civil engineering contracts,* NEDO (free).

8 *Price adjustment formulae for civil engineering contracts — Steelwork: sub-formula,* NEDO (free).

Index

ABC inventory categories, 115-16
Accounts department, relationships with, 31-3
Acknowledgements, 54, 89
Act of God, 106
Administration, timing of supplies, 12
Advice notes, 57-8
Agents:
    import, 146-8
    insurance, 150-1
Aljian, G.W., supplier rating, 169
Analysts, purchasing, 8
Arbitration, general conditions of purchase, 92
Authorisation, letters of, 53
Availability, 4

Bankruptcy:
    of suppliers, 92
    transfer of title, 95
Banks:
    as a source of foreign purchasing information, 137
    guarantees from, 86-7, 154
Bar charts, see Charts
Battersby, Albert, 120
Bill of lading, 146
Black & Decker, 5
Blanket orders, 51
Bluff, in negotiation, 77

Bonds, performance, 87
Brainstorming, 161
Brand names, 64
Bribery, 4
British Aircraft Corporation, quality appraisal of suppliers, 167-8
British Constructional Steelwork Association, price variation formulae, 213
British Electrical and Allied Manufacturers Association, price variation formulae, 206
British Metalworking Plant Makers Association, price variation formulae, 210
Buyers:
    as a source of information on suppliers, 67
    judgement of, 171, 202
    personnel aspects, 4
    qualifications of, 22
    relationships with colleagues, 23-41
Buying: see also Purchasing
    abroad, 133-58
    cost comparisons, 139
    reasons for, 134-5

definition of role, 22
departmental operating costs, 190-1
performance *see* Performance: buying, measurement
stockless, 123-32

CIF, 148
Capacity, of suppliers, 71
Capital:
  opportunity cost of, 12, 111
  projects, order numbers, 50
Card, quality used for forms, 45
Cars, disposals, 61, 189
Cash flow, 84, 85
  timing of supplies, 11-12
Catalogues, indexing of, 62
Centralisation, 5, 8
Certificates of origin, 148
Charts, 99, 101, 176
Classification, stocks, 115-16
Collusion, in negotiations, 76
Commercial vehicles, disposals, 61, 189
Commodity records, 47
Communication, 6, 23-4, 182
Completion:
  general conditions of purchase, 91
  late, damages for, 104
Computers, 37-8
  purchasing research, 173
  role in expediting, 56
Conditions:
  foreign suppliers, 153
  general conditions of purchase, 87-92
    acknowledgement to purchase order, 89
    arbitration, 92
    cancellation, 92
    completion, 91
    definition of terms, 88
    dispatch and delivery, 90
    drawings, patterns and toolings, 90
    force majeure, 91
    infringement of patents, 91
    legal interpretation, 92
    packing, 90
    payment, 91
    prices, 89
    standard of supply, 89
    variations, 90
  negotiations, buying performance, 186-7
  special conditions of purchase, 98-108
    model, 107-8
Consignment notes, 61
Consulates, as sources of foreign purchasing information, 136
Contacts, foreign purchasing information, 136
Contracts:
  annual, 63
  buying, 123
  expediting, 56
  model special conditions, 107-8
  non compliance by purchasers, 78
  order numbers, 50, 51
  price adjustment (CPA), 206
  registers, 56
  renewal, 76
  variations to, 96
Corruption, 4
Cost/s:
  as a percentage of average selling price, 73
  estimates, buying performance measurement, 196-7
  savings, 80
  suppliers, 173, 205
Credit:
  letters of, 144
  notes, stores, 130
  ratings, 86, 173
    foreign suppliers, 139
Critical Path Analysis (CPA), 176-8
Currency:
  effects on prices, 140-1
  exchange rates, 82

payment methods, 141-2
regulations, 151
Customers, effects of buying performance on, 188-9
Customs and Excise:
    clearance, 146
    requirements, 144-5

Damages:
    inadequate performance, 105
    late completion/delivery, 104
De Rose, Louis, supplier rating, 171
Delegation, 23
Delivery, 33
    basis of, 70
    buying performance, 185, 187, 199
    foreign purchase enquiries, 137
    general conditions of purchase, 90
    late, damages for, 104
    notification of, 57, 103
    performance, 25
    supplier rating, 170
Departmental relationships, 182
Designs, registered; general conditions of purchase, 91
Deterioration, stocks, 111
Development, 4-5, 22
Directories:
    as sources of information on suppliers, 48, 67
    foreign purchasing, 136
Directors, involvement of, 20, 22, 194-5
Discounts, 72-5, 83
    original equipment manufacturers, 72-4
    payment, 75
    quantity, 74-5
    trade, 75
    turnover, 74
Discrepancy advice, 58, 128
Dispatch, general conditions of purchase, 90
Disposals, 60-2, 189-90
    cars, 61, 189
    commercial vehicles, 61, 189
    office equipment, 61, 190
    scrap, 61, 189
    surplus stores stock, 61-2, 189
Documentation, 43-63
    special conditions of purchase, 99
Down payments, foreign purchses, 143
Drawings:
    general conditions of purchase, 90
    special conditions of purchase, 99
Dun and Bradstreet, 86
    foreign investigations, 139
Dutch auctions, 77

Economic Development Committee for Building, price variation formulae, 210
Economic environment, 14-16
    purchasing research, 173
Electronic data processing, *see* Computers
Embassies:
    as sources of foreign purchasing information, 136
    as sources of information on suppliers, 67
Emergency orders, 51-2
Empathy, 4
Engineering, relationships with, 29-31
England, *Prof.* Wilbur B., 164
Enquiries, 48, 68-70
    adequacy of information in, 68
    buying performance measurement, 199
    closing dates, 69
    foreign purchasing, 137
Environment, effects on buying organisation, 6
Erlicher, Harry, 160
European Economic Community, 16

Exchange:
  controls, 151
  rates, 82
Exclusions, in quitations, 71
Exhibitions, sources of information on suppliers, 67
Expediting, 24-6, 54-8
  advice notes, 57-8
  contracts, 56
  delivery notification, 57
  critical action, 55-6
  supplier visits, 57
  supplier work load, 56-7
Exponential smoothing, 118-19

FOB, 148
Farrington, Brian, 204
Fearon, purchasing research, 172
Finance, function, 81-2
  bank guarantees, 86-7
  performance bonds, 87
  price, 82-3
    variation formulae, 83
  terms of payment, 84-5
Financial status, 86, 173
Flexibility, 6
Force Majeure clauses, 87, 91, 106
Forecasting:
  price movements, 79
  stock control, 118
Foreign:
  currency, *see* Buying: abroad
  currency, *see* Currency
Forms design, 44
  purchasing research, 173
Free issue materials, special conditions of purchase, 99-100

Gallahers Ltd, 6
Goods received notes, 129
Goodwill:
  effects of buying performance on, 188-9
  timing of supplies, 13
Guarantees:
  bank, 86-7, 154
  special conditions of purchase, 93-4

Hints to Businessmen, 137
Hoagland, purchasing research, 172

Imports, 133-58
  agents, 146-8
  licences, 144-5
  payment for, 151-2
  procedure, 157
  regulations, 144-6
Incoterms, conditions of contract document, 154
Indemnities, 58
  site workings, 100
Indices, 83
  buying performance measurement, 198
  checking prices, 76
  foreign purchases, 141
  price variation formulae, 208
  weightings, 200, 208
Inflation, 83
Information, purchase research, 173
Inspection:
  foreign purchases, 153
  special conditions of purchase, 98
Insurance, 36, 58
  agents, 150
  during manufacture, 96
  free issue materials, 100
  site workings, 100
  stocks, 111
  timing of supplies, 12
International Chamber of Commerce, Incoterms, 154
Inventories: *see also* Stock/s
  categories, 115-16
  levels, 33
  rationalisation, purchase research, 173
Investigators, financial, 86, 139
Invoices, 32

Job descriptions, 23, 182, 195
  stores controller, 131, 132
Job programs, special conditions of purchase, 98-9, 101

Judgement, of buyers, 171, 202

Laboratories, suppliers', 166
Labour, price variation formulae, 206, 210
Language, foreign purchase enquiries, 137
Lead times, buying performance, 187
Learning curves, 163-4, 197
Letters:
 of authorisation, 53
 of credit, 144
Libraries, 11, 67
Licences, import, 144-5
Liens, 95
Line of balance, 174-6
Loss, consequential, 94

Maintenance, Repair & Operating Items (MRO), 124
Make or buy, 10, 65, 77
Management by exception, 9
Manuals, 24
Market studies, 14
Marketing, relationships with, 34
Material/s:
 control, relationships with, 35-6
 handling, purchasing research, 173
 management, 22
 price variation formulae, 207, 210
 requirements, definition, 9
 substitutes, purchasing research, 173
Miles, L.D., 160
Morale, 8, 21
Motor cars, disposals, 61, 189
Multinational companies, 15, 16

Negotiations, 75-9
 planning, 78
 use of the learning curve, 164
Network diagrams, 99
North West Regional Management Centre, 5

Objectives:
 buying performance measurement, 203
 corporate, 4
Obsolescence, 34, 111
Office equipment, disposals, 61, 190
Order/s *see* Purchase: orders
Organisation, 5-9, 20-42, 190, 195
 and methods, 44
 research, 13
 restructuring, 21-2
Origin, certificates of, 148
Overheads:
 apportionment by sellers, 17
 stockholding, 111

Packing:
 general conditions of purchase, 90
 purchase research, 173
 special conditions of purchase, 100
Paper, quality used for forms, 45
Pareto's Law, 9, 31, 51, 199
Patents, 65
 general conditions of purchase, 91
 infringements, 154
Patterns, general conditions of purchase, 90
Payment:
 discounts, 75
 general conditions of purchase, 91
 progress, 84, 85, 95, 143
 terms of, 23, 84
  foreign purchases, 142-4
Performance:
 bonds, 87
 buying, measurement, 18, 181-203
  cost of measurement, 191
  departmental operating costs, 190-1
  disposals, 189-90
  expediting, transport and quality control, 188

failure to meet production requirements, 185
information to management, etc., 187
organisation, 195
outside customers, 188
over-exepnditure, 184
programmes, 203
qualitative, 202-3
quantitative, 196-201
  delivery, 199
  evaluated cost estimates, 196-7
  inter-company/division, 197-8
  market indices, 198
  past performance, 197
  price performance, 79-80, 196
  quality, 199
  sourcing, 199-200
  unpriced orders, 198-9
  value, number and complexity, 200
delivery, 25
purchasing, 26
Perrigo, 177
Personnel, restructuring problems, 21
Planning, 4
corporate, 34
Politics, purchasing research, 173
Postage, foreign purchase enquiries, 137
Preservation, special conditions of purchase, 100
Price/s, 2, 11, 71-9
analysis, 14, 16-17, 162, 205
as a measure of buying performance, 79-80, 196
awareness of by storekeepers, 50-1
basis of, 70, 82-3
changes, purchase research, 173
condition of, foreign enquiries, 137
costs as a percentage of, 73
discounts, *see* Discounts
effects of currencies on, 140-1
forecasts, 4
general conditions of purchase, 89
leaders, 76
negotiation, 75-9
supplier rating, 170
targets, 184, 196
transfer, 15
trends, purchasing research, 173
variation formulae (PVF), 83, 204-12
  foreign purchases, 141
Price Commission, 205
Procedures, *see* Documentation: Systems
Procurement, *see* Buying; Purchase
Product demand, effects on obsolescence, 34
Production:
effects on profitability, 1
timing of supplies, 12
relationships with, 28-9
Profit, of sellers, 17
Profitability, 1
Programme Evaluation and Review Technique (PERT), 177
Programs, special conditions of purchase, 98
Progress:
foreign purchases, 152-3
payments, 84, 85, 95, 143
special conditions of purchase, 98
Publicity, special conditions of purchase, 107
Purchase:
conditions, foreign suppliers, 153-4
orders, 50-1
  acknowledgement, 54, 89
  cost of, 51
  economic order quantities (EOQ), 114
  emergency, 51-2
  letters of authority, 53
  local, 52-3
  numbers, 50-1

order numbers, 50-1
  reconciliation, 54
  unpriced, 198-9
  requisitions, 45-6
  terms of, foreign suppliers, 153-4
Purchasing: see also Buying
  private, 62

Quality, 2
  appraisal, 166-9
  buying performance, 185, 188, 199
  control, 29
    foreign purchases, 153
    relationships with, 34-5
    supplier rating, 170
Quantity, 2, 64
  discounts, 74-5
  surveyors, 85
Quotas, 66
  foreign purchases, 144
Quotations, 48-9, 70-1
  buying performance measurement, 199
  evaluation, 49
    foreign purchases, 138

Rebates, 83
Receivers, 95
Recruitment, 5
Rejection notes, 58
Relocation, 21
Reports, 14
Representatives, as a source of information on suppliers, 67
Requisitions, 45-7
  purchase, 45-6
  stores traveller, 46-7
  travelling, 127
Research:
  purchasing, 8, 26, 35, 172-4, 203
  total buying activities, 13-14
Responsibility, 6

Salaries:
  stockholding, 111

Sales department, relationships with, 34
Sampling, of potential suppliers, 11
Scrap, disposals, 32, 61, 189
Service levels, stock control, 120
Shift work, control of by suppliers, 167
Site work, 31
  indemnities, 100
  smoothing, exponential, 118-19
Sources, foreign, 135-7
Sourcing, 64-71
  buying performance measurement, 199-200
  use of directories, 48
Spares, special conditions of purchase, 105-6
Specialisation, 6
Specifications:
  adequacy of, 70
  foreign purchase enquiries, 137
  restrictive, 30
  special conditions of purchase, 99
Staffing, 190
Standards:
  buying performance, 191-5
    achievability, 194
    flexibility, 193
    influencing factors, 192-3
    organisation approval, 194-5
    period of application, 194
    relevance to purpose, 192
    understandability, 194
  of supply, 89
Statistics, 14
Status:
  foreign suppliers, 139
Stock/s: see also Inventories
  buying performance, 189
  classification (ABC), 115-16
  control, 110-32
    ABC inventory techniques, 115-16
    card for, 126
    levels, 113
    purchasing research, 173
    review level system, 116-17

levels, 28, 33, 35
nature of, check list, 120
reason for holding, 110
reorder levels, 119-20
records, 47, 112
rotation, suppliers, 167
safety, 119-20
timing of supplies, 12
Stockless buying, 123-32
Storage:
of stocks, 11
special conditions of purchase, 103
timing of supplies, 12
Stores:
controller, job description, 131, 132
credit notes, 130
disposals, 189
functions of, 32
issue notes, 130
management, 110-32
relationships with, 33
repair note, 130
traveller requisitions, 46-7
'Stream concept', 2-3
Sub-contracting, 71
special conditions of purchase, 98
Supervision, 6
Suppliers:
appraisal, 164-6
cards, 48
foreign, 139
cost information, 173, 205
development of, 178
evaluation, 10, 29
financial status of, 86
good, definition, 164
international 66
local, 65
national, 65-6
rating, 169-72
records, 47
selection, 11, 49
visits to, 48, 57, 68
work loads, 56-7
Supply and demand, 16

Surplus, stores stocks, 61-2
Systems, 43-63
analysis, 14
contracting, 123

Targets, *see* Standards: buying performance; Prices: targets
Tariffs, 66
Telex, use of in foreign progressing and inspection, 153
Tenders, closing dates, 69
Terms, negotiation, 186-7, *see also* Negotiation
Time, 2, 11-13
is of the essence, 103, 104
Title, to goods, 87, 95
Tooling, general conditions of purchase, 90
Trade:
directories, *see* Directories
fairs, 67, 136
discounts, 75
literature, 136
protection societies, 86
Trading blocs, 16
Training, 4-5, 6, 22
Translations, 137, 138
Transport:
buying performance, 188
departmental relations with, 36-7
purchasing research, 173
timing of supplies, 13
Turnover discounts, 74
Typists, 38, 44

US Navy NAVMAT, 176
Usage rates, 35

Value:
analysis, 35, 159-63, 173
engineering, 159-63
purchasing research, 173
tests for, 161
'Value in use', 30
Valuation, stocks, 113

Variations:
 formulae, 83
 general conditions of purchase, 90
 price, 83, 141, 204-17
 to contract, 96
Vehicles, disposals, 61, 189
Visits, 48, 68

 buying performance, 188
 reports, 57

Wages, stockholding, 111
Weightings, 208; *see also* Indices
 buying performance measurement, 200
Workloads, suppliers, 56-7